WRITE YOUR OWN ADVENTURE

ALL-TEEN SHORT STORY ANTHOLOGY

FOREWORD BY DARBY KARCHUT

Edited by Hannah Smith & Nicole Brouwer

Owl Hollow Press
in partnership with Teen Author Boot Camp

Paperback: 978-1-945654-70-1
Ebook: 978-1-945654-71-8

Publisher's Note: This is a work of fiction. Names, characters, places, and incidents are products of the authors' imaginations. Any resemblance to actual people, living or dead, or to businesses, companies, events, institutions, or locales is completely coincidental or fictionalized.

WRITE YOUR OWN ADVENTURE/ Smith, Brouwer. 1st ed.

www.owlhollowpress.com

To brave creatives everywhere:
May your pursuits always be an adventure.

CONTENTS

Foreword: The Brave Things 7
Deathly 11
Monster Blizzard 19
They're All Our Stars 35
Creatures of the Underground 49
Dangers of the Deep 62
A 'Pun'-believable Tale 76
Aurelia's Box 94
He Held up the Sky 110
Unseen Forces 127
White Capped Waves 131
The Guardians of Time 135
The Republic of Briariia 151
Raven 159
Side by Side 173
Breaking Barriers 188
A Little Mermaid 203
Mindscapers 219
The Trials of Psyche 227
Taking Flight 237
Windkeeper 251

I Rode a Phoenix Once....263
Miracles....274
Honor Bound....282
The Counter Writer....298
Author Bios....315
Finalists....321
Editor Bios....323

Darby Karchut

FOREWORD: THE BRAVE THINGS

"But I suppose it's often that way. The brave things in the old tales and songs, Mr. Frodo: adventures, as I used to call them. I used to think that they were things the wonderful folk of the stories went out and looked for, because they wanted them, because they were exciting and life was a bit dull, a kind of sport, as you might say. But that's not the way of it with the tales that really mattered, or the ones that stay with us..."

—J.R.R. Tolkien, *The Two Towers*

Throughout time and in every culture, you will find the storyteller. The bard. The narrator. The raconteur. The minstrel, the fabler, the spinner of yarns. The stranger who waves us over. Come, come, take a seat. Make yourself comfortable because it's going to be a long and glorious night filled with tales of unknown lands, hopeless quests, enemies defeated, and hearts explored. Of adventures chosen.

While the story's setting may be as varied as an alien planet, a museum in Amsterdam, the ruins of Machu Picchu, uptown Manhattan, downtown Seattle, the Canyonlands of Utah, an inner-city high school, or the courtyard of a medieval castle, the *power* of story is the same. Some stories may feel oh-so-familiar, others will be as new to us as a foreign country, and all will touch us, maybe disturb us, maybe even plant seeds within us that won't germinate for years to come. But, when they do sprout, we will climb that beanstalk, and like Jack, become a different person.

That's what stories do. They change us. They challenge us to be bigger than we are. To be better than we are. To be bolder than we are.

As readers, we live other lives. We see through different eyes and feel with another's heart. Through stories, we experience multiple existences, multiple escapades. All this richness, while living that glorious adventure known as Life. It's enough to make one's head explode.

As *writers*, however, you and I share something extra-special, extra magical, when we put pen to paper. We experience all that a reader experiences, but a hundred times more. A million times more. Sitting in front of the keyboard or notebook, we are doing something that's almost impossible to comprehend: We are *reading* our story as we are *writing* it—it's happening simultaneously. Pretty freaky what our brains can do, right? Writing is addictive, scary, and frustrating. It may alienate our family and friends, and ruin our sleep and our health. It is the ultimate wild adventure. And we cannot imagine *not* saying yes, please, and how soon can we start on the journey?

In *The Hobbit* by J.R.R. Tolkien, there is a scene early on in which stodgy Bilbo Baggins wakes up after a crazy and quite unexpected dinner meeting with thirteen dwarves and a wizard. Rising to an empty hobbit hole, he realizes the dwarves have left, undoubtedly on the quest they had spoken of the night before. And though they had asked him to come along as a member of the expedition, and even agreed to pay him, he declined.

"We are plain quiet folk and have no use for adventures," he had pointed out earlier to the wizard Gandalf. "Nasty disturbing uncomfortable things! Make you late for dinner! I can't think what anybody sees in them."

Yet if we shift from J.R.R. Tolkien's book to Peter Jackson's film version, we see Bilbo racing through the Shire, knapsack on his back, a light in his eyes, and waving his employment agreement (a scene I'm tempted to re-enact every time I sign a new publishing contract), eager to catch up with the dwarves. He has changed his mind and made his choice to embrace the quest. The road ahead and home behind. When asked by a neighbor why he was running, Bilbo shouted over a shoulder: "I'm going on an adventure."

And so he did.

And so do we each time we write.

I've often thought about the sheer audacity of writing a story. What nerve, to think we can put pen to paper (or fingers to keyboard) and craft something another person would want to read. But we're not alone. Never forget that. We word warriors are part of an ancient and noble avocation that's been core to the human story ever since our beginning. Maybe story-telling is what makes us human. It can certainly make us humane.

Studies show that literature deepens our empathy toward others and enlarges our understanding of the world. And it is totally free, reading is; a library card costs nothing. Just think—by writing stories and sharing them with others, we are actually benefiting in a positive way to the world. Good for us. Reason enough to keep writing, my friend.

"You write in order to change the world, knowing perfectly well that you probably can't, but also knowing that literature is indispensable to the world... The world changes according to the way people see it, and if you alter, even but a millimeter the way people look at reality, then you can change it." —James Baldwin, author of *Go Tell It On The Mountain*

Sometimes it's hard to write our story. To write our heart. To choose that adventure. What if people don't like what we've written? What if they sneer at our characters and laugh at our plot? Or, even worse, decide we have no right to tell that particular story just because of who we are?

That's when we remind ourselves that we're allowed more than one adventure in this life. Writers must fight for the right to write more than one story, and even better, write more than one *kind* of story. In fact, all artists have that birthright, to create and express whatever they wish. It's important that we do not allow others to dictate to us what we can or cannot create. True, society may not want your art. Rejection is a given in the book world. I know this from having 102—yes, 102—rejections from agents and editors before landing my first publishing contract. But I believed in Griffin's story. Believe in your story, too.

And, my friend, never write a story because you think you *should,* either because of societal pressure or popular trends. No, write the story you know you *must.* As Richard Wright, author of *Native Son*, said: "The artist must bow to the monster of his own imagination."

We writers (or painters or musicians or designers) are all adventurers. We choose to live the creative life, be it through literature or visual arts or music or dance. We embrace the quest, the journey, the terrors and the joys. Nothing we do in life is more compelling than creating.

So paint your landscape, compose your song, play your tune. Write your story.

Choose your adventure.

Willow Seymour

DEATHLY

I pushed aside the tent flaps and entered, smelling blood. I quickly covered my face with my sleeve and set off through the tent, looking for a man by the name of Adam Greensworth according to the list in my pocket. There were six bodies, wrapped in bandages and lying immobile on cots. Each man's chest moved ever-so-slightly, as they breathed deeply. Except for the man at the far end of the room who lay as still as a statue, his eyes gently closed. As I approached, he started to stir, his eyes fluttering open. His face gaped with recognition and he struggled to get away. Everything below his knee had been amputated, and tightly wrapped, bloodied bandages covered the remaining stump. I reached the edge of his cot, and placed a gloved hand on his leg. He winced in pain, but my touch seemed to calm him.

"Adam Greensworth?" I asked, meeting his eyes. He slowly nodded. I removed the glove from my hand and sat on the edge of his bed. I placed my hand on his chest. He seemed apprehensive, but he didn't pull away. I could feel his heartbeat resonating throughout my body. *Thump, thump...thump.* The pounding gradually slowed until it ceased entirely. With a shudder, the life drained from his eyes. I eased him back down onto the cot. "Rest in peace," I whispered and slipped my glove back on.

My business was done. I turned to leave the tent, but one of the figures was sitting up, staring at me in the dark. Before I could stop him, he reached to his bedside and turned on a lantern, illuminating the room with a warm yellow glow. The young man's skin was marred by dozens of small slashes and scrapes, and his left eye was covered by a strip of bandages. The red hue staining the white gauze told me exactly why he was in the tent. He looked upon me with confusion. Thankfully, none of the others stirred along with him.

"Who are you?" the man drawled, his voice still slowed by sleep. He spoke with a heavy accent I couldn't place; Scottish or Irish. "Why're you creeping around the medical tent at night? You plannin' to harvest my organs? I can still put up a fight, scumbag!"

"I wasn't here." I started for the entrance of the tent. "Forget me."

"Is that an order, you creep?" he accused, sitting up even further. "What's your name?"

"I don't have one," I muttered.

His face contorted in confusion. "Tell me who you are or I'm going to shout and bring down the entire battalion on you," he grumbled.

I stopped and slowly turned toward him, considering my options. I could let him do as he threatened and then disappear, leaving him to rant and rave for his comrades. Then again, that seemed just a little too easy. Despite myself, I remained, standing in the center of the foul tent, gazing down at him.

He stared up at me with confidence and strength in his eyes. "Now, who are you?"

I opened my lips and let the words escape in a seething hiss. "I am Death."

Without a moment of pause, the man countered sarcastically. "Did your parents name you that, or did you think it fit you?" He shook his head, chuckling. "I suppose you fancy yourself an assassin. Ooh! So scary. I'm tremblin', look at me!" He held out his hand, feigning fright.

"I am Death!" I spat. "You will address me as such."

"You're Death," he scoffed, shaking his head in disbelief. "As in, the Grim Reaper?"

"What other Death is there?" I asked, straightening my gloves. He took a moment to think.

"But you're too pretty to be Death," he said, his eyes trailing up and down my figure. I folded my arms over my chest.

"Excuse me?"

"Death is supposed to be some old man in black robes, with a scythe an' a hood. You're a lady, wearing a gown, to boot." He motioned to me with a limp hand.

"Do you wish to see my scythe? I normally only bring it out for the big ones, kings and presidents and the like, but I suppose I could make an exception." I reached toward my back pocket. The man smiled.

"If you show me your scythe, I'll show you my shaft," he said, a sly grin creeping across his cheeks.

"Disgusting!" I scoffed. "You're lucky I have enough on my plate already without another brainless git to kill."

"Why not? Can't you just kill whoever you want?"

"No. There is law and order in death. I am not the one who kills; I am the one who frees souls from their suffering. Once the *mortals like you,*" the word flew from my lips like a curse, "are done with your killing, I bring peace to the dying. If I killed you, it would alter your timeline, disrupting order and causing even more wanton death in the end."

"Damn," the man mumbled. "You've got us all figured out, don't you?"

"Of course," I sighed. "I have no purpose, other than the reaping of souls."

"Sounds like an awful hard life," the man said, looking at me with something in his eye. Pity? Empathy? Something in between, maybe?

"You mortals don't know how good you have it. At least you have an end. I am forever." I averted my gaze to the floor. "It's lonely. The best part is when humans talk to me before they die. They ask questions, look for comfort. I'm the last one to give it to them. It's a moment of solace for us both, before they leave."

"I can't..." He looked confounded. "I can't imagine that. If it's any comfort, I'll talk to you as long as I can." His face was no longer embossed with the confident smile of before. He now sat forward, engaged, while his eyes softened, and his voice filled with comfort.

"No." I sniffed. "It wouldn't work. I can't say that I wouldn't like to, but I'm immortal. You'd be gone in the blink of an eye for me."

The man threw his legs over the end of the bed. He grabbed a wooden crutch leaning on his nightstand and propped his arm up on it. With his shadow filling the room, he hobbled over to me. He looked at me intently with his one eye and stuck out his hand. "The name is MacNeil. I may only be a mortal, but I can't let you suffer by yourself." I did not offer my hand back. He seemed a bit confused for a second.

"I don't do handshakes," I answered coldly. "You would die if I touched you."

"Of course." MacNeil dropped his hand and rubbed the back of his head nervously. "You bein' death an' all, I guess touch is out of the question. Damn shame." He grinned again, winking playfully.

"You are aware that you are quite literally flirting with Death?" I crossed my arms and pursed my lips to hide a smile.

"Maybe I'll get lucky and Death will flirt back," he said as I rolled my eyes. He chuckled. "When you said you don't choose who dies and when, how d'you know what to do?"

"I have a list."

"A list…" He thought for a moment, nodding to himself. He sat back down on the cot, biting his lip. "Who writes the list?"

"No one, it just exists." I nearly grabbed it from my pocket to show him but realized that would be a mistake. "There are dates and names marked on it, so I know where to go."

"Are you sayin' that you have a list for all of eternity? Everyone who will ever die?" He scrunched his eyebrows and looked at me incredulously. "That can't be possible."

"Of course, I do." I smiled, and my chest puffed with the pride of having exclusive knowledge. "I know the death-day of every person in this room. I know when children whose parents have yet to be conceived will die, and their grandchildren, and so on, *Colton*." I made a point to use his first name, so he would know that I had already read and memorized his place on the list.

"I'm going to have kids?" MacNeil said, looking befuddled. "Do you know the name of my wife? Because, I have a lady waitin' for me back home, and if she's the one—"

"I'm not allowed to tell you that." I stopped him before he could get too excited. "That would alter your timeline."

"Of course. I should've realized." He nodded. He opened his mouth to speak again, but stopped when he saw something across the room.

I turned to see Adam Greensworth, laying still on his cot. Unnaturally still. MacNeil had undoubtedly figured out my purpose in the tent that night. MacNeil's face was stained with grief. "You took Greensworth, didn't you?" MacNeil sighed.

I nodded solemnly. "You saw the pain he was in. I couldn't let that continue."

"Poor old sod. Had two lil' girls at home. They'll be missin' their dad."

"Rebecca and Tracy. I know." I said. The paper holding their death-dates burned in my pocket.

"Why now?" MacNeil asked. "Bit cruel, leaving him for so long. He's been groaning' on about the pain for weeks. You could've killed him before he suffered."

"Everyone has their time." I folded my hands on my stomach. "War does not change that. I may not be cruel, but I cannot be especially merciful either." I looked through the tent flap and into the night. "I'm afraid I must depart. The night is coming to an end."

"See ya later," he said, his eyes wide with excitement.

"No, you will not see me again."

"You have to come back eventually. This is a war zone, right? People die all the time."

"I made a mistake tonight, assuming all the injured were unconscious." I readjusted my gloves and sniffed, smiling subtlety. Although he was crude, it was sweet that MacNeil would want me to come back. "The next time you'll see me is when it's your time to move along to the next life."

"But that won't be durin' the war?" His voice was quiet, solemn, as if he was scared.

For a moment, I wondered whether I should tell him anything. "It will be a while before we meet."

"That's the best news I've heard all week," he said, sighing and smiling.

"I suppose it would be." I took a slow step toward the tent's exit, my smile widening as I turned back to give him my final word. He smiled back, which was… startling. No one ever smiled at death.

"Goodbye, Colton MacNeil."

"Bye, Death." MacNeil gave me one last grin. It was odd, but I felt that MacNeil was different, somehow. He was the first mortal that ever meant more to me than another soul to reap. He seemed like he could be a friend. "See you soon!"

With that thought still in my head, I disappeared through the tent flaps and into the dark of the night.

The paper crinkled in my pocket, seeming to echo through the desolate street as I walked along. My heels clicked against the pavement in a staccato pattern as I looked back and forth, searching for the address.

When I first met MacNeil, I had broken so many rules for the only living mortal that knew of my existence. Now, it was all coming to an end. Throughout the decades, what had taken place during our previous meeting haunted me. I could never shake the idea of him in my head. I had turned him into an entirely different creature, by the end. Something to look forward to, a prize waiting on the horizon. At that point, I was not sure if I would even recognize him. Distance is a lens that you do not realize you are gazing through.

My head whipped around as I felt a familiar aura glaring at me from the building to my right. A towering red-bricked apartment loomed over the street. I gazed at the fourth floor where I saw a figure staring down from the window, a colorful shroud-like shape blurring the glass. It was him. I felt my stomach buzz with excitement.

I walked into the stairwell. The listing on the wall offered buzzers for each apartment. My eyes scanned the list until it fell on Room 32: "Colton and Lacie MacNeil." The sign included Lacie MacNeil even though I had taken her a few months ago. I wondered if MacNeil hadn't changed it yet due to grief. I pressed the button next to the names and waited.

After a crackle followed by a moment of staticky silence through the speaker, a voice quavered. "Come on up." I paced up three flights of stairs, before I came to a long, empty hallway. Stepping forward, I counted the doors as I passed, looking for Room 32. As I reached the end of the hallway, the door clicked and slowly swung open.

Inside smelled of faded newspapers and cologne. A small, closed window let in the sparse sunlight and highlighted the disarray. Plates and papers were stacked in precariously leaning towers. An old man with whitened hair, wrinkled skin, and an eyepatch over his eye hunched over in a rocking-chair. He rocked back and forth, staring at the street below through the icy glass of the window.

"Hello, Death," MacNeil croaked, without turning to look at me. "I saw you comin' down the street." He sighed, still rocking. "Has my time finally come?"

"Yes," I answered solemnly.

"I'm ready." He sighed. "I've been ready since the day when I woke up when you took Greensworth." He turned to look at me. "You're still pretty as a rose, even after all these years."

"Thank you," I whispered. My voice was dry and quiet. I did not want this.

"Wish I had time to clean up a bit, before such a fine lady came to visit." MacNeil looked down at his crippled, bone-thin legs. "I never had a beard in my life, but now I can't even lift the razor." He motioned tiredly to the puff of white hair reaching his neck.

"It's fine, Colton. I didn't expect you to do anything special for me." I stepped toward him. "I'm afraid I cannot linger for much longer."

"When you took my wife, I felt your presence. I realized how alone I felt." He sighed and ceased rocking his chair. "Good thing you came when you did. Lacie was real sick, crying herself to sleep most nights. She had something in her brain, makin' her feel pain when nothing was there. She flinched at everything, and couldn't even sit down without hurting'." He blinked slowly. "Did you tell me the truth when you said it's better on the other side?"

I paused. "No."

"Is it worse? Am I going to hell?"

"I have no idea." I pursed my lips. "Only those who have passed know what it's like."

MacNeil closed his eyes. "Damn. My great-grandson will never meet me, then?"

"No." I rested a hand on the arm of his rocking chair. "Your grandson names him Colton, after you."

MacNeil smiled brightly. "My daughter raised him right." He took a deep breath, staring out the window with a crinkled smile. "Well, I'm ready as I'll ever be, love. It's time." He straightened his posture. I knelt in front of him, and he looked down at me, his eye filled with kindness as he searched my face. "You look so much like Lacie."

I reached up, brushing a hand over his cheek. As if with renewed strength, he rested his wrinkled hand atop mine. I leaned down and placed a gentle kiss on his cheek. "Goodnight, old friend." I felt his hand slacken as his breath escaped in a weak gasp. His body fell back into the chair, a smile still playing across his lips as his glassy eye stared out the window. He was finally gone.

I stood, replacing his hand on his lap. I turned to exit, but froze when I heard voices coming down the hall.

"David is a good name though! Nice and simple. Why use a baby book when we can go with the tried and true? There's no need…" The young man's voice trailed off as if he had gotten distracted. "Why is the door open?"

The man appeared in the doorway. I recognized MacNeil's features in the face of his grandson, Arthur. A pregnant woman appeared beside him. It was Maggie, Arthur's wife. "Grandad? Are you in there?" Arthur's voice trembled.

Arthur crept over to where MacNeil sat in his chair. After the old man was shaken and he did not respond, Arthur begged him to come back to no avail. Maggie stood back, covering her mouth in a silent cry. I walked up beside her, looking down at her belly.

"Good morning, Colton," I whispered. Maggie's head whipped around, but her eyes saw through me. She crossed her hands over her abdomen and shivered, as if a cold breeze had passed over her. I started for the apartment's door, pausing in the hallway. Arthur now sobbed silently into his grandpa's sleeve. MacNeil stared into the street, his last smile still etched onto his lips.

I felt something cold and wet fall from my eye and drip down my cheek. I brushed my finger across my cheek and pulled it away. A tear? I had never cried before. The feeling was not a pleasant one.

With a final glance into the apartment, I departed with my eyes still flushed with tears. I had to hurry to attend to the next death.

Elijah Lewis

Monster Blizzard

RAHH!!

A guttural roar pierced the air. Through the whipping snow, little could be seen of anything. I wasn't cold, nor was I concerned about where I was or how I had gotten into such a wintry wasteland. The beauty of the storm fully captivated me.

The sound of distant voices caused me to turn. Several dozen men were standing in a circle, arguing. Others milled around tents half buried in snow.

As I watched, five or so of the arguing party broke off from the others and, grabbing packs and gear, started off from the main group into the blizzard.

Suddenly, the roar echoed through the snow again. I turned behind me to see the outline of something approaching through the blizzard.

Something big.

RAHH!!

I started awake at the sound of my phone ringing. Squinting, I reached out and grabbed it from my nightstand. I saw who was calling, and I groaned. Then, bracing myself, I answered.

"Hey," I said groggily.

"Morning, Logan," came the voice of my boss, Shane Hill. "It's that time again."

I could barely hold back another groan. "How much snow did we get?"

"Six inches. We'll be busy for a while. Do you have everything you need?"

"I've got my snow gear and shovel."

"You should be good with that. Thanks, Logan. I'll be over in a couple of hours to check your work. See you later."

"Yep." I ended the call and looked at the time. 4:17 AM. With a sigh, I stood, flipped on the light and began to dress into my snow gear.

For the past several months battling winter storms had provided my income. Whenever it snowed I had to shovel—no matter the hour. I didn't drive a plow truck. Instead, I'd drive to each of the company's various properties and shovel the walks. It wasn't convenient work, but Shane Hill paid me well if I did a good job.

Once I was done outfitting myself, I grabbed the keys to my beat-up pick-up truck and braced myself to head out into the cold.

The house was silent, my parents fast asleep. I impulsively grabbed an orange from the kitchen table and, slipping it into my coat pocket, headed into the garage. After starting the engine and waiting a moment for the truck to warm up, I pulled out of the garage and drove into the quiet morning snow.

As I drove, something about the snow tickled my memory. Right before Shane called, I had been dreaming, but of what, I couldn't recall. Concluding that I was just tired, I dismissed the vague tug.

I arrived ten minutes later at my first job. This property, a stripmall, was significantly larger than the others. I knew that I would be there for a couple of hours, at least. I hesitated before parking and peered into the darkness at the winter magic.

The parking lot was covered in shimmering, uncorrupted snow, untouched and beautiful. Its reflective light illuminated the area, and every now and then, a gust of wind would blow, kicking up snow and creating a mist-like haze.

I was, as usual, in awe.

I parked my truck on the side of the road, where a plow truck had already come and cleared. I climbed out, and then, removing my shovel from the backseat, began to work.

The entirety of the stripmall's large sidewalks were buried under half a foot of snow. Typically it only snowed three or four inches. I estimated that with six inches, it would take me two hours to finish the walks. I had a snowblower, but during the last storm, it had broken down, and Shane had yet to replace it. So I used a shovel.

I had been working for roughly half an hour, when the snow began to fall again. It started out as just a small snowfall, but in a matter of minutes, it was falling so thickly that I could barely see farther than a few feet ahead. The patch of sidewalk that I had already cleared rapidly disappeared under a fresh layer of snow, and six inches was soon seven, and then eight.

I paused from my work to look into the swirling darkness and descending storm. Something about my dream tugged at me again—like I had seen something familiar. I looked at my watch, and then up in confusion. The world of 5:04 was usually busy at the strip mall—there was a gym located in one of the buildings, and usually people were there by now. But there was no sign of life.

It was as if the world had died.

The snow flew down with greater velocity. My phone buzzed in my pocket, and I withdrew it. A message from Shane instructed me to get out of the storm and head home until it passed. I turned back to my truck when I realized I had lost my sense of direction. In the swirling storm, I didn't even know where the buildings of the mall were.

I began trudging through the snow, hoping to run across some form of a landmark to indicate which direction I should turn—something that shouldn't have been so hard. The snow, not long ago reflecting light, now seemed draped in darkness. Biting, deadly darkness. Darkness that seemed to have swallowed up my world.

I stopped in my tracks. Something was wrong. I should have found something by now, some sign of the building or people. I knew I should stop where I was and wait to be found, but with a sinking feeling in my stomach, I realized that no one would search for me. Shane would assume that I had returned to my truck and headed home. My parents would not wake up for another hour or so. No one would worry about me—until it was too late.

Shivering, I decided to call Shane, and I removed my phone from my pocket. I turned it on and quickly scrolled through my contacts. Then, clicking the call button, I waited.

Shane didn't answer. I tried again, but to no avail. Desperately, I tried the same thing with my parents, yet no one answered.

So I trudged on. My face was to the ground, avoiding the whipping winds and icy particles flying through the air. I had set my shovel down at some point, and the only thing I carried was my phone, as well as the orange I had grabbed from the table. My focus was wholly on pushing my way through the blizzard. Inside my gloves, I felt my fingers numbing, the cold having long since seeped in. The snow was no longer soft and powdery. Instead, it had become hard and crusty, like it had been there for an eternity. I no longer felt cement beneath my feet, and it seemed as if the snow stretched far deeper than eight inches.

Suddenly, the snow beneath my feet gave way. I struggled to pull them out, but my efforts did nothing.

To my horror, I began to sink slowly.

With a lurch, the snow beneath me completely collapsed. I felt myself falling. I scrambled for a handhold, but there was nothing to hold on to. Nothing but crumbling, unreliable snow. All I managed to do was bury myself further.

I stopped struggling and looked around, panting.

I was stuck, wedged in a crevasse of rock and ice. Slowly, I was sinking further and further down. Already the surface was a foot above my head, and the distance was only growing.

RAHH!!

My heart skipped a beat. Every inch of my body froze as I listened for the source of the roar.

Crunch. Crunch. Crunch.

Footsteps.

Crunch. Crunch.

A pause.

RAHH!! The booming snarl was only feet away. Guttural and deep, its voice set off every alarm in my instincts. The sound seemed to echo through my bones, like the world's biggest drum magnified a thousand times.

The sound was familiar. I knew it from somewhere…

Crunch. Crunch. The footsteps were growing distant. Soon, they were altogether silent. I let out a sigh of relief.

Crrraack!

Part of the frozen wall I was wedged in suddenly shattered—and I fell.

I landed on my back with a jolt. I was vaguely aware of my arm beneath me, twisted at an odd angle, screaming in pain. I had heard something crack when I landed—whether it was the floor of ice beneath me, or my arm, I didn't know.

After what seemed like hours, I sat up. My body protested, throbbing in pain, but I forced myself up. If I sat still for too long, eventually I would begin to freeze. My snow gear kept me warm enough, but it wouldn't last forever. I needed to figure out where I was and how to get back home.

Gritting my teeth, I stood. My legs were fine—that was a relief. I tried to move my left arm, but the effort sent needles of pain up my arm. Gasping, I determined it unusable for the present.

My back was bruised, but besides my arm, I was all right. I wanted to lay on the ground forever, but unfortunately, I had to get out of this pit.

I looked around. I was standing in a large cavern that seemed to be made entirely of ice. Behind me, the cave sloped steadily down. With a shiver, I wondered how far it went. The crack I had fallen in stretched above the deeper end of the cave. I was suddenly glad I had not fallen over there.

I looked the other direction. The cave sloped up much slower here, and I started climbing up. Every few minutes I would stop and grit my teeth as pain enveloped me, and then continue as it receded. It was slow going, but it was progress.

The cold dug deeper into me, and I wished I had dressed more warmly. My fingers were numb, and I tried to remember the signs of frostbite. Not that there was much I could do. I had to keep making my way out of the tunnel.

What if there is no exit? a skeptical voice whispered in my head.

I ignored it. If there was no exit, then it didn't matter. There was no chance of climbing out the way I came, and with no food I would starve. Not to mention the cold.

There had to be an exit.

It grew dark. *Surely it couldn't be night already*, I thought, bewildered. Yet the little light falling through the crack above was fading. I was shivering uncontrollably, and I found myself taking more frequent rests.

I paused to readjust my scarf, the only protection I had for my mouth and nose. Suddenly, a fierce gust of wind swept through the cave, picking up my scarf. I scrambled to grab it, but it slipped down the tunnel, racing with the wind. I yelled in frustration and kicked the ice. Instead of causing my foot more pain, however, it stirred only a bit of feeling in my foot, reminding me how cold I was. I groaned.

Then it hit me. My scarf had been carried away by the wind. The crack in the ceiling was tiny—not nearly enough room to admit such a gust. That meant—

There was an opening.

I increased my pace, trying to make use of every bit of strength I had to propel me forward. The tunnel no longer progressed in an uphill slant but was instead completely flat. It felt as if I was travelling through the throat of an icy snake.

Unexpectedly, the smell of roasting meat drifted through the air. Trying not to hope, I quickened my pace. The tunnel curved up ahead, and I could hear voices.

People.

I tried to run, stumbling in my effort. My arm protested sharply whenever it bumped the shrinking tunnel walls, but I pressed on. The thought of a rescue party, and *warmth,* carrying me on.

Finally, I rounded the bend. What I saw was the last thing I had expected.

Five people, heavily dressed, sat around a fire on their packs. An iron pot sat in the flames, boiling soup. On a skewer, a chunk of meat roasted. The people, four men and a woman, were dressed in thick furs, and I noticed several swords leaning against the cave wall.

My heart sank. I had spent my ascent in the tunnel convincing myself that nothing *too* out of the ordinary had happened. Somehow, I had wandered out of the city and fallen into a cave. A bear or something of the sort had been walking around. Not ordinary, but not unbelievable.

But this? This shattered my conviction that soon I'd be okay. I was far from home, in a frozen world. This couldn't be a dream—my arm hurt too much for that—yet it was so bizarre I couldn't help but have doubts.

Something about them was familiar…like I had seen them before. I dismissed the thought almost as quickly as it entered my mind. Of course I'd never seen them.

One of the men noticed me.

"Ha! I told you Orrin had spies!" He leapt from his seat and grabbed a sword from the wall. His companions all stood in surprise.

"Wait!" the woman said. "He's no more than seventeen years old!"

"So Orrin recruits young," the first man said. He had a thick black beard, and was tall enough that his head brushed against the ceiling. "That's *his* fault!"

"Adran, I don't think he's one of Orrin's," another man said softly. He had light brown hair that matched his coat.

"He's not one of the extra hands we brought, is he?" questioned the woman.

"Who are you, boy?" asked a graying man, who looked the oldest.

"I'm Logan Matthews," I said, shocked at how weak my voice sounded. "I was walking around up there," I gestured to the surface, "and fell through a hole into the tunnel. I've been trying to get out ever si-si-since-" my words became shivers.

The man with the soft brown hair gestured for me to approach. "You're freezing!" he said. "We can talk about who you are later."

He moved to sit back down, but the dark-haired man, Adran, interrupted.

"No, we most certainly are not going to talk about this later!" he snapped. "I've fought for this expedition too long to see it fall at the hands of a boy!"

If I wasn't so cold, my mind would have pricked at the mention of an expedition. But, in my current state, I could do nothing but push it to the back of my mind for later.

The graying man sat back down. "Let him warm himself," he said. "Adran, keep your sword drawn, and we can interrogate him beside the fire."

Adran sat down reluctantly with the others.

I approached. Unwilling to part with any of my snow gear, I squatted down by the fire and stiffly pulled off my gloves.

I held my hands up to the flames, feeling the eyes of the others on me, particularly the man Adran. At first, I felt nothing—just the same cold stiffness I had felt for the past several hours. Then, gradually, the warmth began to penetrate my frozen flesh. My fingers ached as the fire warmed them, but simultaneously seemed to sigh with pleasure at the banishment of the long-rooted cold.

Adran cleared his throat pointedly. "Shall we begin?"

"Certainly," said the woman, surprising me as well as Adran. "Logan, you claim you're not employed by Orrin. There are no villages for miles around, and besides our party there were no others in the area. How exactly did you get here?"

"I..." If I told the truth, they wouldn't believe me. Yet by the sound of things, it didn't seem very likely I had wandered here from...wherever these people came from.

How *had* I gotten here? Something otherworldly had happened. One rarely gets lost in a snowstorm and winds up in a world of monsters and ice caves. I had been transported from my normal life to a world completely unknown to me.

"I got lost in a storm," I said. "There was a blizzard and I lost my way. I already told you I fell down a crack in the ice. Since then I've been trying to get out."

Adran did not seem to be buying it, but the soft-haired man was nodding. The graying man had listened while staring at the fire, and did not cease to do so now. The others said nothing.

"I think he's lying," Adran announced. "One doesn't wander up the tallest mountain in Straislind and survive. It's impossible."

"Okay," I said, realizing that my tale wasn't enough. "You want to know the truth? I have no idea how I got here. I'm not even from here, and I've never heard of Straightland, or whatever you called this place."

To my surprise, the fourth man, who had so far remained silent, was nodding. "That happens quite frequently in the Eaquan mountains. Strangers, wearing odd clothing, are known to appear after a storm."

"So, you're saying that this boy is trustworthy, Martin?" the woman asked. She had blonde hair, which spilled out of her hood and coat, and she looked no older than twenty.

"I don't know about trustworthy, but he's not one of Orrin's mercenaries," said Martin. "I doubt he's much of a threat."

I grunted in agreement.

"Well, Logan, welcome to our camp!" said the soft-haired man. "I'm Christopher."

"Sanna," the blonde girl said with a nod. The rest of the group followed: The graying man was Raghnall, Martin, and Adran, who was still watching me warily.

"How long have you been in this tunnel?" Christopher wondered.

How long *had* I been in the tunnel? I reached into my pocket to check the time, but found my phone wasn't there. I cursed under my breath—I must have lost it when I fell.

To my surprise, I found something else in my pocket—the orange I had grabbed before I left home. I didn't withdraw it, though, saving it for later.

"I don't know—several hours, at least," I said.

"Long enough to begin to freeze, certainly," Raghnall said. "Do you feel anything unusual?"

"Well, I think I broke my arm; does that count as unusual?" I said, slightly irritated by their relentless queries.

"Well, I consider it unusual," Raghnall said. "Sanna can look at it later."

"So, who is this Orrin fellow?" I asked.

Adran scowled.

Martin spoke. "We are part of an expedition of researchers," he said, leaning forward. "We set out in search of...a creature." A shiver ran down my spine, and I felt the impulse to look behind me. "Raghnall is our leader and head researcher. He's been studying this creature for years. We've been petitioning for funding for an expedition like this for almost as long, but only recently did we acquire any. We've been trekking up this mountain, Mount Håkon, for three weeks. Orrin was Raghnall's sub-captain.

"Then, last night, the creature attacked our camp, killing one of three men assigned to keep watch. The next morning, one of them confronted Orrin and Raghnall, told them what had happened, and demanded that the creature be killed, instead of studied for research."

"But, if the creature killed a man...doesn't that make it a threat?" I asked, confused.

"I was the third man keeping watch," Martin said quietly. "The creature was only approaching in curiosity. It wasn't until the man panicked and shot an arrow at it that it became violent."

"What happened?"

"Raghnall told him we wouldn't kill it," Adran said. "But Orrin insisted we go after the beast. He claims he's concerned about the safety of his team, but really he wants vengeance. The creature killed his cousin, Clodron. Clodron was a coward," Adran spat. "He brought his death upon himself."

"Clodron possessed several desirable qualities," Raghnall said slowly, "But I will confess his general make-up was lacking."

"Orrin convinced most of our team to take down the beast," Adran continued. "With an exaggerated tale of Clodron's death, it wasn't hard. Then, when we stood by Raghnall, they threatened to kill us too."

"We managed to form a temporary peace treaty—long enough for us to get out." Sanna picked up the story. "Now, we're preparing to search for the creature ourselves."

"Hopefully, we can find it before the others," said Christopher grimly.

RAHH!!

The cry rang out again from outside of the tunnel. Everyone tensed. The haunting roar sent shivers down my spine, and I wished for a weapon—even my snow shovel would have helped me feel more secure.

"The creature," Sanna whispered.

"It's been crying ever since Clodron shot it," Christopher said softly.

"Poor thing," Raghnall said.

"If it's so angry, why risk tracking it down?" I asked.

Raghnall turned to me. "Because we believe that this creature wants to be found." I noticed he was much older than he looked at first glance. He appeared to be in his early or even mid-sixties, and I was suddenly impressed by his choice to brave such an expedition. "Mysterious, huge creatures have been seen near villages on the foothills of this mountain for decades. But in the past six or seven years, they have slowed. Last year, none were seen at all.

"They've never been seen up close. They always avoid humans, and the closest we ever got to one was when we came across a corpse, last year. We began to find more and more corpses. White fur, matted and bloodied, bones in poor condition…we began to wonder what was happening. Finally, we pieced together that some sort of war had erupted between them. The sightings completely ceased. For months, we feared they were extinct.

"Then, seven weeks ago, we saw one. The biggest ever recorded, it appeared outside of a village. It just sat there. Watching. Then, when dawn came, it left. It repeated this routine for three more days. When we tried to approach it, it left."

"It's lonely," I realized. Raghnall nodded.

"If it's the only one left, there are two possibilities we can consider. One, it massacred it's entire species and is the sole survivor; or, two, it, being the biggest of its kind, was left alone during the war, and is now the last. The second possibility is more likely, since it's shown no violent tendencies."

"It approached our camp peacefully," Christopher said eagerly. " But Clodron's hasty attack means we don't know for certain."

"Yes, yes," said Raghnall, sounding annoyed at being interrupted. "Therefore, we believe that it wants to meet us. Communicate, even."

"Clodron ruined that chance," Adran said with a scowl. "Now we have to somehow convince it that we mean no harm. If Orrin kills it…"

"We'll lose a magnificent species," Raghnall whispered.

"What is it?" I asked.

"It hasn't been named beyond 'the creature,'" Martin laughed. "It's larger than a brown bear, but smaller than an eleen."

"A what?"

"An eleen?" Martin frowned. "You know, huge creature with curved tusks and a snake-like nose? Do you not have those where you're from?"

"Oh," I said, realization dawning. "Yes, we have those. We call them elephants."

"Ah. Well, the creature is smaller than those," Martin said. "It has white fur, and walks on two legs just as often as four."

"It's a beautiful creature," Christopher said simply.

RAHH!!

The cry seemed distant this time, and I couldn't help but hear a forlorn note in its bellow.

"Are we ready?" Adran asked. Raghnall nodded.

"We'll eat, and then go," he said.

"Wait, what?" I asked, confused.

"Well, the creature is nocturnal," Martin said. "Therefore, so are we." He gestured to the food on the fire. "This is breakfast."

"You'll have to travel with us," Raghnall said. "We can't leave you here alone, and we can't afford to have someone stay with you."

"I've got a tonic for you," Sanna said. "It's full of herbs and vitamins, and it'll give you enough energy to last the night. I have a salve I can put on your arm too, if you want."

"Sure," I said.

Christopher began serving the soup and meat in small wooden bowls, and Martin gave me an extra dish.

The soup was watery, mainly containing onions and a few thin potato slices. The meat was rich and juicy, and I wished there was more of it. I wondered what animal it came from.

I handed back my empty bowl, not entirely full, but content. As the others prepared to leave, Sanna approached with the tonic. It was an orange liquid in a small glass vial. She uncorked it, and I took it and drank. I nearly choked on the bitter brew. However, I managed to down it, my face puckered at the unpleasant aftertaste.

"The energy will come within the next hour," Sanna said. "Now, would you like me to look at that arm?" I nodded. "You'll need to remove your coat for a moment."

I did so, and rolled up the sleeve of my shirt to reveal my arm. It was twisted and swollen, dark patches on my skin revealing internal bleeding. Sanna frowned.

"It's definitely broken," she said. "This salve will help, but it won't completely heal it. You'll have to seek out a healer. For now, this will do." She pulled out the salve, and began to spread it over my arm. I tried not to wince in pain as my arm was enveloped in sickly green paste. "This should help bring down the pain, too," she said, wrapping it carefully.

"Thanks," I said. Raghnall approached.

"Are we ready to go?" he asked.

Sanna nodded. "All set."

"Great. Let's go."

Wind whipped around me. Snow flew about like shards of glass, cutting sharply. I kept my head down, watching the feet of Christopher in front of me. We had been travelling for three or so hours. Sanna's potion had done its job—I felt refreshed, like I had woken from a long nap.

Suddenly, Christopher stopped in front of me, and I came to a halt. Behind me, Sanna stumbled into me, before too coming to a stop. I looked up to see what was happening.

Through the swirling snow I could see Raghnall pointing at something. I squinted a moment before realizing what it was.

Lights.

"Orrin's team," Christopher yelled, his voice barely loud enough to be heard above the storm. I squinted. I could just make out tents around fires, and the forms of people moving about.

Everyone huddled up around Raghnall. "The creature's tracks led up the mountain the last time we saw them," the older man yelled. "We'll head that way, but we need to avoid Orrin's camp. He has people keeping watch, but if we're careful enough—"

"My friend, you're too late for that," a pleasant voice laughed. I spun around, as did the others.

Behind us stood eight people, all dressed in fur similar to Raghnall and the others. At their head was a man wearing a thick black coat that matched his long hair. Beside him stood a woman with striking white hair, though she looked no older than thirty.

"Orrin," hissed Sanna.

"Sanna! Beautiful as ever." Orrin grinned. He turned to Raghnall. "Well, my friend, I'm afraid our treaty expired."

"You wouldn't kill him, Orrin," Christopher said boldly.

"Christopher, you couldn't stop me if you wanted to," Orrin chuckled. Orrin was deceptively pleasant, and I had a hard time focusing on the fact that he was the enemy. What would have happened if I had stumbled on Orrin, instead of Raghnall? I shuddered.

"Let us pass, Orrin," Raghnall said firmly. Orrin grinned again. In fact, a smile of some form or another never seemed to leave his face. It was disorienting.

"What, and let you save the creature?" Orrin asked. "I can't do that. I owe it to my team, to *the world,* to take down this monster. It's my job." His face hardened. "And you're too blind to see it."

"It approached in peace!" protested Martin. "It wasn't until your stupid cousin—"

"My cousin was wise enough to see the danger in the monster!" Orrin snarled, his smile disappearing. "He was willing to sacrifice his own life in an effort to take down a killer, and in death showed us what needs to be done."

Orrin drew his sword and advanced, and his soldiers followed.

"Martin, give Logan your spare!" Raghnall barked. Martin withdrew a long, thin sword and tossed it to me. I almost dropped it, shocked. Raghnall trusted *me* with a sword?

Suddenly, Sanna charged at Orrin, yelling. Adran and Martin followed, and then Christopher and Raghnall.

Swords clashed, clanging loudly over the wind. A cry rang out as Martin took down the first foe. Soon, the cries, yells, and blades merged into a single fierce sound of battle.

I hesitated, unmoved, sword in hand at the edge of the battle.

This wasn't my fight. I had no idea how to use a sword, and it wasn't my intention to kill someone anyway. I could slip out into the storm, and try and find my way home.

This wasn't my fight.

No, I thought. Raghnall and his team had willingly accepted me into their group. They had fed me, warmed me, and offered me healing. They had trusted me.

Yelling, I charged into the fray.

Orrin and Raghnall were dueling head on, sparks flying as their blades connected. Despite his age, Raghnall showed no sign of tiring, fighting just as strongly as anyone else, if not more.

Sanna fought the white-haired woman, while Christopher and Martin fought a huge man wielding two enormous axes, and a smaller man carrying a long, thin sword. Adran was facing three opponents, barely keeping up with their flashing swords. Beside him lay a man, dead, his beaver-coat stained with blood.

I joined Adran. He barely glanced at me before stepping to the side. Two of the men followed him, while the other turned to me.

I swung my sword, but I quickly discovered that handling a real sword was harder than it appeared in movies, not to mention that having only one working arm prevented me from doing as much.

My foe swung his sword—I lifted mine just in time to knock back the blow that would have killed me. He lunged, and I stepped to the side before bringing my sword down, nearly disarming him. Apparently, this man wasn't a master swordsman either.

Unfortunately, he still had more experience than me, and soon I found myself backing up as the man advanced, swinging his sword dangerously.

I tried to disarm him again, using a technique I had seen in a movie, but he brushed my attempt aside.

"Stupid Aragorn," I muttered under my breath. The man swung. "Always—" I ducked. "—makes it look—" I lunged forward, trying to stab him. He knocked my sword aside, and it fell softly into the snow. "—so easy." I stepped back. The man grinned.

"You're not very good at this, you kn—" Suddenly, Adran appeared. The man spun to face him, but it was too late. Adran's sword plunged through him, and he fell back, dead.

Adran turned to me. "We've got to help Raghnall!" he yelled. I turned.

The leader was falling back under Orrin's attacks. The white-haired woman had joined Orrin, and I realized with a jolt that Sanna was missing. Blood dripped from the woman's sword.

Adran and I charged. We were only feet away when Raghnall stumbled.

The white haired woman lashed out, kicking him in the chest. He fell, and Orrin poised his sword above Raghnall's chest.

"This is for Clodron!" he screamed.

Adran rushed toward Orrin. Before he could do anything, however, the white-haired woman stood and threw a knife at him.

To my horror, the weapon found its mark. Adran collapsed to the ground, gasping as blood spurted from his chest.

RAHH!!

I looked up in surprise.

A hundred or so yards away loomed a huge form. There was no mistaking its enormity, even in the dark blizzard.

RUUuaAHH!!

It sounded angry. It was the roar of a creature beyond hope, that had been abandoned by its kind, that had been shunned and attacked when it sought out friends. It was the sound of a creature that had given up.

Dropping to all fours, the gorilla-like creature charged.

It barreled past me, missing me by only inches. It continued onward, and came to a stop in front of Orrin, Raghnall, Adran, and the woman with white hair.

The woman screamed, but she was helpless as the creature lifted her and, with its huge hand, tossed her into the storm and out of sight.

Screaming hysterically, Orrin swung his sword at the creature's furry forearm. The creature avoided his blow and grabbed him, pinning him beneath its back leg. Orrin screamed as the huge beast drove him into the ground, like a cockroach beneath a heel. In a moment, Orrin had stopped screaming.

Then, it raised its fist to crush Raghnall.

"Wait!" I screamed.

The monster turned toward me. It was then that I finally got a real look at it.

It was huge, barely smaller than an elephant. It had silvery-white fur, which covered everything but its hands, feet and face. Its skin was a dark gray, and long teeth overlapped its lips, like a crocodile. Closely resembling a gorilla, I couldn't imagine a more fearsome creature. Its eyes were a stunning blue, and they considered me with curiosity.

"Wait," I repeated softly. The storm had stopped, abating to the quiet still of night. "He doesn't want to hurt you. He's your friend. He wants peace." The creature began advancing toward me. I stumbled back, trying not to show fear. I scrambled to find something to show peace. My hands sunk into my pockets…

And withdrew an orange.

I held it out. It was a strange peace offering. Part of me wanted to put it back in my pocket and look for something else.

The creature cocked its head. It was only a few feet away now—another two steps and I could touch it. A sort of recognition sparked in its eyes—like it understood what I was saying.

"Peace," I said simply.

The creature leaned forward. It was making a sound—at first, I thought it was growling. No, that wasn't it—it was purring.

The creature took the orange.

It sat down with a thump, shaking the ground. Then, delicately, it began to peel the orange with its massive fingers.

I watched, shocked.

"Thank you," a weak voice whispered. I turned. Adran was lying on his side, soaked in blood. "You fixed—" he began to cough.

"Logan!" I looked up. Sanna was running over, her face covered in blood and snow. I felt a burst of relief to see her alive. "You did it!"

Suddenly, a gust of wind slammed into me, knocking me off of my feet. Snow began to swirl around me in a tornado-like fashion. Struggling, I looked up. Through the snow, I could see that the creature was eating the orange, a smile on its face.

And then, nothing. A whirlwind of snow hid everything from my view as the snow pressed me harder to the ground.

And then, the snow stopped. I sat up, gasping.

I was in the stripmall parking lot. It was day, and a foot of snow covered everything. I stood. *Was it a dream?*

And then, I noticed Martin's sword on the ground beside me.

Megan Riann

They're All Our Stars

I am the oldest person alive who doesn't remember the stars. Technically, I was born while their light still reached earth, but I don't remember much from the first nineteen months of my life. Sometimes I wish I could go back and tell my chubby-legged, diaper-butt self to stare at the sky. If she had known those stars would vanish, maybe her toddler brain would have taken care to imprint their shine in our memory. Or maybe she would have blinked and stuffed her round fist in her mouth. Most days I'm sure the latter is the more likely possibility.

Marcella remembers the stars. Being five years older than me, she was nearly seven when the wave of dark matter swept across our pitiful little Milky Way, snatching and bending their light away from us. I think it's comforting to know the stars are physically still out there, that they have not been torn from us completely. I told Marcella that once and she scoffed. "Avy, does it matter if they're there if no one can see them?"

She usually refuses to talk about the stars, though. Just like she refuses to talk about Mom and Dad and the Dark Sickness. Just like she refuses to do much of anything these days.

I shift my bag to my other shoulder, careful of its contents. Ezra's birthday is tomorrow, which means I don't have time to scrounge up more materials if I break anything.

It's a short walk to the outskirts of Celestial City, or Cel as most of us call it. Beyond our lanterns and torches and makeshift power lines, the darkness is like a sentient being. It embraces me, covering my eyes with thick hands. The moon is a sliver against a black backdrop, and it does little to ward off the night. I wonder if it knows the stars are still out there, or if it feels abandoned, too. The humid air clings to my skin like a layer of sweat as I stop to light my lantern. I flick the match against the igniter with the precision of an action repeated many times before.

The lantern creates swaying shadows, but I'm not afraid. I grew up in a world of shadows.

The gravel pathway eventually gives way to the forest which surrounds Cel. Built in the valley between two mountains, Cel is a small puncture of human life in the midst of nature. Our scientists say that the mountains and forests may have protected us against the wave of dark matter. That's why we have the lowest rate of Dark Sickness on this side of the country at only thirty-two percent. They say we are lucky. I say thirty-two percent of us aren't.

Ezra's dad says we should be grateful that the majority of the black matter didn't reach earth. The main wave occurred between our Sun and Proxima Centauri, the second-closest star to us. We merely absorbed the overflow. If it had been a mere four light-years closer, it could have wiped us out instantly or blocked the warmth of our sun. Or done something else horribly unpredictable to destroy our lives. Even now, after years of our world being saturated with dark matter atoms, no one completely understands it.

Despite the darkness, my steps are sure through the wood. Every night for the past week I've been following the same path. The flattened trail of foliage and the thin scratches on my bare calves attest to that. About halfway there, I find a rock shaped like a deformed circle that fits well in my hand. I place it in my bag to use as a hammer for later.

The soles of my feet are beginning to ache. I've been on my feet most of the day at the public daycare. Like most nights, my work shift ended after dark when the last of the kids were picked up by parents with tired eyes and polite smiles.

Finally, I reach the alcove in the side of the mountain. It's tall enough that I can stand, but narrow enough that I can touch both sides with outstretched arms. It'll be the perfect place for what may be my last birthday gift to Ezra tomorrow.

I set the lantern on the cave floor, kneeling to unpack my bag. I take out the rock and the switchblade first, making sure it's securely shut. I set out the nails next, carefully corralling them with my hands so they don't roll away. In total, they cost me over a lantern's worth of oil; building materials are one of the most harshly rationed commodities. Next, I remove the five square wooden boards, scavenged from a wood pallet at an auction.

The last object in my bag is the heaviest and most precious. *Constellations: An Introduction to Celestial Bodies and Their Arrangement.* The text is dense and surprisingly dull, but the photographs are where the value lies. I flip to the dog-eared pages, checking one more time that my carvings match. At this point, I could probably draw the patterns from memory, although I still stumble over their foreign names.

I catch myself smiling as I work, imagining Ezra's face when he sees what I've created. He'll laugh the way that makes his chest shake, and he'll pull me into a hug and press a kiss to my forehead. Then he'll say my name, drawing out the y, and it'll feel like the sun itself is filling me with its warmth.

Years ago, when I told him the same thing I told Marcella—that I was glad the stars were still out there somewhere—he smiled. I didn't know it then, but I loved him for it. "Of course they're still there," he said. "They're just waiting."

I remember frowning. "Waiting for what?" I asked.

"For us," he said, sweeping his arm across our barren sky grandly. "They're our stars for the taking."

"Avy!"

I yelp as I accidentally hit the hammer-rock against my opposite hand. Marcella stands at the mouth of the cave, her hands on her hips. She's wearing her usual summer pajamas—a plain shirt and loose shorts. More than once, people have mistaken her for being my mother. We share the same square jaw and slanted eyes, but our five-year difference is reflected like two decades in the wrinkles around her mouth and the way she seems to squint sourly at the world. "Mar," I say, standing and rubbing my injured hand, "How did you find me?"

"Did you think I wouldn't notice how you've been sneaking out?" she says, "What do you think you're doing here? Don't you have to work tomorrow?"

I step in front of my project, blocking it from her view. I don't have work tomorrow; I have a much more life-changing appointment. "It's a surprise for Ezra," I say.

She walks closer. "Don't you have enough of a surprise for him already?"

I flinch, face warming. "I don't want to talk about that right now."

She pushes past me. Our body heat combined with the lantern makes the cave feel smaller. Despite my objection, she picks up the gift. It's fully assembled now, a cube with one side open. "What is—are these constellations?"

I nod. "Let me show you," I say. There's no point in pulling it away from her now. She might even like it.

I carefully unscrew the glass covering around the lantern, setting it off to the side. I turn the knob to dim the open flame. It can't be too tall or it'll scorch the wood. I lower the cube over the flame. My heart beats faster. The light shines through the carvings, casting dotted sparks of light on the cave walls and ceiling. I smile wide, covering my mouth to stifle a laugh. It's better than I had hoped. I'm sure the locations and proportions of the stars are askew, but I don't care. With a few nails and careful craftsmanship, I have revived the night sky of the past.

When I look to Marcella for approval, my smile drops. Her lips are pursed the same as when she's haggling for something she thinks is too expensive. I'm afraid to ask, but I do anyway, "What do you think?"

"I think this was a cruel idea." She shakes her head, looking away from my makeshift stars. The dim light creates pools of darkness under her eyes.

My gut twists. "Cruel?"

She waves her hand around. "All this is a reminder of what we don't have. It's a reminder of the Dark Sickness and death and how much we're missing."

"No, it's a—a..." I start, balling my fists as I struggle to come up with the right word, "...recreation! I'm giving him something special. He'll love it."

"Are you sure about that?" she says.

Up until this moment, I would have bet my soul on it. But will he think of death when he sees these stars? Will he be reminded of the wave that killed his mom? Will he see it as a reminder of loss? My face burns as I remove the wooden box. "He'll love it," I repeat. He has to. I know him better than anyone. I should be able to give him something perfect.

She shrugs, which means she thinks she's won an argument I didn't even know we were having. "Are you going to tell him about your diagnosis tomorrow, too?" she asks.

I busy my hands with packing my bag. "I'm not going to ruin his birthday with that."

"Doesn't your boyfriend deserve to know?" she presses.

"I don't want to have this conversation right now, Mar."

"If you don't tell him soon, I will."

My gaze snaps to her. "Don't you dare."

"You have to tell him," she says, standing, "It's not fair to him."

"I will."

"You've known for two weeks."

"Maybe—maybe…" I bite my lip. No, I don't have the energy to talk with her about my plan for tomorrow.

"Maybe what?" she says, narrowing her eyes.

"Nothing," I say, knowing she's seeing through my nonchalant act.

"Avy, don't tell me—"

"It's none of your business."

"It is my business if you're going to act like you have dark matter in place of a brain!" she says, clamping her hand on my shoulder. "Don't tell me you're thinking about going to the clinic."

"It's my decision," I say.

Her grip on my shoulder tightens. "No, it's not. I thought we already discussed this. If you go there, you're going to get yourself killed."

I push her hand away, snatching my gift and the switchblade from the floor. "The Dark Sickness is already killing me, even if we can't see it yet," I say. "The clinic is my only chance."

"No!" she argues, with more passion than I've heard from her in a long time. "They'll kill you in there."

"They'll help," I say.

"I won't let you go."

"It's not your choice to make."

"Do you think this is a joke?" she cries, "Avy, this is your life. There is no cure, no matter what the clinic says they're trying to develop. If you go into that building, you'll—"

"I'll die?" I cut her off. "Because that's happening either way. At least I'm doing something about it, instead of sulking around the house like you!"

She takes a step back. I've wounded her. "I won't let you," she repeats.

I swallow. "Please, leave, Marcella."

"I won't let them inject you with whatever drugs or steroids they put in people," she says, "They're not going to help you. Why can't you—?"

"I've already made up my mind," I say.

She presses her palm against the cave wall. "Don't tell me you've already made an appointment."

I stay silent. I know what's going on in her mind. She's remembering when Mom and Dad were sick. That was before the Dark Sickness had a name, before we knew it was a side effect of too much exposure to dark matter. It was before everyone knew what to expect, before we knew there wasn't going to be a recovery. Mom's brain was the first organ to shut down after too many of its cells were replaced with those of dark matter. Dad suffered longer. It was his kidneys that got him. Marcella isn't ready to watch whatever happens to me.

"What is Ezra going to think?" she exclaims. "Do you know how selfish you're being? You're playing with your life!"

"Leave!" I shout, clenching the closed blade harder. "Just leave me alone!"

She lets out a sharp breath like a period at the end of a sentence. She turns abruptly, her braid thumping against her back. As she walks away, I realize she didn't bring a lantern with her. How did she find her way through the woods without one? Or was she trailing me from the beginning? The thought makes my stomach churn.

She doesn't understand, not really. There is nothing like the terror I felt at seeing the diagnosis written on my medical report. Four words in printed, blocky lettering that squeezed the air from my lungs. "Positive for Dark Sickness."

I needed something real to hold onto, something tangible to show that I was not going to allow the sickness to take me so easily. Besides, the first appointment will probably be a simple meeting. I'm prepared to answer questions about my health and let them run whatever tests need to be taken. It's only the first step. I'll still have time tomorrow to have dinner with Ezra and take him here to show him my gift.

Maybe then I'll find the strength to tell him. No, I'll wait until the next day. There will be enough time to break the news, to find the right words to make everything sound a little less horrid than it is.

I take the gift in my lap, flicking open the switchblade. It's dulled with use, but I'm not brave enough to try to sharpen it. By the light of the uncovered flame, I brush my thumb over the bottom of one of the wooden sides and wipe away any lingering dust. I press the knife into the wood and carve simply:

E, They're ours. —A.

"Avy Yosuke?"

"That's me," I say, standing. It seems unnecessary considering the only other person in the room is a middle-aged, white man who smells like smoke. Room is a generous term for this closet-sized space with two chairs and a door on either side.

The young man smiles, holding open the door for me. He wears old-fashioned medical scrubs like the ones in movies that play in the community recreation room. He looks like a child playing dress-up. It almost makes it possible to forget how awfully real this is.

The hallway beyond is narrow, too, and curves around in the shape of an uppercase "L." Bright lights are lodged in the ceiling every few feet, and looking at them makes dark spots flash before my eyes. Most privately-owned buildings can't afford electricity like that. Doors line each side of the hallway, and I catch muffled voices behind some. I'm surprised by how many people seem to be here. It's just after dawn now, early enough that I avoided Marcella this morning and that I'll have enough time to meet Ezra after he gets out of work.

The man opens a door at the crux of the "L" and motions me inside. The room is much larger than where I was waiting. It's different than the pristine, white-washed doctor's office I go to for medical exams, but it's obvious they were trying to mimic that professional feel on a lower budget. The floor is made of white tile squares and there's a sink, a rolling chair, and a small bed. Three of the walls are painted orange and the other is an off-putting shade of red. I'm not sure who thought that would be a pleasing design choice. My eyes are drawn to the wooden cabinets over the sink. What tools or equipment are inside? My heart picks up speed.

"You can sit there," the man says, gesturing to the bed. The mattress creaks when I sit, and it's lower to the floor than I anticipated. I run my hand over the plastic sheets. The man grabs a piece of paper and clipboard from a drawer and asks me some basic questions about my health and family history. My breath catches when he asks how long ago I was diagnosed with the Dark Sickness. It's the first time I've ever said it out loud.

As he asks me questions, I try to guess his age. He doesn't look much older than I, and I wonder how he's qualified for this job. Did they select willing med students to volunteer here? Or is he a random kid in need of some extra cash? He smiles when he's finished. I want to ask him how many people he's treated before. How many of them have died faster because of it.

"Thank you, Ms. Yosuke," he says. "Dr. Hollingsworth will be with you soon." He stands and shakes my hand. He can probably feel how sweaty my palms are. The door clicks shut behind him.

Dr. Hollingsworth sounds like the name of a slug. I imagine an elderly man with rolls of fat in place of a chin. Maybe he's rich enough to fund this little science experiment. Maybe he's trying to get rich by finding a cure. I'm not sure I'll like him.

As promised, it isn't long before the door opens, again. I was right about Dr. Hollingsworth being elderly, but not about much else. For one, she is a woman. She's about how old my parents would be. Gray hair and sagging skin have found her and sunk in their teeth. However, she smiles brightly when she enters and her thinning brows slope outward like opening doors.

"Ms. Yosuke," she says, "it's a pleasure to meet you. I'm Dr. Hollingsworth." She taps the name tag on her breast before shaking my hand.

"It's nice to meet you," I say.

She sits in the chair, scooting closer. She has the clipboard in her hand, but she doesn't refer to it when she speaks. "I understand you were diagnosed two weeks ago. I'm sorry to hear that."

The sincerity in her tone catches me off guard. "Thank you," I say.

"You made this appointment shortly after, correct?" she says.

I nod. It was the earliest one available.

"I understand my clinic can seem like a desperate place, but I assure you, our work is far from unorganized or sloppy," she says. "From what I've read in your file, you seem like a very promising candidate, and I will do everything I can to help make this process more comfortable for you."

I swallow. "My sister thinks I'm crazy for coming here."

She clicks her tongue. "I'm sorry to hear that. Do you feel crazy for coming here?"

I shake my head. This is how I'm going to take control of my life. I say carefully, "I have a lot of things to live for. I figure this is the way to give myself the best chance."

"That's understandable, Ms. Yosuke." She leans forward, pressing the clipboard into her lap. Her perfume smells like lavender. "I won't lie to you. Our methods have a zero percent success rate. However, with each new development, we are working to improve our methods and find a cure. You never know if you'll be the first one we save."

The words are succinct; she's practiced them many times before. It doesn't bring me comfort. I smile. "Thank you, Dr. Hollingsworth."

"Of course," she says, leaning back, again. "Do you mind if I do a quick examination for some baseline numbers?"

"Sure," I say.

When she opens the cupboard, there are no tools with serrated edges or menacing machines. Instead, she goes through the steps of a normal routine check-up. She checks my heart, ears, eyes, and mouth. I don't know where she could have gotten all this medical equipment; specialty devices like stethoscopes and blood pressure cuffs are usually reserved for government research facilities.

With her cool fingers pressed against my wrist, she measures my pulse. When she reaches the bottom of the clipboard, she signs the paper with large, loopy letters.

"Are there any other questions you need to ask me today?" I say. My heart flutters with post-adrenaline nerves. It seems I'll have extra time to get ready to meet Ezra. I wasn't completely set on the blue dress I picked out this morning.

"No, we're all finished with questions," she says. "I actually have a nurse preparing your treatment as we speak. He'll be back shortly, and I'll have you fill out the consent form."

"My treatment?" I exclaim, "I don't understand."

"I'll explain everything," she says, "It's a simple injection into your vein, and it takes less than a minute. Are you afraid of needles?"

"No," I say, wrapping my arms around myself, "but I didn't think you'd be injecting me with anything today. I thought this was a preliminary meeting."

Her patchy brows turn upward. "I'm sorry for that miscommunication, but no, we operate with only one appointment per patient. We don't have enough resources for the volume of people otherwise."

My heart sinks, pushing my stomach against my ribs. The room suddenly feels too compact. I need to get out and give Ezra his gift and wrap my arms around him. I need to pin my hair up and laugh with him over dinner. I need to tell Marcella that she hasn't been a bad sister at all, that I never really want her to leave me. I lick my cracked lips. "I—I wasn't prepared to get any treatment today. Can I reschedule?"

"You could," she says slowly, "but I'm afraid we're booked for about a month out, and by then it's doubtful our treatments would have any effect at all."

Because by then, I'll be in the late stages, if I'm even still alive. My organs will be shutting down one by one until enough switches flip that my body can't operate anymore. If I'm lucky, my heart or brain will go first. I shiver. "Are you sure?"

She doesn't hesitate. "I'm sure, Ms. Yosuke. You can either take the treatment today or nothing at all."

I look at my hands, rubbing my knuckles. "I—I'm sorry, but I just wasn't expecting to make this decision today." I think of my job at the daycare and all the children asking where I am. I picture Marcella tearing through my room to find where I've gone before accepting the reality. Worst of all, I imagine Ezra opening his birthday gift alone with tears in his eyes. It's getting harder to breathe.

"I understand," she says, "Many of our patients decide against treatment at the last moment. You have nothing to be ashamed about."

With her words, I can feel the certainty of death clenching its fist around my throat. "I didn't say I didn't want treatment."

"So was that a yes?" she says.

I swallow, squeezing my eyes shut. I am dying. I am joining the thirty-two percent. These past two weeks have been emotional agony. Will I be able to handle another month? How will I cope when the physical pain starts? Will I have the strength to say good-bye to those I love when I can't even work up the courage to tell them the diagnosis? I press my fingers against my lips.

The door opens, but I don't look up. The doctor exchanges some words with the nurse, and the door closes again. Metal clinks against metal.

"Ms. Yosuke," Dr. Hollingsworth says, "I do need your verbal and written consent if we're going to proceed with treatment."

I look up, taking a deep breath. She passes the clipboard to me.

As I scan the agreement, the words "...in the case of unfore-seen side effects, including death..." scream off the page. There's a good chance that all this will do is make the date on my tombstone a few weeks earlier. Maybe I'm a coward. Or maybe death will find me either way, and I'd rather meet him on my own terms.

"Do you expect I'll..." I can't find the strength to finish the sentence. I swallow and rephrase. "How long does the treatment take to act?"

"It has varied greatly, but our last few trials similar to this particular treatment have been fast-acting," she says. "Its full effects will most likely be seen in less than a week."

Meaning I'll likely be dead or healed by then. "Will it hurt?" I ask.

Her brows draw together in pity. "Again, it varies greatly between patients, but it is not uncommon to experience discomfort."

Anxiety crawls down my spine and burrows into my belly. But could it be any worse than succumbing to the Dark Sickness? I know my atoms are already being displaced and overrun by dark matter, but it will be different when I can feel the effects. When I was twelve, my neighbor lost his eyesight and the movement of his legs before dying. One person in the newspaper had several severe strokes. My body will lose this battle eventually, and it will likely not go peacefully.

I sign at the bottom of the consent form. My middle name is the same as my mother's. Would she approve of me being here? She's too dead to answer.

Dr. Hollingsworth picks up a syringe from the metal tray. The liquid inside is cloudy like the saltwater Marcella used to make me gargle when I got a sore throat. I fight the urge to gag.

"Now, you will be the first patient to try this particular treatment," she says. She carries the syringe comfortably as if it were as normal as holding a pencil. "Do you confirm that you are here of your own free will and that you are willingly receiving this treatment?"

"Yes," I say. I don't try to keep my voice from shaking. She takes the clipboard from me. I keep my eyes on the syringe.

"Can you lay down for me?" she asks.

I do so. The plastic covering on the bed sticks to my sweaty thighs and palms. From this perspective, the red wall looks closer to the color of blood. Is this where I am going to die? Is this bland, water-stained ceiling going to be the last thing I ever see? Or maybe I will have a whole week. Maybe I'll have time to sink into Ezra's arms one last time. Maybe I'll suddenly collapse in front of the kids at the daycare. My heart beats faster until I'm sure all of Cel can hear it. Everything is moving too quickly.

"Now, it's not uncommon for people to pass out after treatment," she says, "There's no need to panic if that happens; just allow your body to relax."

My shoulders tighten. "How many—Do people usually wake up?" I ask.

She nods earnestly. "The majority of patients wake up within twenty-four hours. It's simply your body reacting and absorbing the treatment."

Just like the majority of people here don't get the Dark Sickness.

"Are you ready?" she asks.

I nod. If I open my mouth, I'm not sure I'll be able to keep the word "no" from leaping out. The plastic crinkles. My hair sticks to the back of my neck.

"If you're afraid of needles, now is when you should look away," she says. She bends over me, pressing her fingers over the inside of my elbow to pinpoint my vein. The pressure feels oddly intimate. I wonder if she believes this will work, or if she's anticipating carrying me out in a body bag.

I watch as she inserts the syringe. There's a sharp sting when the metal first slips under my skin, but it's relatively painless. Dr. Hollingsworth knows what she's doing. A sudden rush of coolness spreads up my arm as she presses the plunger.

I close my eyes.

"Ms. Yosuke?"

My hand is against something solid. Fingers intertwine with mine.

"Avy," Ezra's voice says. He draws out the y. His breath is warm on my cheek.

I open my eyes. The water stains on the ceiling stare back at me.

"Ezra?" I croak. Moisture has left my mouth. How long have I been unconscious? How did Ezra find me here?

"Yeah, it's me. You're going to be okay," he says. "Marcella went to get some food, but she'll be so happy to see you awake when she gets back." He gives my hand a squeeze. I try to squeeze back, but I'm not sure the signal makes it from my brain to my hand.

Something cool presses against my lips. "Drink," Dr. Hollingsworth says. I part my lips, letting the water slip down my desert of a throat. I finish the glass. It gives me enough strength to turn my head. Dr. Hollingsworth sits back in her chair, writing furiously on a clipboard. Ezra kneels beside the bed, his glossy eyes shining with concern as he looks over my face. His tan skin is flushed and dark stubble covers his chin.

I swallow. "I'm sorry," I say. "I—"

"Don't apologize, Avy," he says, brushing a hand over my hair. "I wish you would have been honest with me, but we can talk about that later. How are you feeling?"

How *am* I feeling? I test my feet first, pointing my toes and hearing the crinkle of my shoes against plastic. I'm suddenly conscious of my breathing, the steady in and out of air through my nostrils. An IV trails over my arm and disappears under my skin. Nothing hurts. With every moment, things feel like they're coming into sharper focus. I swallow, again. "I feel fine," I say.

"Fine?" Dr. Hollingsworth interjects. "Ms. Yosuke, you're by no means clear as it's only been a few days, but this is very promising. I don't like to give false hope, but I do think something special is happening here. Do you understand what this means?"

It means I'm alive. It means maybe I haven't made the biggest impulsive mistake of my life. It means I have time to tell Marcella that I love her. It means I get to show Ezra that I will never keep something from him, again. I move to sit up.

"Hey, take it easy," Ezra says softly, pressing my shoulder back against the bed. The mattress lets out a distressed whine.

"I missed your birthday," I say. This time I know my fingers give his a gentle squeeze.

"That's not the important thing right now," he says.

I shake my head. "I have to show you our stars."

Alefiya Presswala

Creatures of the Underground

Blood flows from my ankle and leaves a trail of red on the ground. My ankle has scratched up against one of those incredibly jagged rocks, and the sweltering heat is only making everything more sticky and gross. I'm lucky though. This isn't even the worst of a typical Tagros summer.

Anywhere else, summer is a season to be celebrated. Other countries have large festivals in honor of the summer solstice and everyone is happy forever or something like that. But here in our *beautiful* disease-filled nation of Tagros, summer makes everything worse.

It all started three years ago, when my colleague Uma and I noticed a new type of bug flying around at our workplace, Vesonius Corp. It dug all over Tagros soil, infested kitchens and schools. And it multiplied like hell. By the end of a few weeks, Tagros was completely invaded. We called it the Uzvos. It was actually quite fascinating at first, trying to figure out where these blue and yellow insects had come from, but it quickly became horrifying. People were starting to get sick, with what Uma and I called Uzvosis. The Uzvos contaminated everything they touched, especially land, which was especially unfortunate for the people of

Tagros, because our entire economy is built on agriculture and gardening. I myself am just another daughter in a farming family.

To make matters worse, the heat of the sun made the disease even more contagious. The people of Tagros were entirely too slow to realize this. In fact, the head scientist of our group, Vienna Watts, was the first to pass away. President Braum assigned Uma, a few other scientists from Vesonius and I to search for and study new land in hopes of rebuilding Tagros, and maybe even a cure to Uzvosis.

I replay the president's speech in my head everyday and laugh. I'm not even exaggerating. I laugh every time."Our brilliant scientists, Dr. May Kuliq, Uma Golwic, Atrana Wood, Iniq Blakis, and Karl Obhil are going to bring life back into Tagros. They are going to save us." Except that it's been three years and we have only just found new land that may not have been contaminated. Meanwhile, the population of Tagros has dwindled from a grand population to a pathetic crowd.

Uma is the only thing keeping me going. Truly. She is the happiest person I've ever met, even in times like these.

She comes over and hands me a cloth for my bloody ankle. Her blonde bob shines in the sun and she gives me a sparkling smile. "Tough day, huh?"

"No, no! What makes you say that?" I start wrapping the cloth tightly around my wound.

Uma helps me up. "Come on, we're so close. I can feel it. We are so close to a huge breakthrough."

Yeah, right. I search through my tools and grab three little baggies to fill with land samples. We have been digging in a territory of Tagros called the "Mud Mountains." It's basically a section of land that's covered in huge mounds of dirt, and as far as we know, every single pile could consist of a different type of soil. Our job is to dig through the piles, take samples of the soil, and then analyze it.

I've been working on a mound of soil for the past week. It's reddish-brown and there are little golden speckles distributed throughout. I'm calling it Teslica Soil. I'm digging and filling my baggies, digging and filling, digging and filling, and suddenly, I see something move. It's not the usual worm or centipede that you're expecting to find. It's something faster, more excited to be moving.

I quickly tie my curly hair, which is now extremely frizzy, up in a bun and lean down closer to try and see what is in the soil. Another one of those creatures scurries rapidly through the dirt and in an attempt to crouch down and capture it, I fall right into, face-first. The Teslica blends into my scalp, which is the same color, but there are some very easy to see maroon patches all over my light brown skin.

"Damnit!" I brush the red particles off my legs as I get up. "Stop laughing, Uma."

Uma giggles and hands me a water bottle. "What's tripping you up?"

I shake my head. "I'm not sure. I thought I saw a new bug, but it's so fast. I don't know. Maybe I'm going crazy, maybe I've finally been infected by the Uzvos." I pretend to dramatically fall over.

"Hey. Not funny. Who knows, maybe you did discover something. You should report it to May."

"Sure thing," I say to Uma, saluting her sarcastically.

Uma smirks and leaves me alone with my shovel. Something in my gut is telling me to stop thinking about the thing in the soil and just go back to analyzing my samples, but there's another part of me that wants to figure out exactly what it is.

I grab the shovel and start digging where I had been before. I dig for hours and hours and hours, and still nothing, not even one flicker of movement from that little bug, or whatever it was. Soon, Uma and the others start to pack up their things.

"Atrana, we're going back to the lab. It's been a long day, we all deserve some rest," Dr. Kuliq says to me. She took over after Vienna died.

I nod and tell her, "Uh, I think I'm going to stay out here a little longer. I'm not too tired."

"Are you sure?"

I nod again.

"Okay. Be careful. Don't stay out too long, and if you find anything, I'm the first to know."

I watch them leave and wait until they're all completely out of Mud Mountain territory to start digging again. As I dig, my mind wanders back to the day that Uma and I actually discovered the Uzvos. We reported it to Vienna and she was so excited. Uma and I, we were only interns, and we only had the internship with the incredible Vienna Watts because my aunt was her sister's best friend. She was so ecstatic about our find that she immediately gave Uma and I promotions and let us start working with May, Iniq, and Karl, the current members of our team.

Vienna became like an older sister to me. She was truly incredible, she balanced her work, personal and social lives so well together, and she was always up for a new experiment. She also always had some type of purple item, besides her dark violet glasses, whether it was a purple shirt, or small purple earrings, something was always purple. Vienna Watts was the first to pass away from Uzvosis. Uma and I were devastated. It was like a piece of ourselves had just disappeared. Actually, Vienna passed away just a week before my parents and Uma's brother. And while Uma worked on finding new sciences and cures for Uzvosis, I wallowed away. In fact, the only reason I'm at this job right now is to honor Vienna.

We haven't really made any progress in the last few years, but Uma always says we're super close to getting there. *Bullshit*, is what I think, until suddenly, I bring up my shovel to throw aside another chunk of Teslica, and then I notice a little group of bugs I've never seen before. They are metallic looking, and they give off a light purple shine. There seem to be about five of them, and every single one scurries and scrambles across the shovel hurriedly in all different directions.

I've found them.

I quickly grab one and put it into one of my baggies and then continue to shovel. Just then, my shovel hits something hard, something that almost sounds like some type of stone or rigid material. I jam my shovel down into the ground, and there's the sound again, but it doesn't look like anything is there.

I bend down and feel around the Teslica. There's definitely a hard surface, so I brush away any excess Teslica until all I can feel is the smooth, hard surface.

Well, that's strange. I know that there is no more Teslica where I'm touching, because it's definitely glass or some type of transparent stone, but it still looks like there's Teslica there. It's almost as if someone wanted whatever is buried under here to blend right in. *Very strange.*

I can hear Dr. Kuliq's voice in my head right now, telling me not to do this. "Atrana, focus on what your task actually is."

But then I think of Vienna and her curiosity. She would definitely want to know what's under there.

I take a deep breath and hit the surface hard with my shovel. When that doesn't do the trick, I start jumping up and down on the hard exterior, trying to make even a crack in it. Even that doesn't do it. Whoever buried this *really* didn't want it to be found. I look closer at the stone and notice that one of those new purple bugs is scurrying across the surface. And then I realize that they're cutting an opening in the stone or whatever it is. It's almost as if they've revealed a secret trapdoor to me. There's no way their little legs are so powerful. Or are they? There's numerous amounts of possibilities, to be honest, because I know absolutely nothing about these bugs, which I decide to call Imorters. I grab a water bottle, a notebook and pen, my baggie with the Imorter in it and hop through the opening in the stone.

I hear a scratching sound and look up to see that the Imorters who opened the stone for me are now closing it, and wherever they move, they bring Teslica soil with them, to cover the stone up.

How are they doing that? More importantly, where am I and did the Imorters just block my only way out?

I can't even answer those questions because it's so dark in this room, dungeon, wherever I am. I start to panic and thoughts of dying out here run through my head. Atrana Wood, get a grip, I think to myself.

I crouch to the ground. Maybe I can feel around and figure out what my surroundings are. The shine that the Imorter gives off makes it the slightest bit easier to see, so I bring it down to the ground with me. I see red and gold speckles. Definitely Teslica soil. I can work with that.

I get up, and using the Imorter as a miniscule flashlight, I start walking, and just like that, there is light. Wherever I am, it's high tech. Only a genius would be able to make motion sensor work in a place like Tagros, much less underground. As I walk, I notice the walls are made up of Juhes rock, a sturdy gray material only found in Tagros. Good choice, mystery genius.

There are fluorescent green dash marks drawn on the Teslica, but not in a straight line. The dashes twist and turn, like a warning to only step in those certain spots. I heed the "warning" and hop from green to green.

As I'm walking, I realize that this is a tunnel, and it definitely belongs to a scientist or a mathematician of some sort. There are equations, arrows, question marks, descriptions covering the Juhes rock walls of the tunnel. I keep walking until I reach a fork in the road. The pathway breaks off into three separate ones.

I look around me and take in the sights. It's absolutely beautiful. There are three glass boxes, and I think I can see more if I go further ahead. The boxes are filled with amazing looking creatures, but none that I've seen before, which is even more fascinating, because this is quite literally, my entire life.

I can see myself in the glass. It's like a strange mirror. I can barely see my pupils in my dark eyes but my hair is bigger and curlier than ever, thanks to the Tagros heat. My skin is covered in random patches of Teslica. I look like I've come straight from hell.

My curiosity about the new animals around me tears me away from myself. The cage straight in front of me is filled with bird-like animals. They have long, sharp, cotton candy pink beaks, with blinding yellow bodies that are covered in scales, rather than feathers. Their eyes are pure, extremely white. They don't chirp or squawk, they just kind of hum. Interesting. The label on the cage names them as Rhaccas. They are so enchanting. I step inside the cage, which turns out to be a very stupid move on my part. I try to be quiet as I observe them, but I accidentally step on a branch on the bottom of the cage and one of the Rhaccas turns it head. I freeze, being careful not to make one sound. It only stares at me, though, so I start moving again, observing and taking notes as I do. Then I hear it. The humming sound that I heard from the Rhaccas is getting louder and louder. I am in the middle of the cage, and all six of the Rhaccas have their heads turned toward me. The white eyes that I thought were so elegant before I stepped in here have officially become creepy. Their humming collectively becomes louder and louder, and suddenly all six Rhaccas are flying at me, full speed. They scratch at my arms, legs, face, and even pull out chunks of my hair. What are these things?

I scream for help, but evidently, there is nobody else down here. All of a sudden, out of nowhere, the Rhaccas completely stop and fly back to their perches. Thank the lord, the heavens, everything up there, except for the fact that my notebook is completely shredded, and the gray joggers and shirt I had on have many, many holes in them. Oh, and half of my hair is missing.

Next.

The glass cage on my right has some type of veiny plant in it. It's a light blue color and it's moving constantly, even though there is no wind or force that could cause it to move. Magenta berries grow off of it. The label on the cage says "Dirae." The Dirae look magical. They shimmer in the light and it's so beautiful, even more beautiful than the Rhaccas. Of course not having learned my lesson with the Rhaccas, I step instead the Dirae box. The Dirae wraps itself around me gently, its many branches tickling the scratches that the Rhaccas left. I'm giggling and my mind is wandering. It's like I'm in a dream or a fantasy and all my wildest desires are coming true, but the funny part is that all I'm doing is standing in the middle of a Dirae plant. It pops one of its berries into my mouth. *Wow.* This is incredible. The berry has a tangy, sweet, spicy flavor all at the same time. I think I even taste some Salytyr acid, a rare juice native to Tagros. This feels like an out of body experience, I think I might be losing my mind.

Something bites my arm—I think it might be the Imorter in my pocket—and all my common sense comes rushing back. I realize I don't know one thing about the Dirae and whether their berries are safe to eat. I quickly spit the remaining bits off my tongue in an effort to not get poisoned. Bad idea. The Dirae seem to take this as an offense and it wraps its arms around me extremely tightly. The dream is over and this has become a nightmare. The Dirae's arms keep closing in, until I'm gasping for air. Just as I feel like all life is about to exit my body, the Dirae lets go, just like what happened with the Rhaccas. These creatures obviously have an instinct to kill, so why aren't they doing it? And where did they even come from in the first place?

I step away from the Dirae, and turn to my left, where the glass cage is *filled* to the brim with Imortems. The cage almost seems to be vibrating and the Imortems seem to be jumping around, gaining more energy by the second, but honestly, the cage is so filled with them, I'm not even sure how they have space to move. The label actually says "Stekij," but I think Imortem rolls off the tongue nicer. "Look," I say to the one in my pocket, "it's your family!" I wonder how the Imortems can breathe in that container. Maybe they don't even need to breathe to be able to live. Who knows? Definitely not me.

I step closer to the glass, but not inside, because I can't really know what to expect. Each one seems to be smiling; they look so friendly. I make sure not to fall for their appearance because their actions may not be so friendly. This time, however, they come to me. The Imortems cut through the glass, just like they did when I was still above ground, and surround me. They form a circle around me and spin very fast, and they don't really make any type of sound, but they seem happy. I can feel it. The huge colony of Imortems forms the shape of an arrow and starts moving through the tunnel.

We pass hundreds, maybe even thousands of cages, all filled with exotic animals and insects. None of them are native to Tagros and I've never heard of them being from any other nation either. We pass creatures similar to snakes, birds, lizards, ants, even dogs, but none of them are quite what they resemble. There's always a different trait that they have, something very different from what they look like. I wish I had my notebook. Uma and May would kill to see this.

Finally, the Imortems halt a few feet away from a glass cage. There's green dashes leading This one's far away from all the others. It has a sheet covering it and there's no light shining on it, but I can hear violent, rattling sounds from inside. I would know that sound anywhere. Uzvos.

I can feel my heart beating rapidly. Is this where they came from? If it is, we're even farther from finding uncontaminated land than I thought. The Imortems give me a slight nudge toward the cage, and I'm cautious, making sure I only step on the green dashes. I pull the sheet off the cage, and as soon as I do, all the Imortems scurry away, except the little one in my pocket. The Uzvos snarl and growl at me, blue and yellow flying everywhere, making tiny spots of green.

I stare at the cage. Just like the Imortems, there's so many of the Uzvos that they barely have any space to move. How is this *possible*?

I can't take my eyes off of them. A wave of defeat crashes over me. This whole time, I've been digging through Teslica and all other types of soil to find any sources of contamination and its been under us the entire time. The cause of Tagros ruin all started here. Maybe if I'd been quicker in finding this place, so many people wouldn't be dead. Maybe—wait. What in Tagros is that?

The Uzvos are devouring a black leather notebook and its pages. Has somebody been down here before? Maybe the person who owns these creatures?

I try and think about how to get the notebook. I have to see what's in there. For all I know, I could be trapped in here forever and nobody would know. That notebook could be my only chance at survival.

There's no way for me to get the notebook without opening the cage door and potentially releasing the Uzvos and getting myself killed. Unless I can open the cage without the Uzvos noticing.

I urge the Imortem out of my pocket and point toward the very bottom of the cage. The Imortem seems to know exactly what I'm saying, but won't move. "Come on! You brought me here!"

The Imortem cuts a hole in the glass, small enough for me to grab the notebook and pull it out. But the Uzvos notice me and they don't chase after me but my right arm is covered in bites once I pull it out. Three years of studying these pests and how to cure ourselves of them, and I've finally been infected. On a more positive note, I've gotten ahold of the notebook.

I pour some water on the places where I know for sure the Uzvos bit me, but the tricky thing with these bugs is that some of their bites are invisible, so you never really know just how infected you are. I bend down and lean my back against the Juhes rock.

The Uzvos poison is already starting to set in. My eyes are burning and I feel slightly fatigued, but the worst is yet to come. Soon there will be red, burning, itching spots all over my body, wherever the Uzvos touched me. And then, I will become incredibly dizzy, so dizzy, until I eventually go blind. Blindness will be the last stage in my deterioration before I finally die.

Good lord. This can't be the way I go. Oh, but it is. I, Atrana Wood, the girl who spent her entire career studying wild bugs and plants, the girl who *discovered* the Uzvos and spent three years studying them, gets attacked by a swarm and dies underground, alone? I can already see the headlines in the Tagros Tell-All. What a complete embarrassment.

I am weak, but nonetheless, I am still curious. The Imortem crawls onto my knee, as I open the notebook, the bundle of paper that I am going to lose my life for. I hope it's worth it.

Several pages of the notebook are torn, but purple ink covers the pages. The Imortem crawls onto one of the pages, and when it gets up again, there is a blotch of purple ink. All this writing has been done using an Imortem. Imortem ink. How interesting. I wonder what else these creatures can do.

I start reading the pages. The beginning is observations about animals I actually know about: uhnias, likuys, etc, etc. But then the entries get a little weird. There are entries about classified entries from Vesonius Corp. Stuff that only people like Uma and I should know.

Today, I created a monstrosity. The Rhaccas are insanely violent. They look like majestic animals, but the way they attack you is terrifying. It's quite possible that they would be amazing killers. I've been breeding different creatures and I'm trying to make them friendly, so that they are loyal and they can protect you. But every single one turns out fine until I do something to offend it. Only the Stekij are completely loyal to me.

Another entry, two weeks later:

Uma and Atrana discovered my insect today. They called it the Uzvos and they were so excited when they brought it to me. Quite frankly, I was extremely excited too. In my excitement, I gave them both promotions. Not that they were undeserved, of course. Uma is always ready for something new, and she has an amazing work ethic, and Atrana is brilliant. She has a way of noticing things that nobody else does. The Uzvos will help fertilize the soil and make the Tagros economy and industry even better. Hopefully everything goes as planned.

My heart drops, and it's not just because of the Uzvos poison. Vienna Watts created all of this. This is *her* lab. She bred these animals, for what purpose, I don't know, but what I do know, is that she created the Uzvos in her lab, and she spread the disease. If I felt defeated before, I definitely feel it even more now.

I run my hands over the pages, over her words. It makes so much sense that she was the first one to pass away. She spent the most time around them. I flip the pages, and touch all the words.

Something is happening. I'm not in my head anymore. I think I'm in Vienna's. The Imortem ink has somehow caused me to see Vienna's memories in her point of view as I read and touch the ink.

I see 20 year old Atrana, jumping up and down while showing Vienna the Uzvos. She already knows what it is, but she's just as excited. I see her walking through this lab, writing down observations on the Juhes rock when she's run out of paper.

And then finally, I see Uma and I walking into Vienna's office at Vesonius, breaking the news of Uzvosis, how five people are already injured. I see Vienna, rushing to this lab, trying to grab an Uzvos, and getting bitten instead. She knows it's basically over, and for the next week, she covers every red spot with makeup. But she doesn't give up, instead she starts working toward a cure in her last week of life.

In her head, I notice equations, notes, scribbled with black paint on Juhes. I need to figure out where that location is. Before I can, I double over in pain. Those damned tiny bugs. Groaning, I open Vienna's notebook back to where I was and touch the ink, hoping to be sent back to her memories again, but it doesn't work.

Oh no. It looks like I'm going to have to find it all on my own. I stumble around, looking for writing on the Juhes surrounding me, hoping to find anything similar to what I saw in Vienna's memories. Red spots are starting to show up on my legs, and it's becoming increasingly difficult to walk, so I decide to crawl. I finally find the word Uzvosis written in big, bolded black letters in an area where there are no cages at all, in a corner across from the Uzvos.

There are symbols written that I can't understand at all, or maybe they're numbers and letters, and the Uzvos's poison is really starting to settle in but this isn't good at all. Red spots cover my hands and fingers entirely, but I don't realize this until I've rubbed them into my eyes in an effort to understand Vienna's notes better.

I fall backward and collapse onto the ground. This really can't be the way it ends. I refuse.

I get back up and stare at the black writing again. Vienna definitely *was* using some secret type of code, so people wouldn't steal her ideas, but I don't even need to crack it.

The main takeaway that I get from her notes is that the Uzvos mainly consist of a chemical called Kewadr, which acts as a fertilizer when released into Tagros soil, but as a poison when released into blood.

Vienna's notes tell me that the only way to reverse the effects of the Kewadr is to put two other substances—Turae and Kiher—all mixed together into the body.

I ponder on this information for a little while. Those three elements are so difficult to find, much less mixed together. The antidote is nearly impossible to come across.

Except it's not if you are the company who produces Tagros's supply of Salytyr acid. Turae and Kiher both appear in Salytyr acid, which is also one of the ingredients in the magenta berries that the Dirae tried to feed me earlier!

I'm so excited I can barely breathe. That, and I still have Uzvos poison running through my veins. All I have to do is get to the

Dirae, take the berries and get out of here and tell May and Uma. How hard could it be?

Very hard, apparently, because a snake like creature that somehow has legs has gotten out of its cage. It's moving toward me, and it doesn't look too happy either.

"Okay buddy, it's okay, we're all friends here. We're happy, we're friendly, we all just want to get along." The thing hisses at me.

"Okay, okay, we don't have to be friends." I let out a nervous laugh, and this time the thing growls at me. And of course, with my luck, at that exact moment, my body goes limp, and I fall to the ground. *You've got to be kidding me.*

The beast scratches my face deeply, which will definitely leave a scar, but that's the least of my worries right now. As I'm struggling to get loose from this snake thing that's now wrapping itself around my leg, I hear a huge racket in the background. All of Vienna's creatures are banging themselves against their respective cages. One by one, the cages start to tip over and break, and the creatures are free. Vienna, if you're up there, what the *hell*?

Creatures fly, crawl, and slither toward me. The Usvoz cover my scalp and bite me everywhere. I scream and yelp in pain, but it's no use. Nobody can even hear me, and these animals definitely aren't getting off me anytime soon. It's either I die from my Uzvosis, Vienna's creatures rip me apart, or I get to the Dirae and survive.

My head is spinning, and all I can is a rainbow blur of colors around me, but I keep moving. The animals are weighing me down, and I feel like molasses, so so slow, but I keep moving. I just have to keep moving.

I get to the Dirae, and just like the others, they have also broken their cage. The Dirae wraps itself around me, so tightly that the other creatures have to let go of me so that they don't meet the same lovely fate that I'm about to.

The Dirae squeezes and squeezes and squeezes. I struggle to grab one of its berries, and I'm so close but at the last moment, the Dirae moves it away from me. It's like it's laughing at me, reveling in my misery. How evil.

At this point, my arms are flailing anywhere and everywhere, in hopes of grabbing just one berry, just to take this painful, burning sensation away from my body. My vision is blurry and fading. I can barely see where anything is, or what's even happening around me. I realize this is it. It's happening. Wow. Is that the light?

Nope. It's my Imortem! My dear Imortem, my saving grace! It flies toward me, with a magenta berry in its mouth. Immediately, I swallow and let it float around my system. The berry is starting to soothe the burning and itching, and some red spots are even fading away, but my body goes limp, and I fall over, my eyes closing.

Maybe the berries didn't work, maybe I was wrong about the Salytyr acid being in them. Maybe—

I open my eyes slowly.

Uma, May, and the rest of my team are staring at me as I lie on the ground. Am I dead? Is this heaven? Or hell? No way Uma would be in hell. Mayb—

Uma's voice stops my thoughts from racing all over the place. Her smile washes a wave of relief over my body. "What happened to you? You're so tense, Atrana."

She's right. I unclench my fists, and five magenta berries roll out. The team helps me slowly get up. The red spots are gone, and I can see perfectly. I smile.

"I just went on a little adventure."

Lenicka Lee

Dangers of the Deep

Rules to Follow When Sailing the Deep:
1. Always have a Blessed travel with you, when possible. They give you the Earth Mother's blessing on your journey and their Totems help guard you from creatures that target thoughts.
2. Never speak unless absolutely necessary. Any sound can draw the attention of the Deep.
3. Keep a large supply of paper and bottles. The Deep cannot understand our language, so any messages written could potentially save you from a horrible fate.
4. If a creature locates you, hide first. It may be following its own instincts and not controlled by the Deep. If it attacks, be prepared to fight it off.
5. Never swim in unnaturally dark water. This is the domain of the Deep and it will not hesitate to destroy you for trespassing.

Good luck on your voyage, brave traveler! May you accomplish the impossible.

The ship had been beautiful. A brilliant, three-masted ship, *The Landguard* had been the pride of the shipyard. She'd sailed a few weeks ago, determined to prove the Deep could be beaten.

Now she floated into harbor, masts broken and burned, with no sign of her crew anywhere. Her glory was reduced to ashes. The sight of her was enough to chill any heart, for she was a testament of the Deep's victory.

Elix could not tear his gaze away, an old, familiar ache rising in his chest. His brother had captained *The Landguard*. Rhoden had been so proud, so excited to sail the Deep. Now he was gone, with no story to explain how or why. Just like Dad.

Elix was very aware of his resemblance to his father, with the same blond hair and dark brown eyes. He even carried his father's sword, a parting gift given a few months before his father's disappearance. It had been a little over a year since Veltner, owner of the shipyard, was lost at sea. Elix's mom, Anya, had taken over, but it would never be the same. Now the same tragedy had happened to Rhoden. But this time it was worse, because his ship had found its way home without him. There was no doubt of his death.

The pain in Elix's chest spiked when he realized he needed to tell his mom. Already, he could picture the despair in his mother's eyes that she would desperately try to hide behind a wall of suppressed emotions. Her sadness would rival his own and, to be honest, he wasn't sure if they could handle more heartbreak. At least when his father went missing, Rhoden had been present to mourn with them.

Finally, he forced himself away from the burned ship, letting the dock workers handle the salvaging. His leaden steps took him toward his mother's office. He hesitated in front of the door with his hand poised over the knob. Steeling himself, he twisted it and stepped quietly inside.

His mom didn't notice his entrance. She huddled over a stack of paperwork at her desk. The past year had not been kind to her. Her dark hair had grayed, and her eyes had lost their spark. Life was returning to them slowly, but now he feared she would lose the glint again. He cleared his throat. Startled, his mom looked up from her writing. She took one look at his haunted expression and immediately paled, highlighting the dark circles under her eyes.

"The—" Elix coughed, not sure if the words would even come. "*The Landguard* has returned to port."

"What?"

He looked down and his voice was barely a whisper as he said, "Damaged and unmanned."

"Unmanned..." she repeated. A wild desperation illuminated her face and she shoved past him at a dead run.

"Mom!" he called.

Debating for a second, he bit his lip before running after her. He chased her back to the docks, before she collapsed in the sand within sight of *The Landguard.* She moaned, her tearstained face refusing to look anywhere but at the burned ship.

"Not my son too. Please, not him," she said.

Elix blinked away tears of his own and settled into the sand next to her, wrapping her in a hug. Her sobs shook them both. He whispered, "We'll be okay, Mom. We got through this once, and we'll do it again. We'll be okay."

He said the words partly to convince himself. Taking a shaky breath, he offered silent prayers into the Earth beneath his feet. *May the Earth Mother receive your soul with joy, Rhoden. And may she protect us.*

The next day, Elix tried to resume normal life. Everywhere he went, there were pitying faces. The sad looks didn't fill the hollowness inside. He focused on his task, overseeing the preparation of a small vessel for ocean travel.

"This is useless, and you know it," one of the dockworkers said, a little too loudly, halting his labor. "Sure, sure, ocean trading is the next step of civilization. But there won't be any civilization left if the Deep kills us all."

Elix winced but held his tongue. The worker continued.

"You know what happened to our dear Anya's own husband. Now she's lost her eldest son too. This job will end with the death of us all, mark my words." The worker looked in Elix's direction and spat. "You or the ma'am's next and I won't be dragged down with you. I quit."

The worker marched away, ignoring the entreating voices of his companions. "What a bunch of idiots you all are. Go die, if that's what you want so much."

Elix was too empty to do much more than watch him disappear around a building. There were always those who disagreed with their mission. Rhoden had always... The wounds were still too fresh. He realized everyone was looking at him.

"Carry on," he muttered, turning and walking away himself.

Trying to console his sore heart, his distracted wandering led him to the beach. A fundamental piece of his life was gone with no compensation. He found he couldn't blame the dockworker for his decision to walk out on all this. Sometimes he wished he could do the same. But too much of his life, and his family's life, was invested in making ocean travel possible. Two family members were victims of that investment and he hoped that would be final price they had to pay.

Ocean travel was necessary. Society was expanding and ocean trade allowed for convenience beyond that of overland travel. Society had been crippled long enough by the fear of the Deep, a being that dwelt in deep water. Fear of the Deep had become synonymous with the fear of where it lurked and often people referred to them interchangeably.

The Deep was created long ago during a dispute between Tivona the earth goddess and Urrio the sea god. The gods' existence in spiritual forms severely limited their capacity to affect the physical world. In an attempt to overcome this physical barrier, Urrio created the Deep, an independent off-shoot of his power. The Deep lived in the physical realm, controlling the minds of anything submerged in water and bending their wills to its darker one.

The Deep was more beast than person and didn't understand human language. It could not communicate, and it only acted instinctually, so Elix hoped it could be conquered.

Standing at the shore, he gathered his resolve, trying to decide what his family and their shipyard stood for. There would always be doubters, like the dockworker. And there would probably be more casualties too. He winced at the thought. He wished Rhoden, the fire of the mission, could be there to spur them on. Elix drew in a deep breath, realizing how much he missed his brother. Getting used to his absence would be harder than he thought.

The crashing waves seemed to challenge him, laughing at him with the force of their pounding. They housed the one thing his culture feared more than anything. He straightened and issued his own mental challenge to the waves.

Something caught his eye. Amid the pounding, an object floated, eventually pushed to shore only a few feet from where he stood.

It was a bottle, with a piece of paper inside.

He stumbled closer to pick it up. There was some water inside the bottle, so the paper was thoroughly drenched. He could make out the still legible writing, despite the ocean blurring the ink.

He ripped out the cork, dumping out the water. Not wanting to tear the paper by forcing it through the mouth of the bottle, he searched for something to smash open the bottle. The bottle shattered completely against a rock, and he kneeled in the sand to retrieve the paper from the broken glass. He brushed the shards away and gingerly laid the message out flat on the rock. His heart pounded as he deciphered the scrawled words.

Dear Family,

I do not know whether this message will even reach you, but I pray it does. My ship was attacked by beasts of the Deep that we have never seen before. The creatures had completely translucent bodies, appearing as small humanoid figures made of water. We tried to speak to them, but they made no answer. I believe them to be some form of water sprite that ventured too far down and was taken and controlled by the Deep.

The sprites swarmed my ship, outnumbering my crew of fifteen by at least ten. Half of the beasts targeted us, and the other half concentrated on our lanterns, seeming fascinated by the flickering light. My men started dying. Their swords were useless against the sprites, who attacked by drowning them in their watery bodies. The first beast smashed a lantern on deck, igniting my ship almost instantly. The fire spread quickly as more lanterns were destroyed. The beast I was fighting knocked me into the ocean and immediately I felt something pulling me deeper. I fought, slicing the water beneath me with my sword. I hit something and the water around me was briefly illuminated by the glowing scales of a sea serpent. I frantically sliced again as the light faded and was rewarded with a hiss of pain. I swam for the surface and miraculously, the serpent let me go.

When I surfaced, I found I had been pulled much farther than I realized. My ship and crew were now a distant blaze on the horizon. Their death screams still haunt me. To my left was a small island that I swam toward. The serpent had injured my leg, so my progress was slow, but eventually I made it to shore.

I do not know the final fate of my crew, but it is likely that I am the lone survivor of the destruction of the Landguard. I had a compass in my pocket. From what I can gather of my star chart memory, I am far beyond the reach of anyone. I estimate my island has coordinates around 1500 degrees west, 800 degrees south, though that likely means nothing to whoever finds this message.

There is not much food on this island, and it is very small. I managed to fashion this message from the few supplies I scavenged. It's likely that it will be destroyed by the same being that destroyed my ship. I will not last long, even if the Deep does not come to finish me. This is my last goodbye. I hope someone finds this message and can tell my family my fate.

My name is Rhoden Garner. I captained the Landguard on its final journey. I pray the Earth Mother protects us all.

Elix couldn't breathe. There was a date at the top of the letter from only a few days ago. Rhoden was alive. Rhoden was *alive.*

For now.

What were the chances that I would find this letter? Elix drew in a shaky breath and whispered a prayer of thanks. He reverently picked up the letter and stumbled back to the shipyard. He slowly gained speed, the hope flaring within pushing him forward. He had to find his mom. He ran to her office, throwing open the door, but it was empty. He spun around, searching for her.

He guessed she would be praying in the Cave of Repose. He turned and barreled his way to the cave in the mountainside nearby. The mountain overlooked the shipyard, one side steeply dropping into the ocean while simultaneously protecting the cove around the yard. The Cave was located where sand met stone in a direct line from his mom's office.

He held the precious piece of paper close as he stooped in the small entrance to the Cave. Blinking in the dim light, he walked further into the tunnel, turning a few times until he reached the Cave of Repose. In the pitch black, he knew the way by heart. He slipped through the small hole in the wall into the perfectly spherical cavern. The space was lit by one candle's flickering light, illuminating his mother. She knelt with her face to the dirt in prayer and ignored his presence until he knelt beside her and took a few calming breaths. Together, they felt the Earth pulse around them for a few quiet moments.

He gently placed a hand on his mother's shoulder. "Mom. He's alive."

As soon as she'd read the message from Rhoden, Elix's mom prepared to set sail immediately. He protested at first, aware of the danger in the ocean. One shared look confirmed that they had to try to save Rhoden. She had never gotten the chance to save her husband from whatever fate had befallen him. She wasn't about to miss the chance to save her son.

Rhoden had taken their most experienced sailors on his ill-fated voyage, leaving Elix and his mom the most qualified for sailing. Neither wanted to risk their last remaining family member's life by trusting untrained hands. They decided to set sail with just the two of them.

The ship, *Shorewarden,* had already been prepared to sail a short voyage and it was small enough to be manned by two. Elix's mom wanted to prove to the sailors that the ocean could be traveled safely. More importantly, she wanted to get Rhoden back.

Enough rations were packed for a round trip for three people. By the third hour of evening, *Shorewarden* had set sail for the coordinates Rhoden provided. They estimated roughly three days out on the Deep before reaching him, give or take some time making up for error.

Elix paused to watch the land fade from view even as the ocean floor drew farther and farther away beneath him. If he focused, he could feel the way the water moved the top layers of sand, but the Earth beneath remained just as solid as it always was. That feeling was grounding, comforting. Maybe, if he focused a bit more, he could—

"Elix! Snap out of it and finish rigging the sails!"

His concentration clicked back into place. "Ah, sorry." When he'd finished fixing the sails, he leaned against the rails. They traveled in silence for a few minutes, enjoying the evening light dancing over the blue waves. Even though they weren't over deep enough water, any conversation felt dangerous. Old habits took over and they communicated silently with just a glance. There was no need to risk speaking.

They sailed for a few more hours until night fell. Elix took first watch at the helm and adjusted their heading somewhat, then closed his eyes and allowed his concentration to plunge to the ocean floor below. His inner eyes watched the varying landscape of the sea floor. Sensing both the deck beneath his feet and Earth beneath a sky of water felt almost like flying.

He opened his eyes, studying the stars above. The night was clear, and he could see for miles along the rolling waves. Only a few people could sense the Earth the way he did. And others could do far more, controlling the Earth itself. They were known as Blessed: ordinary people granted some of the Earth Mother's power. Legends spoke of a particularly powerful Blessed that had raised the very mountain that protected their shipyard. At a young age, Elix had become Blessed. Despite the years, he was still trying to figure out what that power let him do.

At the very least, it made sailing much more disconcerting because the surface of the Earth was so far away. In deep water, his abilities seemed stretched thin as he tried to reach for the Earth's presence from a great distance. He rubbed a thumb along the edge of the blue stone tied to a cord around his neck. It seemed to vibrate in his grip. Every Blessed carried a Totem, the symbol of their connection to the Earth, and the stone was his.

Something was knocking against the hull.

Tap, tap, tap.

Elix held his breath, not daring to move. The light tapping was probably from some creature, wondering what this hunk of wood was doing in the ocean. Or a malicious thing had come to destroy them. At the moment, there wasn't a way to tell, so he tried to make as little noise as possible. He hoped his mom didn't shift in her sleep.

Tap, tap, tap.

Gradually, the knocking moved farther up the port side and then stopped. Elix exhaled, keeping his breathing as shallow as he could. Something splashed and the tapping resumed where it had left off.

Tap, tap, tap.

There was a scraping sound as something brushed against the hull.

Tap, tap, tap.

A murmuring followed the final tap and then there was a splash as whatever paid them a visit swam away. Elix thought he caught a glimpse of fins disappearing underwater. He practically sank to his knees with relief, gasping for air. That could have gone terribly wrong.

The rest of his watch was uneventful. He didn't even bother to tell his mom what had happened when she came to replace him. Quietly, he made his way below deck and fell asleep.

Dense sheets of fog covered the visible ocean the next day. At best, there was only thirty feet of visibility, though the fog shifted and swirled. Instead of burning away with the heat of the sun as the day wore on, the fog grew denser. Relying solely on their compass, they hoped they were at least headed in the right direction.

Around midday, the fog grew so dark that it was a second night. Light couldn't pierce this kind of fog, so they didn't bother lighting lanterns. The sea floor was now so far away that Elix could sense it only as a small buzzing in the distance. It did not bode well.

Something flashed in the corner of his eye.

He whirled, narrowing his eyes at the fog. He signaled to his mom that he'd seen something, not taking his eyes from the spot. Just as he was about to give up, two white spheres appeared directly in front of him. The glowing orbs pierced the fog, seeming to draw near. A sharp intake of breath told him his mom had noticed them too. More appeared all around them, in pairs.

One pair dulled, then brightened again, almost as if they had *blinked.*

The orbs were the eyes of creatures that surrounded them in the fog, and they were coming closer.

Elix scrambled away, knocking against a spare board in his haste. It clattered to the deck. There was a beat of silence while his mom looked at him with fear-filled eyes.

Then a blood curdling shriek pierced the air. Followed by another, and another. The screams were unnatural, and they increased in volume until the fog was filled with them.

"Get below deck. Now," his mom ordered, abandoning attempts at silence.

He didn't hesitate to obey, practically throwing himself into the hold. Before leaving the deck and from the corner of his eye, he saw long, dark green tentacles grip the railing.

Down below, he scuttled into the far corner behind boxes of supplies. His mom dropped down after him and settled into a different corner. They waited in tense silence.

Above deck, the screeching continued, but the noise couldn't muffle the sound of their ship being boarded. Thumping and crashing reigned.

The door to the hold opened.

Tentacles slithered inside, reaching for them. A thud. Something had joined them.

Elix ducked his head, pressing a hand over his mouth to muffle any sound he might make. Peeking over the edge of the crate shielding him from the beast, he stared at what was in front of him.

Two milky eyes protruded from a mass of tentacles that vaguely resembled a ball of seaweed. He couldn't tell whether the creature had a solid body or if it was literally made of appendages. Slowly, the tentacles crept forward, curling around a crate. The creature hurled it to the floor, splintering wood and scattering supplies. He watched as it smashed crate after crate against the hull.

There were only so many crates protecting him and his mom.

Suddenly, the tentacles making up the creature's body parted right beneath its eyes, baring red-stained teeth. Then it shrieked. In the close confines, the sound hurt Elix's ears, but he didn't dare move to cover them. In a swift movement, the creature gathered all the food from the broken crates and disappeared back to the top deck with a final scream.

The screams above slowly died away.

Elix waited a few more moments to be perfectly sure the creatures were gone before venturing top side. Glancing at his mom, he nodded and crept quietly from his hiding spot. He drew his sword, just in case, then climbed the ladder.

The fog was gone. And so were the creatures. Elix finally allowed himself to breathe normally and sent a prayer to the Earth Mother for protecting them. It seemed the beasts, whatever they were, had not been controlled by the Deep. If they had, they would not have stopped until all humans on board were dead.

He sheathed his sword, then climbed down the ladder to give his mom the all-clear. Together, they surveyed the damage. The helm was broken. Not completely, but it severely limited their ability to steer. Much of the railing was destroyed and their supplies were depleted by more than half. Rationing would have to be tight, especially on the return trip with a third person.

They had gotten off very lucky. Now, the difficulty of their voyage was significantly increased.

A day later, Elix was enjoying the peace. They hadn't seen or heard anything after the tentacle creatures' attack. Slowly but surely, they were coming up on the coordinates in Rhoden's message, and thankfully, the ocean floor had drawn closer, hinting at the possibility of an island nearby.

The sun beat down directly overhead, reflecting off the crystalline water. Elix thought it was beautiful, despite the deadliness looming beneath the waves. Dead ahead, he caught sight of something on the horizon. He squinted and saw what looked like another ship.

"Ghost ship," his mom whispered directly in his ear.

He jumped, turning to look at her. He hadn't realized she'd stepped away from the helm.

She continued. "It's not really there. Not anymore."

He motioned for her to be quiet and gestured at the waves. Who knew what could be lurking below them? She gave him a look that seemed to say, *Shut up. I am being quiet. Just listen to me.* She rested her head against his shoulder and continued her whispered dialogue.

"They say that ghost ships are illusions created by the ocean in memory of those who have fallen in her waves. Almost like she wants to atone for the atrocities committed by the Deep." Her voice was soft and wistful as she said, "She's giving those sailors another chance to brave her waters." She trailed off with glassy eyes.

Elix knew she was wondering if somewhere out there sailed a ship in memory of her husband. His father.

In silence, they watched the ghost ship until it passed from view.

The island was in sight.

Like Rhoden had written in his letter, it was incredibly small. However, it was large enough to still be a pain to search.

Elix's body practically itched to touch solid ground again. He grinned at his mom as they silently guided *Shorewarden* as close as they dared with the damaged helm. The ship was small enough to not need a raft, but they had one anyway because swimming even in shallow water could be dangerous. They anchored *Shorewarden* and rowed ashore, ready to find their lost family member.

As soon as Elix's boots hit sand, he nearly cried with relief. He paused to relish that all was right with the world again. Except, something seemed off. He shook away the feeling of dread. His brother was here. Everything was fine.

"Everything all right?"

Elix startled at the question, still used to silence on the waves. "Uh, yeah. Yeah. Just getting used to being on land again."

His mom nodded. "C'mon. Let's go."

There was a fringe of trees ahead. They struggled through the sand, but before they even reached it, a figure walked out of the trees. It was Rhoden. He looked the same, if a bit worn and scruffy. His dark hair was matted and covered his eyes. Elix grinned, an immense weight dropping from his shoulders. Rhoden was still alive! He shouted and ran closer, but Rhoden didn't seem to notice. He was muttering something and looking at the ground.

Again, Elix was struck by the feeling of wrongness. The strong emotion stopped him in his tracks while his mom ran ahead.

Rhoden put his hand out to stop her. "Wait!" She stopped instantly.

His voice was strained, as if he were trying to say words but other ones were forced out instead. His eyes looked different. Normally blue, they now seemed too dark.

"Rhoden, what is it?" his mom said, desperation leaking into her voice.

A pained, animalistic whine escaped Rhoden. "He got to me first! He got to me first!" His eyes were squeezed shut. "He read my message! He read it. The Deep! The Deep read it! He found me. He's taken me. I'm his. He's coming! He's coming!"

Elix went cold. Rhoden's body started contorting and his voice became shriller as he repeated the last two words over and over. *He's coming.* Then Elix understood that two different voices were struggling for words. Two different wills were fighting for control of Rhoden's body. Only one would win.

Somehow, the rules about the Deep had changed.

"Rhoden!" his mom screamed.

Elix was frozen in shock, not wanting to believe what Rhoden was saying. But his mom ran closer, desperately trying to save her son from some unbeatable power.

"I CAN'T FIGHT HIM!" Rhoden screamed, his voice full of pain and anguish. There were tears streaming down his face.

The change was obvious as the Deep took full control. Rhoden's body instantly relaxed and the words he'd fought to keep at bay stumbled out.

"Kill them. Kill them. Kill them."

When Rhoden opened his eyes, they were completely black. His gaze locked on his mother.

"Kill you," he whispered.

Time slowed. Every detail focused in sharp relief as dark water exploded from Rhoden and shot toward his mom. She screamed and tried to run. Spines of hardened water speared her body and covered her from head to toe.

It was over instantly.

"NO!" Elix's limbs unfroze and he stumbled forward a few steps, falling to his knees.

As the dark water retreated and revealed her pale form, her eyes stared sightlessly into the bright sky.

A sob escaped his lips. "Mom, please don't leave me too."

The Earth beneath him shuddered.

He tore his gaze away from her corpse to look at what used to be his brother. The *new* being had the gall to grin at him.

"Now you."

Elix's sense for the Earth around him flared. As the water rose, Elix gritted his teeth, sinking his hands deep into the sand, and tore open the Earth beneath him. He plummeted into the hole he had just created, resealing the Earth behind him. Falling far, he knew he would survive.

The Earth would protect him.

Cushioned by dirt, he felt reassured by the warmth of its caress. Briefly, he felt removed from all the pain and confusing thoughts. If only he could have used this newfound power to save his mom as well. Already the flare he'd experienced earlier was waning. He had saved himself, but she was gone.

He replayed her death over and over, trying to find a way he could have prevented it. Everything hinged on the fact that he had been too late. Fear had crippled him. He'd failed his mother and had been too late for his brother. At the start of their voyage, they had such high hopes that the three of them would return home together as a family once again. Now, he was the only one left.

For several long moments, he was in too much shock to feel anything. Soon, sobs racked his body.

The Earth whispered that it would take him home while he cried. Someone needed to tell the world that the Deep had learned how to send its presence onto land. The Deep could read and understand language. Rhoden had called it a *him*. Someone had to figure out what that meant.

Society was in so much more danger than before.

Urrio watched the boy disappear into the hole. Tivona had given him some of her power then. What an unpleasant surprise.

At least he remembered her name. He'd only remembered his own a few weeks ago.

The body he inhabited still struggled weakly against his control, its spirit simultaneously mourning the death of the woman and celebrating the escape of the boy. Urrio snuffed out that spirit.

His ability to perceive his surroundings dramatically decreased as the body collapsed next to the corpse of the woman. This was only a temporary setback.

Memory was returning. He could understand more every day, but the progress was slow and frustrating. Though he wasn't sure how yet, he had achieved the impossible. He had been a purely spiritual being, yet here he was, slowly becoming physical. He brought his power back to his fledgling body in the ocean. His power only partially obeyed.

Eventually, he would regain all he had lost by choosing to abandon his spiritual existence. He would also gain a body, his ticket to becoming more than he had previously been. Until then, he hung in limbo, existing in both spiritual and physical realms. It was taking forever, but luckily, he was patient. He settled comfortably into the beginnings of his body, listening to the thoughts of those brave enough to sail deep into his terrain.

They would all be gone soon. After all, they were right to fear a god.

Sarah Bartholomew

A 'Pun'-believable Tale

Chapter One
I'm *Knot* at the End of My Rope

"So, what's on the menu for today, chief?" Speck asked as she took a seat at their kitchen counter.

Red blew the hair out of her queenly face before responding. "Let's see…eggs, bacon, waffles, and a green smoothie for you." Her breath came out in short bursts as she expertly whipped the bowl of eggs she was holding. Her wrinkle-free apron was already splattered with breakfast food.

Speck whistled. "You know, I don't know much about this sort of thing, but I assume in most groups it isn't the fearless leader that does the cooking."

Red blew the wisps of hair out of her face again, then carefully poured the egg whip into the already warmed-up pan before her. "Yeah, well, I like to cook. Besides, you do all the cleaning. Pass me the cheese, would you?"

Speck sighed dramatically. "Sadly, 'tis true. But in moments when I feel overloaded, I just think about how *grate-ful* I am for cheese."

"That pun wasn't even very good."

"You're right. It was, sadly, *tear*-able," Speck said dramatically as she pulled a piece of paper out of the pocket of her denim jean jacket and ripped it in half.

"I still can't believe you carry paper with you just for moments like this."

"And I still can't understand how you're *knot* at the end of your rope with me."

Red sighed but was smiling as she dished food out onto the elegant teal plates that were neatly arranged on the counter. Her face fell when she looked at the four empty seats beside Speck. "Where's Willow and Abigail?"

"Well, Willow probably went to work early, and you know how Abigail gets." Speck finished.

"Oh. What's she done this morning?"

"Well, you know how she is. This morning she told me, 'Verily, I pray thee, disturbeth not me for at least an hour more, for pressing matters I am attending to. Ah, yes. Pressing indeed.' She followed this by a deranged laugh and snapped at me to not touch anything, before magically blasting me out of her room and wizarding the door closed."

"Oh, so nothing too bad. She's always ornery when she's working on something."

"I suppose. I just wish she'd stop talking like she's been force-fed Shakespeare."

"Did I hear someone say Shakespeare?" a voice asked as the door opened and Michael stepped inside.

"Ooooh! Michael! I meant to call you and ask how your play went, but I forgot. Red made a *feast.* You can tell us how your play went while we eat." Speck squealed, starting to drag him into the kitchen.

Red interrupted, firmly guiding Michael back into the hallway. "Sorry, house rules. Males are not allowed in any rooms. Just hallways."

"I still don't understand that rule," Michael muttered under his breath, but allowed Red to sit him down on the rich brown wood that was their hallway floor.

"I did make a bit too much food, so I'll whip you up a plate." Red said as she turned away from him and dished up a plate of eggs and waffles. "Want any bacon?"

"Yes, *please.*"

Red took Michael over a plate and turned to Speck. "Speck, would you be kind enough to take a plate to Abigail?"

Speck's face fell. "But I want to hear about Michael's play."

"I'm sure Willow can tell you all about Shakespeare. But right now, I need you to take a plate to Abigail."

Speck sighed as she grabbed the plates and shuffled out of the room.

"You know," Michael said, "You really should attend High School. You'd learn so much."

"High School? Sounds useless. And boring. And stressful. Besides, most of the world still refuses to accept that magic exists. I'm not going to sit in a science class while the teacher spouts off explanation after explanation about what can clearly be identified as magic, and thus defies logic."

Michael grinned. "Sometimes I wish I could just pack up my textbooks and come live with you guys. It'd be a nice break from the real world."

"Don't say those words."

Michael frowned. "Which words?"

Red mouthed, '*real world.*' "Abigail would have a fit if she knew you said that. She's still trying to convince herself that it doesn't exist."

"Oh...Okay," Michael said, puzzled, before wolfing down his waffles. Meanwhile, Speck was walking up the spiral staircase and the cramped, dark hallway that led to Abigail's den. She knocked on her door, opening it without waiting for an answer.

Abigail was hunched at her desk, her hair a rat's nest and her eyes aglow with a crazy light. Her staff glowed orange beside her, and she didn't seem to realize that someone had come in.

Speck hesitated for a moment, wondering if she should come back, but decided against it. She coughed loudly to alert Abigail that she was there, and disaster struck.

Chapter Two
Spell Shenanigans

"Just came back to get my car keys," Willow said as she stepped through the door.

"Your car keys or your sword?" Red asked suspiciously at the same time that Michael asked, "Why do you need car keys if you travel by portal?"

There was a pause, and then she said abruptly, "How can I hack my way through history without a weapon?" Willow ran into her room.

They heard a loud clattering sound, followed by frantic yelling. Michael was on his feet in an instant, but Red remained calmly loading their magical dirt-powered dishwasher.

"What was that?" Michael asked, his voice tinged with worry.

"Oh, nothing. Probably just Willow rehearsing something in her armory. Movie industry, you know."

But Willow came out of her room a moment later in full armor, a long black sword attached to her waist. "What was that?"

"That wasn't you?"

"No. It seemed to come from Abigail's room."

"Let's check it out!" Red said. They quickly rushed to Abigail's room, where the door was already open, the dim light illuminating Speck, who looked horrified. She had her hands over her mouth as Abigail yelled, "Nay, verily, nay!" and crawled across the floor picking up pieces of what looked like a large orange crystal.

Red felt a sinking sensation. "What happened?"

Speck looked like she was on the verge of tears. "Well, I...I coughed to let Abigail know I was there, and...and..." Her voice faltered.

Abigail stood up, but instead of looking angry or horrified, she just looked...lost. She was staring at the pieces of crystal in her hands. Red scanned the room, and her gaze locked on a broken twist of wood lying splayed on the stone floor.

"Forsooth! The fault is mine." Abigail seemed to realize with detached emotion that she was speaking like Shakespeare, and she made an effort to stop. "I was too distracted."

But then the blood drained from her face. "Oh, no."

"What is it? What's wrong?" Red asked in panic.

"I-I was working on a spell! It had been dormant in the staff, but it wasn't complete! It...it wasn't complete! Oh, no, no, no!"

"What? What does that mean? What's going to happen?" Red asked.

"I don't know! That's the point! It's a rogue spell, I have no idea the impact it will have!"

"What...what should we do?"

"I don't know! Maybe I can still contain it before it drains from the crystal shards! Maybe..." Abigail trailed off, rushing to her desk, putting her hands over the shards and shouting incoherently, her voice rising louder and louder. "Shalmarkikzalashiouk!"

"How is she doing magic without her staff?" Michael shouted.

"Most of her magic was stored in her staff, but she still has some residual magic!" Red shouted back.

Red watched wide-eyed as an orange glow started to fight to get out of the crystal shards, and blue light from Abigail's hands fought to contain them. A roaring filled the room, and she had to yell to be heard over the tumult.

"Michael, stand behind Abigail to steady her! If she falls, we're all done for!"

Michael, who had been standing just outside the room, seemed to be going into shock. His eyes were wide. "But what about the hallway rule?"

"To blazes with the hallway rule!" Red shouted, hands over her ears. "Help Abigail!"

"Shalmarkikzalashiouk!"

Another lurch rocked through the room and Abigail was thrown to the floor. The world exploded into orange light.

Chapter Three
This is 'Pun'believable

When they came to their senses, they found themselves sprawled across a rocky battlefield. The sounds of fighting came from a few hundred feet away. They groaned.

"Where are we?" Speck asked as she leaned against Abigail, her arm over her eyes to block out the sun. "I feel like I've been asked to crush root beer cans."

"What?" Willow asked, frowning.

"You know, because this situation is soda-pressing."

"Well, I guess I walked right into that one."

"Really, guys, where are we?" Red asked.

There was a long silence, and they all looked at Abigail, who remained silent, apparently deep in thought.

"Anyone got a pen?" she finally asked.

Michael sighed before handing her one.

She started compulsively clicking it and murmuring under her breath. They could hear the odd word here and there. "Most of my magic gone…teleport…puns…effects…no other option…don't have enough left… Willow… Willow!" Abigail suddenly jerked her head up. "We don't have Willow."

They all looked around, hoping Abigail was wrong.

"Where could she have gone? She was right by us when we teleported!" Red said.

"There's no other option," Abigail said abruptly before standing up and striding away. "Stay here."

They sat dumbfounded and confused for a few minutes, waiting for Abigail to come back.

When she did, they bombarded her with questions, but she simply gestured for them to follow her. After a while they arrived on the top of a tall bluff and looked into a sheer valley below them, where the source of the noise was.

Below them, an army made a racket struggling to get in formation but bumbling into each other and collapsing from exhaustion, while, on the distant horizon, red sunlight glinted ominously off the armor of an approaching army. If the army directly below them didn't get their act together soon, they would be slaughtered. And there in the front lines, yelling for the men to get in formation, was Willow.

They all gasped, and Abigail moved to sit a few paces away. They all clustered around her, waiting for her to say something.

"Forsooth! Danger lurks…*ahem… So here's the deal. Willow is trapped in the middle of a pun. She's taken on the role of general, and she will be slaughtered unless we can figure out the pun." Abigail bit her lip.

"How do you know that?" Michael asked.

"I used nearly all my magic asking the enchantment that created this spell what was going on."

"What sort of spell was in your staff?" Speck asked suspiciously.

"Well, that is to say…Forswear, forsooth! Nay, I have done no wrong. I pray thee, hark unto my words. Wherefore thou questioneth me? For anon there is pressing danger, not a legion away. I feign calm, but alas, I…I…"

"Goodness, Abigail! What spell was it?" Willow asked.

"Well…it…I don't see why that's important.

"It's very important, Abigail. What was the spell?" Red said firmly.

Abigail had no choice now. "Well, I was getting really annoyed by all of Speck's puns. I wanted to cast a spell that would prevent her from saying any more puns around us. But only around us!"

"WHAT?!" Speck burst out.

Red stepped in. "Abigail, that was unkind. But there are more pressing problems right now."

Speck closed her eyes and took a few deep breaths, trying to control her anger. "You're right. Sorry."

Abigail nodded. "Now, we need to figure out the pun. Willow's life is on the line!"

"Yes!" Speck shouted excitedly. "We need inspiration, valor, strength, and courage! But most importantly, we need puns!"

Chapter Four
The Problem with Sleep Deprivation

"Come on Speck, think!" Speck told herself for the billionth time. They were laying belly-down on the jagged rocks that littered the landscape, their heads peeking over the cliff.

"Let's go over what we know one more time," Red said calmly. "You can do this, Speck."

"One," Willow said. "There are a ton of soldiers down there, and they are not able to fight the other army."

"Two," Michael said, "They're bumbling around. We don't know why, but a lot of them are falling to the ground and going to sleep, so it could be sleep deprivation."

"Ah, alas, sleep deprivation. An illness that plagues the great populations all over the world. Even the mightiest woman often falls under its tricky spell," Abigail muttered darkly.

"Soldiers. I don't think they *are* soldiers," Speck muttered. "They have full armor. And look at their shields! They each have a crest, so they must be knights. But what's the question? Without the question for the pun, I can't figure it out!" Speck started to hyperventilate.

Willow nudged Abigail. "I think we may need your magic again. Speck's right. If we can't figure out the pun's question, we aren't going to be able to solve this thing."

Abigail grimaced. "Very well, I'll figure it out."

She walked a few paces away, placing her hands on the ground once more and muttering under her breath. When she got back, she looked a little ill.

"The magic told me that the question has something to do with why the army can't fight the other army. Also, I learned the army has been there for almost a week."

Speck nodded and started to murmur, rocking back and forth. "It's on the tip of my tongue. The *tip* of my tongue. Quick, start naming synonyms for knight and tired."

There was a general bumble of words. "Warrior, exhausted, soldier, fighter, troop, officer, drained, sleepy, sleepless, drowsy."

"Um…Speck?" Willow said.

"Quiet. I'm trying to think."

"Well, I think you're gonna want to know this."

"What *exactly* is so important?"

"Well, it's just that the soldiers in the other army are big. And faceless. And made of fire. And a few of them are walking toward us."

They all leapt to their feet and spun around, Abigail putting herself in front and raising her hands. Now, they could tell that the soldiers hadn't been glinting red from the light of the sun, but that they were made completely of fire. Their black leather armor was somehow supported by heat and air. The five beasts fixated their empty, eerie faces on the friends.

"Um…what should we do?" Michael asked, his voice quavering. The soldiers had stopped, but there was no telling how long that would last.

Acting as one, the five fire figures raised their arms in a jerking motion and pointed them at the group.

"Everyone, stay behind me!" Abigail shouted. Blue light shot out of her raised hands just as the strange soldiers shot at them with fire. The blue light kept the flames at bay, but now the army had almost intercepted Willow's troops.

Speck started to tremble. She had never done well under pressure, and now lives were at stake. Closing her eyes, she shut out everything and let the words swirl around her brain. *You are the queen of puns, Speck. You can do this. Why can't the knights fight the army? They can't fight because they're tired. Tired. Sleepy. Drowsy. Sleepless. Exhausted. They haven't slept for days. They haven't slept for nights. Nights. Knights? Knights. They were sleepless knights. They couldn't fight because their army had too many sleepless knights! Knights, nights!*

"I have it! I have it! The army can't fight because it's had too many sleepless knights!"

The soldiers dissolved, Abigail slumped, and the world turned black.

Chapter Five
A Deadly Situation

"I'm beginning to hate teleportation," Red groaned.

This time they landed in a heap on top of one another, in the middle of what seemed to be a pitch-black graveyard. They disentangled themselves and rubbed their bruised limbs.

"Augh. Abigail, how many more of these are we going to have to go through?" Speck asked.

There was no response.

"Abigail?" Michael whispered, looking all around, then stating the obvious. "Guys, Abigail is *gone*."

Each of them looked around, hoping he was mistaken. But he was right. The grumpy wizard was missing.

Willow groaned and rubbed her head. "What happened?"

"Well... Actually, it'll take too long to explain now. We'll catch you up later," Speck said. She turned to Red. "I assume that since Abigail is gone, she's the pun?"

"I guess." Red looked worried.

Willow looked beyond confused. "What?"

"I'll give you the rapid-fire version," Michael said. "Basically, you were a pun. Once we figured your pun out, we were sent here, where we now have to figure out the next pun. Since Abigail is gone, we assume she's the pun. Any questions?"

Willow looked like she had too many to count, but she remained silent.

Speck shivered. "It's creepy here. And cold. Let's hurry and figure this out."

"Agreed," Michael said.

Suddenly, two voices came from around the bend in a narrow path that twisted through the lurking trees cutting through the graveyard.

"Bu-bu sha's alive misses," a deep, rough, accented voice said.

"I don't see how that makes a difference," a high, sharp voice answered as a tall woman and fat man that matched the voices perfectly came around the bend. The group immediately noticed the wagon the man was dragging behind him. And the bound and gagged figure that struggled within.

"Oh, my goodness! Is that Abigail?" Willow panicked.

"Shhhh!" Red shushed.

"Yess, mem. I'm just here ta follow orders. Yesser. Yess, yess. Whever ya shay," the fat man said.

The two figures stopped next to an open area, and the woman pointed to their left. "Just make sure not to dig here in this nice plot, you fool. You can bury her over there by the bushes and weeds."

"Yess, missess," he said, and the woman walked briskly down the path. The man started digging the hole, deepening it impossibly fast.

"We have to do something," Michael said. "It isn't like last time. There are five of us and only one of him. I say we overpower him."

"I agree," Willow said approvingly. "A frontal assault all at once. My favorite type. Weapons encouraged." They nodded, and she said, "On three. One…two…three!"

They all surged forward, but the man didn't even turn around. Out of the blue, black vines exploded out of the ground, wrapping around the five friends and restricting their movements, just feet away from the man and the struggling wizard.

The black vines started to squeeze, and Speck cried out.

"Speck! We'll have to *Oof try the pun approach!" Red shouted, but a thick tendril wrapped around Speck's mouth and muffled shouting ensued.

The man finished digging the hole and grabbed Abigail by the collar of her deep blue wizard cloak. Muffled shouting now came from Abigail as well.

"Speck can't talk, guys! It's up to us! Let's think. Quick!" Michael shouted, struggling to get words out as a vine compressed his chest.

The man flung Abigail into the pit, then started filling it, one small shovel at a time. Luckily, he started at her feet.

"I don't know if this is important, but he dug the grave in the wrong place." Willow panted. Because of her armor, she was spared the brunt of the crushing force, and could speak freely.

A vine wrapped around Michael's mouth and he struggled to breathe through his nose.

"I-It's up…to…us!" Red gasped to Willow. "I'm…hopeless at puns! It's a…grave. Grave. Grave situation? No. Maybe…*Augh! I…don't know!"

A tendril wrapped around Willow's mouth, leaving Red alone. She looked around in panic. Abigail sounded like she was sobbing in fear behind her gag, and the dirt was already up to her chest. Abigail looked at Red, her eyes begging Red to pull herself together and figure it out.

Red didn't know what to do. Despite all the books she read, she was hopeless at word play. She focused with all her energy. *He dug in the wrong place. Grave…grave…*"I've got it! It's a grave mistake!" She shouted just before the tendril covered her mouth. The world turned upside down and they were falling…falling…falling.

Chapter Six
It's About Time

This time, they ended up in a strange sort of workshop, but only Willow noticed right away. The rest were lying face down on the rough stone, drawing deep gasping breaths.

Now unbound, Abigail was on her hands and knees and sounded like she was hacking her guts out. They could make out a few words in between coughs. "…never…sleep…again… of…all…the…puns…never…again…"

"Are you all right, Abigail?" Speck asked.

Abigail waved them away. "I'll be fine in a moment," she said, and they took a minute to look around.

The workshop had narrow windows on one side of the room and heavy wood doors on the other. Willow walked over and tugged on the door viciously. "Locked," she said. "Or at least too heavy to move."

They looked around at each other. "This time Michael is gone." Speck said. "How many more of these are we going to have to go through, Abigail?"

"No telling," Abigail whispered. Her voice sounded weak and raw. "It seems like we all have to take a turn."

Speck groaned and Red sighed.

"There's something I don't understand," Red said. "What are the rules here?"

Abigail shrugged helplessly. "Honestly, I'm not sure if there are any."

Suddenly, a noise came from the chimney and a dusty figure fell out, skidding several feet. He got up, rubbing his head and beaming. It was Michael.

"Michael!" Willow shouted, but Michael seemed not to hear. He walked over, still beaming robotic-like, to a desk in the southwest corner of the workshop.

They walked over and started to shake him. "Michael, wake up! Snap out of it," Speck said. But Michael continued on, oblivious to their shakes and shouts.

Finally, Willow tried ripping him from his chair and throwing him across the room. They all looked at her accusingly, and she shrugged. "Nothing else was working."

Michael just got up with a smile and walked back to his seat.

"What is he working on?" Red asked.

"I'm not sure, but at least nothing life-threatening has happened yet," Speck said.

"Great," Abigail growled. "Now you've jinxed it. Have you no sense?"

They ignored her comment and continued watching Michael's hands at work. He was busy drawing strange symbols with chalk all over a strip of leather.

"Abigail, you'd better get over here. Strange symbols are your specialty."

Abigail grumbled but shuffled across the room and fixated her eyes on the strange symbols.

After a moment of intense study, she had an answer. "Those symbols represent characters that used to be on magical clocks."

"Er, guys?" Willow said. "The wood in the chimney just lit itself."

"Great," Abigail muttered. "This'll probably be the second time today we're almost roasted alive."

"If we focus, that won't happen. Let's just think of the pun. Abigail, do you have enough magic left to ask for the question?" Red asked.

Abigail shook her head. "It'll take me days to recharge. But maybe this one doesn't have a question, like the last one."

"All right, let's think. Speck, we'll need all of your pun brainpower for this," Michael said.

"We need to hurry. The logs in the fire keep multiplying and they're moving this way!" said Willow.

They all made sure that what she said was true. What was once a small cooking fire was now a blazing bonfire. Every time a new log appeared with a *pop*, it tumbled off the stack in their direction.

"Why does there always have to be imminent danger?" Speck groaned.

"I love it!" Willow beamed. "Though it would be more fun if I had someone to fight."

"Hark!" Abigail shouted, apparently not having the energy to hold back the Shakespeare any longer. "Not far hither 'tis roaring flames. Wherefore do you bicker like squabbling children? Thinkest thou, all of you, this situation amusing?!"

They sobered, and Red looked relieved. "Thanks, Abigail," she said.

"Mention it not," Abigail replied. She sat down, looking a little queasy.

"Can I have a quiet moment while I think?" Speck asked. She started to murmur under her breath. "Belt...leather? Is it about the leather? Or the jumping fire? No, it must be about the belt. Clock. Belt of clocks. Belt of time. No, belt can't be the right word. Whip. Whip of time? I guess that wouldn't work either. Whips make nicks in skin. Nick of time? I don't think that will work either. That one wasn't bad, though."

The fire got closer, heading toward the girls and the oblivious Michael. The heat became oppressive, but the girls refused to move.

"Make haste, make haste," Abigail whispered, but quietly, in case she broke Speck's concentration.

The flames were fifteen feet away. Then ten. Red tried tugging Michael away from his task. Willow joined her, but no matter how desperately and viciously they tugged, this time Michael seemed magically glued to his seat. The girls refused to leave him. Everyone else's eyes were glued on Speck, whose face turned desperate. The heat mounted, and so did the tension.

Finally, Red asserted, "I'd rather not solve this one in the nick of time like the last ones, if you don't mind. It's getting kind of old."

"I...I can't do it!" Speck sobbed.

The fire was three feet away. Then two. All they could do was tug on Michael and watch the bonfire grow closer and closer with a horrified sort of fascination. Then, just as a log tumbled down, down, down, straight at Willow who had stubbornly put herself in front of Michael in an effort to protect him, Red shouted, "Waist of time! Waste of Time! It's waist of—"

Red was cut off as the world started spinning and spinning and spinning into a blur.

Chapter Seven
Why 'It' Should Never Be Trusted

When they came to their senses, they were in what seemed to be a wagon of straw. They were gasping like landed fish. Abigail was muttering between desperate breaths. "Frikin'…fetch…freak… flippin'…"

"I assume since I don't remember anything, I was the last pun?" Michael groaned.

They nodded.

Once they had their breath back, they climbed out of the wagon, which was parked in the middle of what seemed to be the courtyard of a stone castle. The space was filled with people, not with peasants, villagers, or guards, but with clowns. Some were juggling, some were unicycling, some were smoking, and some were just sitting down laughing hysterically. But they all had a few things in common. All of them were carrying bloodstained weapons. Plus, they looked insane and evil, their makeup smeared and their hair sticking straight up. They were also all frozen in place and staring eerily at the four friends.

Once the teens noticed this, they stopped in their tracks. "Er, guys?" Michael asked behind them, his heart sinking. "Is Speck gone this time?"

"Yes," Red said, her eyes fixed on the clowns.

"Great," Abigail muttered. "Just back away slowly. There's a door behind us to the left. Slowly, slowly, that's it."

The friends shuffled back until they reached the door. "All right," Red said, placing herself in front. "Abigail, you open the door, and the rest of us will remain facing the clowns. No sudden movements."

As slowly as she could, Abigail turned around and slowly pulled on the big brass handle on one side of the door. Softly, then harder. "Uh, guys? It's locked."

"Just to be clear, if something goes wrong the plan of attack is a full-on frontal assault. Use of lethal weapons is encouraged, but it you're squeamish you can stay behind me. I'll be happy to chop these clowns to bits," Willow said.

Suddenly, the door, that had been locked a moment before, burst open, and Speck, in full clown uniform, jumped out, graciously opening the door for them and bowing low. Bedlam ensued. The clowns in the courtyard screamed as one and rushed toward the friends, swinging their weapons about like maniacs.

"This is why you can't trust clowns!" Michael shrieked before being yanked inside by Speck. The rest of his friends sprinted after him, and Speck shut and locked the door behind them.

They sprinted down a narrow stone hallway lit by torches just as the sound of wood being hacked to bits erupted from behind them. Speck ran in front, her clown nose falling off. She came to a halt, made a comical stop gesture, then pointed to a room to their right. They skidded to a stop and ran inside the indicated room. Speck shoved the heavy, wooden door closed and barred it with a spear from a rack that was to the right of the door.

"Now *this* is an armory!" Willow shouted excitedly, scanning the room.

Speck shook her head violently and put a finger to her lips.

They were indeed in a spacious armory, racks and racks of swords, spears, axes, shields, bows, arrows, and all manner of anything and everything pointy arrayed neatly from floor to ceiling everywhere in the wide chamber.

Just then, a loud crash came from the back of the armory, and row after row of weapon racks fell in a domino effect, each tumble creating an enormous racket. When the dust settled, Willow stood at the back of the room, her eyes wide, limply holding a cool-looking wavy sword. "I-I'm sorry," she stuttered. "They had a Flamberge Arming sword. I must have p-pulled too hard removing it from its stand."

"Well, there goes our element of surprise," Abigail said, just before the point of a spear appeared on their end of the door, and several clowns' insane laughter sounded outside.

Speck waved her arms to get their attention and smiled at them before gesturing to the back, where a door stood unnoticed. Speck got there first to hold the door open, smiling and gesturing graciously. As they escaped, they heard the armory door explode behind them. They found themselves in another courtyard and ran for their lives, evil clowns pouring from the door they had just exited. As they reached the heavy double doors that guarded the main entrance into the castle, they pushed with their combined weight but could not get them open.

Speck started hugging everyone and picked flowers from a nearby flowerpot to give to all of them.

"What is she doing?" Red asked, dumbfounded.

"She's not in control of her actions! Get behind me and Willow and think of the pun! Now!" Abigail yelled before raising her hands against the approaching clowns.

Willow stepped beside her, a wide grin on her face. "I've always wanted to do this."

As the first clowns reached them, Abigail created a sword out of blue light and drove it into a clown's chest, dissolving the clown with a blood-curdling scream. A knife juggling clown came toward Willow, and she dropped low, swinging her sword at the clown's legs as several knives flew to where she had been standing a moment before. Abigail took care of another clown by stabbing it in the thigh. Michael winced appreciatively.

Abigail yelled for everyone to move back. Willow, who looked to be having the time of her life, stepped away from the chaos. Abigail gathered all the magic she could muster into her hands and slammed them on the ground. Every clown within twenty feet dissolved as Abigail kept her hands on the ground, muttering very fast. After a moment, she stood up woozily just in time to viciously slash the first clown of the next wave. She yelled behind her, her voice cracking with strain. "Don't focus on the other clowns, the pun is about Speck!"

The friends started a heated discussion in the background. Abigail's light whip started to flicker, and Willow stumbled, barely catching the dagger of a clown on the flat of her new sword.

"I don't mean to rush you. I love you guys, so no pressure, but HURRY UP!" Willow screamed.

The conversation behind them grew even more animated, and just as a sword began its whistling, deadly ark for Willow's head. Her sword started raising too late to block it.

"Nice Gesture… Nice Jester!" shouted Red. The world swirled and they were all turned inside out.

Chapter Eight
I Don't Carrot All

"This better be our last one," Speck grumbled.

They groaned and sat up in some kind of concrete warehouse. Before them was what looked like a circular aquarium with no water inside. Sitting inside at a table dressed in a hippie outfit and shoveling broccoli in her mouth was Red. Across from her was what looked like a baseball pitching machine.

"I'm confused on so many levels," Michael said.

They all agreed. They didn't see what was dangerous about this situation. Plus, seeing Red in a hippy outfit was beyond strange.

"Let's hurry," Abigail growled. "There's gonna be danger soon. If not to us, then to Red."

"You're just a ray of sunshine, aren't you?" Speck said.

"Absolutely not. I hate sunlight."

"Let's focus," Speck took charge. "Everyone, shout out observations."

They scooted their backs against the cold concrete. "Well, Red doesn't seem to be enjoying this experience," Willow noticed, and the others agreed. With every bite she shoved in her mouth, Red grimaced.

Then the baseball pitching machine started to hum. "Here we go," Abigail said.

The machine's hum got louder and louder until it was a deafening roar and they were all forced to cover their ears.

The machine's noise reached a climax and it shot out a… steak. Then another. Then another. A steady stream of them shot out, all aimed directly at Red. The meat seemed to swerve at the last minute, missing her by millimeters, but they kept coming in droves. Soon the problem wasn't the steak hitting Red, it was the steaks rapidly piling up at her feet.

"Where are they all coming from?" Speck shouted.

"It doesn't matter! Start thinking!" Abigail shouted. "She's eating vegetables. Is she a vegetarian? She's wearing a hippy shirt, is that significant? The steaks keep missing her. What is important about that? Think, Speck, think! You're supposed to be the Queen of Puns, Remember?"

Speck closed her eyes and blocked out the world. *You're the Queen of Puns. You're the Queen of Puns. You're the Queen of*

Puns. "Aha! I know what it is! Red becoming a vegetarian was a mistake—a missed-steak!"

The world turned outside in and they found themselves sitting on the ground of Abigail's cold stone room in complete and utter shock.

"That's it. I'm never coming over again," said Michael, and they all started laughing hysterically. Once they started, they couldn't stop.

"I feel cheated. Those weren't even very good puns," said Speck.

"Agreed," they all chorused.

Abigail frowned. "I swear if I hear another pun this week, I'm going to throttle whoever says it myself."

"Absolutely," they all laughed.

Red smiled and looked at them all happily. "You know, we really are pretty great."

They all smiled, and Michael asked tentatively, "Does that mean we can get rid of the hallway rule?"

They all laughed.

Trenton Morrison

Aurelia's Box

Normandy carefully maneuvered the toggle that rested in the palm of her hand. The airship glided above dense jungle. This was the tenth day Normandy was on this trip, and the cost of hiring out the hot airship wasn't the only thing making her sweat around her collar.

"Your parents left you another letter, Lady Callisto." Clement informed. Normandy tried to ignore Clement as she breathed in the moist, jungle air. She closed her eyes for half a second, absorbing the rays from the rising sun. Over Clement's voice, she faintly heard the jungle itself. A quiet rustle of foliage was overpowered by creaking branches and strange sounds.

"Lady Callisto?" Clement prodded. Normandy groaned and opened her eyes, preparing herself for her parents' consistent letters of disappointment.

"What do they have to say? Cut out the parts where they plead for me to return home and ignore any mention of me dishonoring the family."

"In that case, your parents have nothing to say," Clement said with a flat voice.

Normandy perked up. "Delightful!"

"How long are we going to continue, Lady Callisto? A three-day mission has turned into a week and a half long excursion," Clement asked.

"I won't stop until I find Aurelia's Box," Normandy said, stubbornly.

"What will you do if you don't find it in a month? Two months? What if in a year from now you are still chasing a legend?" Clement asked. Normandy remained silent.

"Clement, can't you feel it? When we are down in the temple, can't you feel the… magic? The power the natives whisper about is there! Don't tell me it doesn't intrigue you."

"Whether it intrigues me or not is not the question. The question is how long your parents will keep supporting this chase," Clement reiterated.

Normandy tore her eyes from the jungle below and looked at Clement. He was a tall man, much older than Normandy, with a few gray hairs mixed into his orderly mustache. Instead of his usual waistcoat and jacket, he wore a long tan cloak. It was made of aged leather and had her family's crest inlaid in gold on the breast pocket. Glaring at the crest, she hoped the day would come soon when she could finally be free of her mother. After all, Clement was her mother's servant, charged with serving Normandy.

"I need this, Clement," Normandy said, turning back to steering the airship. "I need to prove myself to my parents! To all of Hollow Port that I am more than just the heir of Callisto. That I am more than just a social bargaining chip! I will find Aurelia's Box, and it will make things right." Normandy pleaded, staring straight ahead. A stone structure was growing on the horizon.

"If you say so, Lady Callisto. Just keep in mind that your mother spent years searching for magical artifacts. Do you think you can do better than her, and at a younger age? We've only been here for a few days, where she has had years." Clement sighed. They flew in silence, approaching the jungle temple. The temple seemed gigantic from the outside. Hiding under its façade was a massive labyrinth. It proved to be the most threatening part of the entire mission.

←→

Though the air was warm and dense, Normandy felt a chill as the airship neared the ground. Clement tossed down a rope, and Sariah, one of the ground crew, reeled them in, until they touched down. The chill of magic present made the hair on the back of her neck stand on end. As she met Clement's eyes, he shivered.

"I never said I didn't feel it, Lady Callisto. Just expressing my worries that you are getting caught up in the supernatural." The ground crew moved around them, tying down the flying machine. Clement undid the door to the basket and let Normandy out

Normandy surveyed her workers. Instead of being employed by her parents, they were hers. First, she stumbled upon Ryker, and the rest of the team came with him. This group of people was the only current proof of her independence, and she hoped to add Aurelia's box to that list.

There were fifteen men and eight women. The men wore short sleeved buttoned up shirts with suspenders. A few had their suspenders in place on their shoulders while others let their suspenders hang at their belt loops. They greeted Normandy with polite "good mornings" and "G'day Lady Normandy." No one called her Lady Callisto. After spending days getting to know them and breaking through social barriers, they finally opened up to her about their friends and family members. Most of them had only each other. Also, she knew each of their names, which was not appropriate for one of her station. Clement was not impressed with her social efforts.

"How was your night?" Normandy asked as she approached the arched temple entrance.

"They came again. But as with previous nights, they don't get close enough for us to see them," Ryker replied. He had gotten into the habit of reporting to her every morning. Clement stayed behind, overseeing the management of the airship.

The workers stayed just inside the temple for the night. The plan had been for Normandy to stay the nights as well, but she had only stayed the first. After that first night... well, they learned to not trust the magic. Normandy shook the shadows out of her mind as she stepped into the entrance chamber of the temple and her surroundings changed. She left the jungle behind and was consumed by the true majesty of the temple.

The walls were made of giant stone blocks, aged to a pale yellow. Emerald vines snaked over everything. Natural light poured in the first tunnel from skylights placed in the ceiling. The giant hallway made Normandy and her small band seem inconsequential.

"Lady Normandy, the Natives have left a representative to speak with you." Ryker appeared beside her, sounding amused.

"Representative? No more messages?" Normandy asked. Clement wordlessly appeared at her side. She spared him a glance and he nodded, reassuring her that the flying machine was in good hands.

"I think they are concerned their messages aren't getting through," Ryker said. They passed the camp set up in the first atrium. Tents, piles of smoldering cooking fires, and laundry drying on clotheslines filled this room. Plus, the excess of torches. Lines of lit torches clung to the walls, even though the skylights let in plenty of light.

That first night with only three torches had been disastrous. Too many shadows.

"Where is the native?" Normandy asked.

"He is waiting at the entrance to the Dark Tunnels." Out of the corner of her eye, she noticed Ryker seemed to have a glassy look on his face. "My Lady Normandy," he added finally. "The Native is kind of odd," he said with a shiver. Ryker fell back as she left camp. Clement moved in closer.

"Did you see the distracted look in his eyes?" Clement asked.

"You think the stories are true? Of all people, Clement, I wouldn't take you for a believer," Normandy mocked.

"I acknowledge the magic, Lady Callisto. You need to acknowledge that it only exists in this temple. The real world just is *not* like this," Clement pleaded.

"Who is to say that there isn't another temple like this out there? Here, let me see that torch. You have the territory claims from Hollow Port, right?" Normandy asked, taking Clement's torch. She basked in the warmth as the temperature dropped a few degrees.

"I have all legal documents needed to allow our search of this structure," Clement said. Normandy let the conversation die as they went deeper into the temple.

To Normandy, it felt like magic infected the air itself, sucking the heat and warmth out of everything.

The moist air had turned dry, and sound echoed a lot more. Nothing physically changed. Light still poured into the tunnel from holes above, and the vines seemed more plentiful further into the temple. Even after ten days of entering the temple, the change still unsettled her. They entered the second and final atrium before the Dark Tunnels. This atrium had six interconnecting tunnels, the main one leading in and five leading into narrow, shadowed passages.

"It appears you have been ignoring us Normandy." A boy's voice pulled her attention away from the captivating atrium. Normandy couldn't place the boy's age, but he was short with wide eyes and an innocent tanned face. Standing on top of a staff, he loomed over Normandy. She tried to ignore the boy's strange air of superiority. She would have preferred to ignore him all together, but at this point that wasn't an option.

"You will address my mistress as Lady Callisto, Native." Clement glared at the boy, meeting his wide eyes. She was grateful for Clement's height and strong presence beside her.

"Lady Normandy is fine," she replied and then felt a chill of magic. Was it coming from the boy? It vanished in a second, and the boy lost his balance and landed on the ground with abnormal grace. Standing at his true height, he was barely five feet, but it did nothing to take away the authority he seemed to project.

"What's your name, Native?" Normandy asked.

"I am afraid you wouldn't comprehend my name if I told you, so you can call me Blaze. My people won't respond to 'native,' Master Clement and Lady Normandy. You can call us the People of Legend," he remarked. He held out his hand to shake. Normandy took it and found his handshake powerful and steady. He noticed her lack of commitment in the handshake.

"I apologize Lady Normandy. Am I shaking your hand the correct way? The others found it reassuring when I gave a strong handshake." He looked concerned. This look of worry put Normandy at ease, more than the handshake ever could. Blaze appeared harmless, but his eyes pierced her.

"You have a message from the People of Legend?" Clement asked.

"I do." Blaze stepped back from Normandy and Clement.

"Speak or let us return to our business," Clement said.

"Are you sure you should be interfering with this temple?" Blaze asked with a twinkle in his eye.

"We are very sure. We have a document signed by the Hollow Port court that gives us territorial responsibility of this temple and a claim to any spoils found inside. A document that was offered to your people centuries ago, but you refused," Normandy said.

"Fare Golt is no one's territory, Lady Normandy. It belongs to the Shadows, as I am sure you have experienced?" His eyebrows raised and eyes squinted as if he was smiling, but his mouth just smirked. Reading his emotions was hard.

"Your message, representative Blaze," Clement said, more firm.

"I am delivering a warning." Blaze's face fell flat. "If you find Aurelia's Box, do not open it, do not remove it from this temple, and do not break it. Failure to do so will likely result in all of your deaths." His face was absent of the mild humor that had been present for the conversation.

Normandy felt a sudden chill. Blaze's childish smile returned. His dark, almost black eyes reflected bright green for a second. With a flash, Blaze ran off the way that they entered, spinning his staff nonchalantly.

"If I wasn't more careful, I would almost consider that a threat, Native." Clement called after him as Blaze laughed.

"It is a threat. I'm just the one informing you of it," Blaze said. Clement and Normandy watched him leave.

"We could arrest him Lady Callisto," Clement said.

"I don't think he means harm," Normandy said.

She tried to shake it off, but the chill settled deeper, getting under her skin. Knowing the chill wouldn't leave until she left the temple only spurred her motivation. "Let's get to work," Normandy said turning back to the tunnels.

With eleven able men, they split up into three teams. Each person had a torch, which was their only defense against the Dark Ones. Normandy joined the three-man team to divide everyone equally. Clement stood behind Normandy, just like her parent's shadow.

"You know the drill," Ryker addressed all of them. Normandy used Ryker to lead the men. It was proper for her to have a middle man considering her rank, even if she did prefer them to call her Normandy. "Keep a map, mark where you've been, mark tunnels that lead to dead ends, don't get lost, and don't let your torches go out," Ryker continued. Clement motioned to her that he wanted to talk privately. As they retreated toward the Dark Tunnels, a few men glanced at them but didn't say anything.

"Are you sure Ryker should be trusted with so much control over the men, Lady Callisto?" Clement asked.

"I trust him. He expresses as much determination as we do to find Aurelia's Box. I doubt he would turn against us," Normandy replied, watching Ryker.

"You never know," Clement murmured, watching Ryker with narrowed eyes. "Your mother wouldn't approve of people having more control than you on your own mission."

"That's fine with me," Normandy sneered, leaving Clement to receive instruction from Ryker.

Splitting up, Normandy led her group into the tunnel they had been venturing down every day. She held her torch in front of her. The Dark Tunnels were a lot smaller than the entrance tunnel and two atriums. Normandy could touch both walls at once if she tried. The descent was unnerving, and she took a deep breath of relief as the channel leveled out.

The chill neither increased or decreased, whatever spell lay over the place was at least consistent. Walking in silence, their footsteps were strangely loud against the stone. They moved quickly, passing shadowed passages they had previously explored.

They ignored the Dark Ones or tried to. Ten days of exposure, had yet to make any of them used to the Dark Ones. At the first sighting of one, Willis, the youngest explorer, jumped, and let out a small yelp.

No one knew what the shadowed beings were. All her group saw was a cloud of gray smoke or mist drifting across their path, the creature hidden within the cloud. The Dark One kept walking across the intersection in front of them, its pace speeding up as the light neared it. The light would evaporate the clouds, which scared whatever was inside and usually made the Dark One flee. This aspect of the creatures had kept the explorers safe, but also prevented them from discovering what they actually were.

During the first night in the temple, the Dark Ones had emerged from the tunnels and attacked. The explorers hadn't had enough light to evaporate any clouds completely and had barely fended the Dark Ones off. Those who had been unfortunate enough to be caught up in one of the creatures' clouds, had been able to see glimpses of them. The reports they had collected the next morning of the descriptions of the creatures ranged so wildly in appearance, that they couldn't decide exactly what they were facing.

Normandy forced herself to not break pace as she walked past the Dark One. The others didn't have as stalwart resolve. Clement was the only one who didn't at least shiver, but Normandy noticed his face was white with terror.

As they continued deeper into the tunnels, Dark Ones appeared more often. If the Dark Ones didn't retreat or started to gravitate toward the explorers, then her men retreated.

"Intriguing? Isn't it?" Normandy laughed, giving Clement a sly look. Her voice was loud and shaky in the tunnel.

"Lady Callisto, I find the prospect of our death lacking humor," he said.

"Wait? Where's Willis?" Normandy asked, looking at the three torches behind her. The boy was gone. They all turned back, looking down the way they'd come. Light shone out of the previous passage they just passed, and Normandy remembered seeing a Dark One down there.

"Wil—" She was cut off by screaming. The light in the tunnel flickered out, and the piercing scream left an even more piercing silence. Everyone paused, straining to hear anything.

"No." Normandy broke the silence. "No, no, no!" she yelled in frustration. For someone to die on this mission would put shame on her, and her name would be stained with this death. Guilt immediately followed this thought. *Shouldn't I care more about my explorers?* Conflicted, Normandy pushed past the others to the tunnel where Willis had last been seen. Rushing around the corner, all she found was a dead torch. On the wall, a crimson handprint stained vines and stone.

Normandy started breathing rapidly, the chill in the air squeezed her throat tight! Her heartbeat made a frantic song in her ears. She witnessed her collapsing future in a single, bloody handprint.

Yelling pierced through her broken thoughts. Normandy turned rapidly, a different kind of fear taking over. Normandy ran back to the others and found Clement backing away from two corpses, while two torches sputtered on the ground.

"What happened?" Normandy yelled, the three deaths weighing on her.

"The other one isn't dead," Clement said stepping over the bodies to Normandy. "The disappearance of Willis was a trap meant to lead you away from us. The other two men tried to bribe me when you had gone. From what I can tell, they have sided with Ryker. I told you he had too much control."

"You killed them?" Normandy asked, feeling numb.

"I did what was necessary to protect you, Lady Callisto." Clement's face was stern, his hands weren't even shaking. He wiped a bloody knife along the back of one of the bodies, cleaning it, then hid the knife in his coat again.

"You have a knife," Normandy said, feeling woozy. She wasn't feeling so well, and she tried to sit down.

"Let me get you out of here before you rest. I know you will feel a lot better out of this temple." Clement supported her under her shoulders.

"I'm fine." She pushed Clement away. "We have to find Aurelia's Box." Normandy said, taking a few deep breaths, then standing up straight.

"Don't be irrational, my Lady—"

"Don't patronize me! We are going to find the box. This is the best chance to search while the other men are distracted. They will probably come back and check on the others to make sure the job was done, and if we leave, we won't be able to get back in here without going through them." Normandy turned away from Clement and continued walking.

"Yes, Lady *Callisto*," he said after a minute, accentuating the Callisto. Normandy shot him a glare, but his face was flat of emotion.

"Let's hurry. If we're doing this, we don't want them to find us." Normandy ran down the passage. Clement reluctantly followed.

"Someone's coming!" Clement gasped in surprise. "Ryker has come to finish the job," he stammered, but something in his voice sounded unsure.

Normandy looked back and saw torches. She ran around a corner while Clement followed, running past Dark Ones in their retreat. Normandy took random turns where no Dark Ones lurked. Behind them, the light grew brighter. Suddenly, the floor gave way beneath them and they plummeted into darkness.

←→

Normandy awoke with a pounding headache. She tried to move.

"Don't move, Lady Normandy, you might have an injury I didn't find." The voice sounded familiar. Looking around in the darkness, she saw only one torch lighting the rubble around her. She couldn't see Clement, but she saw a boy that looked like a mummy. He wore layers off wraps, and his strange clothing made it harder to recognize him.

"Blaze?" Normandy asked. The dark eyed boy nodded.

"What happened? How did you get here?" Normandy asked, laying still. She had a wrap on her left wrist, where she only felt a dull ache. Another long one wrapped down her right leg and ankle.

Blaze was a few feet away, kneeling next to what looked like a pile of rocks. The rocks were moving.

In the dim light, she thought she saw the small Native lift one of the boulders, at least as tall as the boy himself. Closing her eyes, she wondered how hard she must have hit her head in the fall. When she opened them again, Blaze was dragging Clement out of the rubble

"Is he dead?" Normandy asked, feeling a stab of pain.

"No, just unconscious. It seems like he is less injured than you."

"Why are you helping us?" Normandy asked.

"If Hollow Port men die near my people's land, I don't doubt that the People of Legend will be blamed for their death," Blaze said.

"How long have you been spying on us and following us?" Normandy demanded.

"Since the first day," he said.

"You travel without a torch?" Normandy asked.

"I have my ways," he said, finishing with Clement and coming around to Normandy to help her sit up.

"Where are we?" Normandy asked, as she looked around the room. Her headache was fading. What exactly did Blaze do to her?

"You found the original atrium of the labyrinth, and you found Aurelia's Box," Blaze said, his voice unreadable. Normandy saw the room as Blaze pulled her to her feet. It was an underground atrium, larger than the ones above. The item she had been searching for was in the middle of the room on a pedestal covered with vines. Aurelia's Box was smaller than she imagined. While she stepped toward the pedestal, Blaze helped Clement wake up.

Suddenly, Normandy became aware of the chill in the air. The same chill that consumed the whole temple emanated from the box. Another, duller cold came from Blaze. Normandy tore her eyes from the box and looked back at Clement and Blaze. She felt the cold from Blaze abruptly vanish. Glancing over her shoulder at him, she saw him helping Clement sit up and he gave her a perplexed look. She turned back to the box.

Aurelia's Box was a handspan wide, and she needed two hands to pick it up. The box was a milky white with emerald inlay. The marble carvings on the box were vines, impossibly small. They encompassed the entire box covering the lid, wrapping on and around the lid. Inspecting it, she didn't notice any breaks in the vines, which meant the lid was sealed to the box by the carved vines.

Normandy laid a hesitant hand on the box. She shivered at the untamed magic raging inside. Its dark origins should have unnerved her, but it didn't. Touching the box's power granted her a vision of the magic spreading across the world. All she had to do was open the box. To her shock, the marble vines on the box started moving. Normandy watched as the marble vines on the box wriggled, pulling away from the lid.

The stories told of an evil inside this box, but it was just magic! Magic that would change their world forever. She flinched as images of magical battles expanded in her mind, then mystical wars. In her vision, land broke before the power of the box.

"Open me!" The power of the box entered Normandy's mind. It had been injected with the power in the box, and she couldn't think.

"Have you ever wondered about the Dark Ones of Fare Golt?" Blaze was suddenly standing next to Normandy. "Back in the time of legends and magic, there was a great sorcerer whose name was Aurelia. She saw the evil and spite in the magic of the world. After watching the evil consume everyone in her family line, Aurelia swore to trap that power. She spent the rest of her life collecting magic and sealing it inside this box. Taking on an impossible task, she did well, but didn't get all of it. The leftover magic in the world attacked people and turned them into monsters."

Normandy felt a primal hatred toward Blaze hidden inside the box.

"You have magic. I can feel it, so don't deny it. Who are you?" Normandy asked.

Blaze continued, "Aurelia took the magical monsters, and through a series of complicated rituals, sealed them and all the left-over magic inside her family's home. The house was expanded into a temple, a labyrinth built to guard the place. The monsters that survived became bipolar creations, spending their time either docile or aggressive. When Aurelia left, she enchanted the temple with a final magic command that kept the temple from decaying. The command made a shocking amount of vines grow over the years, but kept the temple from falling apart."

"Who are you?" Normandy demanded as her hand trembled on the lid of the box.

"I am Aurelia's direct descendant, as are all the People of legend. Aurelia's long life of sorcery made her soul intertwined with a small part of the power, and her connection passes down to only one of her children each generation. My child will take Aurelia's connection from me."

"Why didn't you tell us this earlier? Why didn't you stop me from touching the box?" Normandy asked, her voice shaky.

"Most of the explorers that came were scared away by the Dark Ones. Your determination and will drove you further than others ever went. Honestly, I doubted you would get this far," Blaze said.

"Why can't I let go of the box?" Normandy whispered the question.

"I don't have an answer for you."

"I came to prove myself," Normandy said, her hand growing steady on the box. "I came to prove to my parents and all of Hollow Port that I am more than just the heir of Callisto!"

"How would you best prove that? I doubt you will prove yourself by ending the world with magic." Blaze almost laughed.

Normandy narrowed her eyes and tore her hand from the lid of the box, which felt like dropping the world off her shoulders. The magic left, leaving a hole inside. Normandy felt exhausted, and she almost fell over. "I knew you could do it." He said grinning.

"What am I going to tell my parents?" Normandy shook her head. "Where are the other explorers?" Normandy mumbled into her hands. "They are still searching for me and Clement and want to kill us and take Aurelia's Box."

"Kill you? I've been watching all of you. While the others say nothing but positive things about you, they aren't too fond of Clement," Blaze said, helping Normandy stay on her feet.

"Where is Clement?" Blaze asked. Normandy and Blaze turned to where Clement had been laying in the rubble of the collapsed hallway.

Normandy and Blaze walked over but didn't find him in any of the rubble. The single torch was still wedged between some rocks.

Blaze picked up his staff, which had been leaning against the wall.

"Lady Callisto." Normandy and Blaze turned back to the pedestal. Apparently Clement had recovered. "I don't know what to do, Lady Callisto." For once, Clement looked hesitant and unsure. Blaze took a step toward Clement. "Stop there, Native! I am going to take this box and deliver it to June Callisto," Clement said, hardening his resolve.

"Clement, don't touch it," Normandy warned.

"You're not my master, Normandy," Clement said, defeated. "My master, June Callisto, spent a lifetime searching for something like this, and she charged me to bring her any magical items we might find." Clement growled and then grabbed the box before running away. Clement moved shockingly fast, his long legs taking him far. He took one of the four dark doorways leading out. Blaze and Normandy took off after him. Normandy had a clear enough mind to grab the torch before plunging into the Dark Tunnels.

"Clement! What did my mom tell you?" Normandy yelled after him.

"Lady June Callisto told me to bring her any spoils we might find and to prevent your success if necessary," Clement said with a stern voice. She imagined his stone cold face as he betrayed her.

"My parent's letters?" she asked. Clement actually laughed.

"They don't care about you enough to send you letters. I fabricated those to wear down your resolve. I also killed those two explorers, since I hoped that you would leave if you thought we were being hunted by our own men."

Normandy was shocked and tried to boost her speed.

"I didn't want to have to go this far. Sorry, my Lady." She followed the sound of his voice around to the labyrinth's upper layer. Dark Ones kept clear of them, but Clement must have been out of his mind to be running these corridors blind.

"The men never turned against us! It was all your fault!" Normandy yelled. Blaze started glowing next to her, light rising from his skin. His magic was a dull thread compared to the complex weave of Aurelia's Box.

"Your parents thought that they'd punish me for your lack of decorum by assigning me to you. By bringing them your spoils and fulfilling my mission, they will restore me to my status as head steward."

"Is your only aspiration in life to be a servant?" Blaze asked as they ran. "That is kind of sad."

Clement went silent. Normandy stopped speaking, focusing on the sound of Clement's footsteps.

"What is this voice in my head?" Clement inquired.

"Don't open it!" Normandy yelled.

"I am going to try to intercept him. Catch up as fast as you can," Blaze intoned. The wraps slowly lifted off his skin. Animated by some unseen force. The cloth grabbed the walls and floor, and lifted Blaze off his feet, then he shot forward, lengths of tattered cloth shooting out and propelling him faster. He easily outpaced Normandy as a glowing whirlwind of cloth. His single vein of magic was being used efficiently.

As Normandy ran in silence, the torch in her hand grew heavy. She heard Clement yell, and then a grunt from Blaze, but nothing else reached her ears. Normandy followed a light until she eventually found herself running up an incline. She erupted into the second atrium with skylights. The natural light burned her eyes. Panicking, Normandy wondered where they were. Clement erupted from a tunnel across the room. He looked calm and collected despite being chased by a magical being. Normandy threw aside the torch as she sprinted for the exit. She had come out closer and easily beat Clement, and she blocked him with her arms extended. Seconds later, Blaze emerged from the tunnels. Whips of cloth lashed out at Clement, but he put his hand on the lid threateningly. The glowing whips of cloth slowed.

"Stop! Stop the voices!" Clement screamed.

"If you try to open that box, you will die. You will also release an angry power to the world that has been waiting for revenge since the time of legends," Blaze said.

Clement turned to Blaze.

Clement's back was to Normandy, and she saw the hilt of his dagger sticking out of his jacket. No, she couldn't! She couldn't kill Clement!

"I don't know if I want to be a servant for the rest of my life. One thing hasn't changed: I always do as I am told," Clement said.

Normandy could almost hear the box begging to be opened. And she couldn't let him open the box. Shaking, she lunged forward, pulling the knife from his coat. It was still tinged red from its last victims. Clement's body tensed and she stabbed him in the back before he could react.

Normandy backed away shaking, letting go of the hilt of the knife. Tears welled in her eyes as Clement's body went limp. What had she just done! The ivory box tumbled from his grasp. Normandy tensed, hoping the box wouldn't break against the floor! One of Blaze's wraps snatched it from the air. Clement's body made a dull thump on the ground. Normandy found herself sinking to the ground. She had just *killed* Clement! The one person that had supported her no matter how stupid her decisions. Clement who had taken the brunt of her mother's disapproval. He was dead, lying in a jungle temple.

Blaze lowered his body to the ground; the glowing wraps were fading and recoiling around his body. Aurelia's Box landed in his waiting hands as the last of the wraps slapped around his wrists. It seemed to have no effect on him. He looked at Normandy.

"You did what you had to," Blaze said, regret in his eyes. He offered a hand, but she waved it off.

"I just killed my only family, Blaze. I know I probably just stopped the next apocalypse, but it was Clement!" She felt numb as tears spilled down her cheeks. "Not only that, but my family will never accept me back into Hollow Port. I murdered one of my mother's higher servants! And I wasted my family's money and time gallivanting into the wilderness looking for treasure. Plus, Clement had killed three of the other explorers!" Normandy exploded as the four deaths weighed heavy on her heart. How did Blaze not understand the severity of her sins?

"Clement's death was very unfortunate, and I'm sorry it had to come to this. You don't need Hollow Port's acceptance, and you certainly don't need your parents. From what Clement said, they want you gone anyway." Blaze sat next to her.

"What are you saying?" Normandy asked.

"Leave. Put all of that behind you. You have a group of men that have already given up on Hollow Port, so take them and go. Send those who don't wish to leave with you back to Hollow Port and have them declare your death," Blaze said, shrugging.

"Where would we go?" she asked.

"There are more myths out there then Aurelia's Box, since the magical wars left lots of relics worth your attention. Become a legend," he said, as if they were discussing a simple weekend getaway. His words rang through her mind. Could she become a legend? Normandy forced a smile and looked up at the square of sky above. The smile was fake, and she knew it. The sky outside was dark and dreary, but it was hers.

She was free of the expectations of Hollow Port and her family's negative expectations. The memory of Clement's death was always going to walk with her, and in front of her?

"Tell me about some of these legends."

Emily Carlisle

He Held up the Sky

The storyteller wore the golden robes of a market performer, exuberant sleeves and a steep neckline trimmed in metallic bronze threads. He was twenty at most, with a sharp jaw and bright eyes. His smooth chest was draped in a single emerald necklace, its silver chain flashing in the broad daylight. Strands of short, bone-white hair drifted over his brow and the tops of his ears. Pale skin crinkled at the corners of his storm cloud eyes when he laughed. Multiple rings on his fingers sparkled in the sun, all the phases of a silver moon and one of an eclipse because he liked how it made the children whisper and imagine.

The storyteller's voice was like the song of a siren, alluringly beautiful. "And he leapt, straight into the sky, where the power of gravity and the ocean could no longer reach him." He spread his hands, eyebrows raised and a daring smile playing on his lips.

I crossed my feet at the ankles, observing from my usual front-row seat on the warm cobblestone street. I watched as the children crept closer bit by bit, the infamous story having reached its climax. Their eager shadows loomed over the storyteller's stall, dulling the silver and gold ribbon twining through the wooden pillars holding everything up. The carved sign set into the face of his stall was inscribed with the pattern of feathered wings, spread wide open and intricately detailed.

"He knew that once he touched the very sun itself, the world would become open to him, and freedom would finally be his. No more angry father or watching the crashing waves from his solitary bedroom window. His father's inventions would be the tools to his escape." His face grew serious, eyes flashing. Like the skilled performer he was, he drew the silence out, the anticipation grabbing them by the ear and pulling them closer.

"Icarus would fly."

The smaller children clapped their approval, smiling and getting to their feet. I stayed sitting, watching them gather themselves and prepare to leave.

At first, I couldn't believe it. I could never understand why he liked this part so much. Yet when he taught me to truly *see* the people around me, it grew to be my favorite part too. The wonder was so raw… I could feel it in the air all around me. A child was the only creature who could truly believe something. Only their hearts could create a story out of the words, transforming it into something that only they could really touch and see.

It was a powerful thing.

"He did not fall!" His voice rose over the crowd, and he paused, waiting for them to settle down before speaking again. "No, he rose higher than us all. Icarus touched the sun and it changed him. His wings became pure light, fusing to his back. The winds breathed life into him and gave him the strength to fly forever and ever. The Icarus the world knew existed no longer. Thus, a creature of the sun was born, and the skies became his."

The applause was deafening this time, filling my ears. I smiled at the storyteller, and he grinned back at me.

It was best for the people to believe that this was the true ending.

After the crowds spilled out, spiraling into the rest of the market's pleasures, I got to my feet.

Atlas grinned at me, sliding off his last ring. "Hello, you."

"You look like you need a break."

"I do. And *you* need to get out of the sun." He offered his arm to take me back to my house. Yet as soon as we touched, a bolt of static electricity zapped me, stealing my breath. I released his arm.

He paused. "Well… that's new."

"Nevermind me. How are *you* feeling?" I took him in, from his sharp facial features to the lean and subtle muscle cording his body. He looked the same as usual. While he'd always been odd, with his stark shock of hair and pale skin, things had been…happening lately. Inexplicable things.

"I'm fine," he said with a shrug.

I frowned.

His eyes met mine. "I've been hearing…voices."

"Voices?"

A dry laugh. "I know this sounds crazy, but the voices… they're talking about my brother."

Icarus, who had flown into the sky and never came back. Not exactly brother of the year material. "He's been gone for years. You've never even met him."

"I know," he said, voice strained. "But I know exactly what he looks like. I can picture him so vividly, Mayris." He ran a hand through his hair, mussing it into its usual chaos. "It's not just that, either. I feel…restless."

On the way to my home, I filled his ears with nonsense about my favorite books, the song I'd picked up on the lyre, even my progress with wood carving. Not once did it feel like his mind has drifted or that he'd gotten distracted. His presence was constant and loving, so I'd learned that I really could tell him anything.

I shoved my hands in my pockets as we rounded a bend, passing a thick copse of trees.

My house came into view. First the thatched roof, then the sharpened branches I'd placed around the perimeter to ward off unwanted visitors. Three of four stone walls were blanketed in crawling ivy, while the front door was a piece of driftwood. Both front windows were boarded up. To any random bystander, it would appear abandoned.

The door groaned as I shoved it open with a hip. Dark, gritty stone floors were bare and cold through the soles of my thin sandals. We padded through the living space and turned on the lanterns at each corner of the room. Flickering light bathed the chairs and rickety table nearby. A few shelves of wooden figurines were illuminated, different woods carved with varying degrees of efficiency. The terrible, half-deformed looking ones were my handiwork. A whole shelf full of rough-hewn horses, dogs, and willow trees that looked more like deranged demons crawling from the depths of Hell.

The rest of the shelves were full of Atlas's art. His trees swayed in an unseen breeze, and his horses cantered playfully across the wall. A falcon poised mid-dive, each feather so detailed you could feel every individual grain. He had this fascination with mythical creatures, and he'd taken up feverishly carving them this past year. There were multiple centaurs with bows and arrows drawn, long hair flowing behind them. A fiery phoenix rose from its own ashes. A fist-sized hydra glared menacingly. Atlas had even carved a dragon from wood the color of sunshine with magnificent wings and a large, toothy head so heavy I had to carry it with both hands.

However, my favorite was the palm-sized girl with long curly hair, sitting on a river rock with a big grin on her face. *Me.* He'd carved me, and somehow that meant more than anything else ever would. I had been working on a similar one of him ever since, though it was taking me a lot longer. Something told me that a demonic Atlas wouldn't be the best gift.

My stomach growled.

"Soup?"

I yelped, whirling around. The voice had come from the kitchen, where I'd neglected to turn on any lanterns. "Who's there?" I tried to make my voice sound bigger and more brusque.

Atlas stepped in front of me, the air humming with electricity.

In the dim light, I slowly made out details. A tall, muscular figure emerged, and I took a step back. Golden skin flashed in the light and warm brown eyes met mine. The lanterns seemed to flare brighter as he drew closer. I was transfixed, yet painfully aware that staring at him was putting me in even more danger, but I just—I couldn't stop.

The man—no, *boy*—stood in front of me. Hair, the color of golden-brown dinner roll crusts, was unkempt and windblown. Good heavens above! He was shirtless for no apparent reason and absently nurturing a bowl of soup. Loose drawstring pants hung on his hips and he was barefoot. Despite the somewhat bulky muscles surrounding his frame, he looked to be around the same age as me and Atlas, maybe a little older.

Full lips tilted into a smirk. "This is the amazing Mayris, hm?" Fear thrummed through my veins as he leaned closer. "I don't see it."

Coming up short on weapons, I shoved his chest. "See *what*?" I snapped. I managed to succeed in pushing him back half a step, if only because he was shocked.

He chuckled, dimples appearing. "I stand corrected."

"Who are you? What are you doing in my house?" I jutted my chin out, glaring fiercely.

He stepped back, running fingers through his hair. Plopping himself onto a chair, he leaned back. "I came here because you have quite a reputation to uphold. My curiosity, as usual, got the best of me. I've heard a lot about you." He shared a meaningful glance with Atlas.

I placed my hands on my hips. "What on earth are you talking about?" A thought dawned on me. Maybe the half-naked man was crazy. "Are you lost?"

"Uh, no," he said, squinting. "I'm not lost."

"What are you doing here?" asked Atlas sternly.

The other boy smiled. "I'm here to see you, of course."

"You...know Atlas," I said.

"I should hope so," he said, examining the shelves of wood carvings with care, running a finger along the dragon's scaly brow. "I am his brother, after all."

My heart started to beat double-time as the air thinned. "You're Icarus?" I choked out. Somehow, hearing his story for the majority of my life and actually placing a face to the name were two entirely different matters.

Icarus cocked an eyebrow at me. "Obviously."

"I-I don't—"

"Listen," he drawled, holding a hand out to silence me, "I've come a long way to get here. It's been... a while since I last had to suffer through human customs. Can't we just cut to the chase?"

I swallowed and that endearing, dimpled grin appeared once again. What was 'cutting to the chase'? How about we cut to the part where he answers what in heaven's name he was doing in my house?

"Excellent." Icarus clapped his hands. "I need to speak to both of you immediately."

"It's late."

He scoffed. "Sleep is for the weak."

This was my house and I got to make the rules. I changed the subject. "How exactly did you find my house?"

He sighed. "Atlas and I are connected through our thoughts. When I checked in tonight, it was your house that I kept seeing, over and over again."

"That's impossible..." I trailed off. Really, hadn't stranger things already been happening lately?

Smirking, he ruffled my hair. "You're a little dense, aren't you?"

I ducked away from his touch. "What are you talking about?"

"Let's talk to *him* and find out," he suggested.

I scowled. "Fine."

Atlas dropped down by the hearth, pearly hair catching the light. He sat motionless with his head bowed. I caught my breath and approached slowly. Eyes closed in thought, his ivory lashes fanned against his cheeks. His brows were furrowed into deep valleys and his mouth pressed into a thin line.

I reached out. "Atlas?"

Silver eyes snapped open and he scrambled away from my touch, the look of concentration evaporating. "I'm sorry for keeping things from you, Mayris."

I pressed a fist into the folds of my dress. "Um, well—"

As if reading my thoughts, Atlas's gaze shot past me, straight to Icarus, who inched closer to our conversation.

"Hello, brother! Welcome back to reality," Icarus said cheerily. "Have a minute?"

Those eyes narrowed and Icarus chuckled.

Atlas turned to me, softening. "Are you okay?" he asked quietly. I blinked when he took my hand in his, running a thumb over my knuckles. No shock.

"Yes," I said, catching whiplash from the different emotions he put off. "I'm fine. Are *you*?"

He gritted his teeth. "I don't know."

Icarus threw an arm over both of our shoulders, nearly pulling us in for a group hug. "This is really nice," he sighed. "Got room for one more?"

Atlas knocked his brother's arm off his shoulder, looking positively venomous. "What are you doing here?"

"We need to talk." He turned a dazzling grin to me. "This one appears very clueless about this whole ordeal. Should I fill her in, or will you share the news?"

Atlas stilled. "You will do nothing of the sort."

Icarus's grin grew wolfish. "I think she deserves to know, since you both are so…close."

"What's going on? Does this have anything to do with your voices, Atlas?" The questions rushed out.

Icarus raised a brow. "Voices?"

Atlas's gaze darted between us. A muscle in his jaw twitched.

I pressed my lips together, waiting.

Icarus let out a monstrous groan. "This is painful to watch."

Atlas stilled. "Brother…"

"Listen, kid," Icarus started. It took me a moment to realize I was *kid.* "What he means to say is that he's been keeping gigantic secrets from you and he's really very sorry."

I blanched. "Excuse me?"

"Don't worry about it, Mayris," said Atlas gently. He snagged a look at his brother. "Clearly he's spent too much time up in the clouds."

"You're not being fair to her—"

My brain was definitely lagging, but I didn't like that tone in Atlas's voice. "What are you keeping from me?" I asked him slowly.

If he was pale before, he looked positively dead now.

And he said *I* was a terrible liar.

In a flash, a look of fury stole over Atlas's face as he turned to his brother. "You have no idea what's going on!" he said harshly. "Stop trying to rope her into things that aren't even certain!"

"Not certain?" Icarus laughed. "Do you even see yourself right now?"

My breath caught in my throat. Atlas's eyes, they had *changed.* Those stormy grays had lightened to a bright silver, the pupils elongated into dark slits like…

Like a snake.

"*Holy Hera*," I breathed.

He took a shuddering breath, then marched into the kitchen, out of sight.

I turned to Icarus, trying to ignore my shaky knees. He stood, staring at the door with an odd look on his face. Then he smiled.

"Well, I don't think I did that right. I've forgotten how…*messy* human emotion can be," he said. "I'll be back tomorrow morning. I think…I've done enough damage." His smirk spoke the silent *for now* behind his words.

While I continued standing there, staring like an idiot, he continued, "He needs you."

I blinked. Right. Of course. Atlas was clearly suffering in some way, for something so big I couldn't yet understand it. I swallowed, slowly entering the kitchen.

Atlas sat on the table, massaging his temples, eyes scrunched shut.

"I don't mean to be insensitive, but..." I trailed off. He tensed. "I'm really, really hoping you don't have a forked tongue." I grinned. "Or do you?"

He blinked at me with normal, *human* eyes. A slow smile played on his lips. "No forked tongue," he replied with a laugh. "You are absolutely mad, Mayris Demetriou. Do you think me a snake?"

I tapped my chin. "So far, all signs point to yes."

Atlas shook his head, still smiling. His eyes dulled with serious thought. "You might be closer to the truth than you think."

"How so?"

His smile vanished and I immediately regretted asking such a forward question. I'd never seen him so off putted before. What if he got too nervous and closed himself off even more? However, I didn't take it back. The question needed to be asked.

He pulled out a seat for me and I sank into it, watching as he did the same for himself.

"We are called Draconis," Atlas stated simply, running a hand through his already mussed hair. "A race of people intended to protect nature and keep it balanced. Dragon-shifters, to put it plainly."

"You're...you're a dragon?"

He met my eyes. "No, but I believe we might have accidentally started the whole myth of them." He gave me a small smile. "We're all over the world, but most concentrated in Europe and China."

"So many..."

"Nature is everywhere." He nodded. "It is a Draconis's job to be the opposition to all things. Most powerful are the sun and the moon Draconis. Light and dark. Life and death."

My brow furrowed. "And you believe you are one of them? Shouldn't it be fairly obvious?"

"Unfortunately, I was not so lucky. I was created. I have no parents, no family." He paused, considering. "The sun and moon Draconis are the only two of our kind that are chosen. While others are born into this life, two are carefully selected and thrust into it without warning." His jaw clenched. "There is no choice in the matter."

I considered my words carefully. "You're so angry. Were you chosen?"

Our eyes locked together like magnets. There was such sadness in those gray depths. An ocean of fear and uncertainty and...repulsion. "I was meant to be the opposite of the sun, to balance him out." His voice was a coarse whisper. "Icarus was chosen. The sun elements loved his confidence and curiosity. When his wings melted and dripped feathers into the sea, he really did fall. He plunged into the deepest part of the ocean and before he released his last breath, the elements decided to create him anew. Such a large gift for his hubris."

The air thinned as I struggled to respond. This must mean that Atlas... my Atlas... was the moon Draconis. The opposite to Icarus's sun. "I don't understand. Do you mean you're the moon, Atlas? The darkness to his light? That couldn't be farther from the truth."

"But you're wrong, Mayris. That *is* who I am." His laugh was short and harsh. "I only exist to bring destruction and opposition, don't you see? I am the monster of this story."

"Enough with the doom and gloom!" I snapped. "You're wrong. Look at the children's faces when you tell them a story in the market. You bring wonder and light."

"You think much too highly of me."

"No. I don't." I rolled my eyes. "Good Zeus, Atlas, I never took you as the brooding type."

His eyebrows lifted. "What?"

"This isn't you." I reached a hand toward his cheek but rested it on his shoulder instead. "Trust me. I *know* you. No cursed element can change that."

Atlas slumped over and buried his face in my shoulder, arms wrapped around me tightly. It was like an electrical shock jolted through my system and through my arms around his shoulders. His soft hair and smooth skin brushed against the bare skin of my neck, his voice rumbling through me when he said, "How is it that you're so perfect?"

I was ridiculously glad he couldn't see my flaming face. "Flattery will get you nowhere, sir." Holy Hera, what was I even saying? "Er." I coughed. "I am far from perfect."

There was a *whoosh* and a loud *thud* as a new voice said, quite smugly, "This is just too pure." A fake sniffling sound. "My heart is full."

Atlas and I jumped apart so fast I nearly tilted my chair over. Its legs hit the ground again with a scrape. I glanced to the open doorway where the night spilled in on a crisp breeze that brought goosebumps to my arms.

Icarus's broad form filled the doorway, where he stood barefoot and shirtless, his arms crossed. He smirked at us, gesturing nonchalantly. "Ah, young love."

"Shut up," I choked out, my embarrassment palpable. "I thought you said you wouldn't be back until morning."

"I did say that," he amended with a nod, "but then I got bored." He collapsed on the chair beside us, its wood protesting under his weight.

"Why are you here?" asked Atlas.

I realized then that we still had no clue as to why Icarus had bothered coming back to this place. It didn't make sense that a powerful Draconis would linger here. If I had wings, I knew that I would fly away and never return, as long as Atlas was beside me.

"Well, I wanted to put this off for as long as I could, but it couldn't wait any longer." Icarus scratched his neck, trading a glance with Atlas. "There's been a lot of commotion lately. Something about Daedalus getting too close to King Minos and his daughter, Ariadne."

"Wait, Daedalus? Isn't he your father?" I asked him.

Atlas stiffened, but then Icarus answered, jaw tight. "He was no father to me."

I nodded, closing my mouth. Obviously not the time.

Icarus forced a smile. "Anyway," he drawled. "Dear old dad is not the best at maintaining friendships. He helped the king's wife cheat on him and conceive a monster. A half-bull, half-man creature, crazed with bloodlust. I can imagine the king was quite horrified." He chuckled. "That was what sent us on the run. Daedalus made these wing contraptions and told me to fly away with him." A dark smile. "Guess they didn't last too long in the heat."

"I have been hearing rumors," added Atlas, eyes thoughtful. "People say that there have been a lot of disappearances recently. Servants and young girls who wander after dark and never return." He paused, dread consuming his features. "Do you think..?"

Icarus lowered his drawn eyes. "Yes. My sources tell me King Minos has been using them as sacrificial victims."

"You're telling me the king is kidnapping girls as bull food?" Bile rose in my throat as I thought of all the times I'd been out at night, all alone. They could have grabbed me at any time…

Atlas pulled my hand into his. "I wouldn't have let them get you, Mayris."

"But what about all those other girls?" I glanced down at my hands, clasping them together tightly. Holy Hera, they were probably dead.

Icarus gave me a somber look. "It's horrible and disgusting, I know. That's why I came here to ask for your help."

I watched Atlas from the corner of my eye as he shifted uncomfortably with the new details. "You want to fight the Minotaur?" he asked incredulously.

Icarus glanced up at him. "Yes." His lips curved. "Will you help?"

"I will," I said resolutely, while Atlas gave a resounding "Definitely not."

A hint of panic edged into Icarus's gaze. "Don't tell me you're scared?" A small laugh. "Unfortunately, you don't have a choice. The Minotaur is a freak of nature. It offsets the balance. We must kill him."

Atlas raised his chin but said nothing else.

Wrapping an arm around my shoulders, Icarus grinned at me, looking wicked. "Well, kid, can't say I saw you coming." He looked at us both. "We leave in the morning."

He strode into the night, saluting me before the door shut after him. There was a large gust of wind, and I knew he was long gone.

The palace of Knossos was a sprawling mess of squares and pillars, like a child got carried away with their building blocks. Each section was layered like a cake, some tapered like steps and others at a steep incline. Crimson pillars were accented with black swirls and dips in the stone. Gaping windows in the tan stone showed guards and servants rushing about to fulfill their duties. Mosaics and murals depicted lions stretched out on their haunches, swaying stalks of wheat, and snoring bulls, favoring the color red.

The first crests of morning sunlight bleached the walls, catching flecks of micah. Goosebumps skittered across my arms as Icarus led us through a lone black door, so far apart from the rest of the palace's chaos that it was almost a completely different building altogether. The door had been left unlocked, so Icarus pushed it open, a sharp creak splitting the air. Cool, humid air collected on my skin, like a dead man's breath. Earthy stairs declined steeply, and soon faded to darkness.

"This is the entrance to the labyrinth," stated Atlas, narrowing his eyes.

Icarus grimaced. "It's lacking Daedalus's usual flair, isn't it?"

I walked past the boys and took the first step into the maze's gaping maw. The stench of musty earth and stale air swelled with each breath. Atlas grabbed my arm, his warm presence over my shoulder comforting and constant. He pulled me to face him, looking deep into my eyes.

He was so close I could hardly breathe. A flicker of a smile crossed his face and suddenly my back was against the wall and I could practically *taste* him, holy Zeus—

"You know, we could die down there," he said in a low voice. "Maybe get savagely ripped to pieces."

I glanced up through lowered lashes. "Wouldn't want any regrets."

And he kissed me.

He kissed me like his life depended on it, like he was a drowning man desperate for air. I tugged him closer, threaded my fingers through his hair. His lips were like moonlight and fireworks and that candy you've always wanted to try but were too scared to. The kiss seared through my frayed ends. The rips and tears in my heart and mind were mended in this one moment, this moment where I realized I could never live without him and his touch ever again.

We broke apart and I nearly melted all over the stairs. I propped myself against the dirt wall behind me and tried to regain my composure.

Tucking my hair behind my ear, Atlas smiled and turned away, disappearing down the stairs.

"Need a moment, kid?" Icarus smirked. "Was it everything your poetic thoughts imagined?" He fluttered his lashes. "*Oh, his lips were like the fuzziest peaches!*"

I covered my mouth. "Hades, no!" I shoved his arm. "You're so weird."

He winked. "Welcome back to reality." He gestured ahead, into the darkness. "After you."

←→

Down in the tunnel, the walls seemed to have eyes and ears. More than once I felt an invisible touch on my shoulder, skeletal fingers probing my mind and my thoughts. The feeling that we weren't alone, that we were being *stalked*, was impossible to chase.

Between the lit sconces, the darkness was all encompassing, making it hard to breathe. I kept track of Atlas by grasping his hand and we followed closely behind Icarus in the lead, where he commandeered the whole quest. He seemed to have a natural compass inside of him, pointing the way, because we never took a wrong turn. Not even once. I couldn't help but wonder if the labyrinth acted like a submissive puppy to Daedalus's blood running through his veins.

We found ourselves in a massive corridor, the floor a never-ending mosaic of the sun and each phase of the moon. Each design was big enough to fit a small house, and they circled each other like an abstract solar system, their tiles glittering.

Crossing the tiles, I heard moans and earsplitting shrieks. Catlike wails filled the room with agonized noise. The air was filled with a steady drumbeat of pounding and clanging metal. There were dozens of cages stacked on top of each other. Each was strapped to the walls with chains. Reddish stains wrapped around the lower levels from either rust or blood. Inside each one, the living remains of women, screeching and snarling, rocked the cages and slammed their faces against the bars.

Horror crept up my throat as I clasped my hands over my ears, the sound becoming too much. The sheer anguish in the air gripped my lungs and squeezed. Icarus looked pale, and his gaze was turned to the sun mosaic along the floor. Atlas hefted me upright from where I'd unknowingly sunk to my knees. I clung to his arm, trembling and following Icarus's gaze.

There she was. How could I have missed her? She was the grand trophy among them all, displayed in the center of the room.

The beautiful girl was dressed in golden threads that clung to her generous curves and gleamed brightly like polished chain mail. Tears dripped from her round, heart-shaped face. Freckles sprinkled across her cheeks and nose. Bottle green eyes rimmed in black and purple bruises peered out from a matted mess of long black hair. Her bloody fingers wrapped around the bars of a cage so tall that it cast shadows over us.

Her chapped lips parted. "*Icarus*!" she screamed.

Time stopped. Sound was nothing. Everything fell apart.

Icarus was so fast I didn't see him move. He gripped the bars, his entire body trembling as he gazed into the girl's face. He was saying something, scrambling to reach the girl as she sobbed, blood dripping from her fingers. She clutched her face and clawed at her hair. Icarus' hands glowed over the bars, heat filling the room and searing the metal. The bars bent outwards with a creak. He gently held her hands away from her body before she tore herself apart. Cradling her against his chest, their bodies fit together perfectly.

Until she dissolved into ash.

Icarus stumbled backward like he'd been stabbed. He stared at his hands that were now stained black. Her remains sifted through his fingers, bones clattering at his feet. The entire scene around us collapsed, the cages morphing into mounds of sand. The prisoners turned to ash while the sound of shifting sand filled my ears. Skeletons decorated the ground, scattered haphazardly across the room.

Staring down at us, a giant animal skull decorated the wall. Long horns curved over the massive bull's head, the whole thing larger than my entire arm span. Glassy, *human* eyes glared out at us.

A sick sense of wrongness climbed up my throat.

I lurched after Icarus at the same time that Atlas darted ahead of me, arms pumping. The air was so cloudy with ash that I tasted it on my tongue. Icarus remained motionless, repeating the same words with remorse.

"*I'm sorry.*"

I wiped the ash from his cheeks as he stared at nothing. "Icarus," I pleaded. "Wh— Who was she?"

The ground beneath our feet shook with the force of an earthquake. The walls themselves warped and wobbled, spinning around us. I pulled him down and Atlas wrapped his arms around me, shielding me from the oncoming dust storm. It all settled in a rush, and behind my scrunched eyelids light flooded my senses. The clamor stilled.

Slowly, I opened my eyes.

Icarus, Atlas, and I were crouched around each other on cool grass. The long strands tickled my feet as I took in the scene around me. Atlas and his brother staggered to their feet, the ash in their hair drifting like fallen snow with every movement.

We were not alone.

Two men and a girl faced us, dressed in brilliant fineries. Everything was gold— the threads in the girl's black braids, the crown on the older man's head, and the embroidered animal hide on the younger man's back.

I rubbed my eyes from the sudden brightness, removing the grit. The people came into focus and I nearly collapsed. The beautiful girl from the cage stood mere feet away from us with her fingers intertwined with the young man wearing the hide. The older man bore the seal of the king, and his familiarity slapped me in the face.

We stood in the presence of King Minos and his daughter, Princess Ariadne. But who was the stranger beside them, holding the princess's hand?

Atlas stood beside me, touching a hand to the small of my back. His pupils were slits as his eyes narrowed. "Your Majesties," he said softly. "To what do we owe this honor?"

Icarus stepped forward, every inch of him shaking and trembling. "Why?" It was one question, but the emanating heartbreak was enough to pierce my soul. As he moved even closer, the young stranger tensed over his sword hilt. "What is this deceit?" Icarus' voice cracked.

Minos ignored Atlas and motioned toward the man dressed in skins. He drew his sword and advanced to Icarus, leveling it at his head of messy brown locks.

"This is Theseus," said the king, his voice soft and deep. "My dear son-in-law. He slayed the Minotaur, you know." His face hardened. "Kneel."

Icarus fell to the earth, hunched over himself. Even with a sword at the back of his neck, he peered at Ariadne, a fallen angel looking up at the sun. "Ari?" His voice was small.

She regarded him with an expression devoid of emotion. I felt a brief flash of pity as her eyes seemed to fill with tears when she quickly glanced away. That feeling disappeared when she wrapped a hand over Theseus's bicep. Icarus' heart shattered into a million pieces, crushed under her heel.

"What do you mean, the Minotaur is dead?" I demanded, coming to Icarus's side.

King Minos's eyes flashed to me and his lips quirked. "Theseus fought for the freedom of his people. As was his right."

Atlas massaged his temples, his eyes glowering at the king. He shifted uncomfortably, and when he spoke again, his voice came out rougher than usual. "Brother, you said there were sacrifices. Missing people."

Icarus glanced down. "I lied."

"Why?"

"He said..." The air grew noticeably warmer. "He said they had Ari. That the Minotaur took her as a sacrifice."

My eyes widened. "Why trick us?"

The king chuckled darkly. "I am owed a great debt. A retribution." He strode to Icarus, lifting his chin.

Icarus's eyes glowed like twin suns, and the hairs on the back of my neck rose.

Minos clicked his tongue. "Ah, ah. Control yourself."

Theseus drew another sword and scissored them on either side of Icarus's neck. "Shift forms, Draconis," he said through gritted teeth, "and you lose your head."

"Do you know what it feels like to be a victim of your father's psychotic inventions?" barked Minos. "Do you have any idea how it feels to watch as he ruins your entire life?"

Icarus growled and I shivered. "His inventions *killed* me," he said, referring to his plunge in the sea.

"Hm. And yet here you are." The king shook his head. "You should have died." He pursed his lips and gave a nod to Theseus. Atlas leaped forward and I cried out as I reached for him. The swords began to close, as Minos said, "Son of Daedalus, say hello to your father for me."

Midair, Atlas began to Shift.

White fire consumed the field around us, enveloping his body in a haze. The ground quaked and the skies darkened. Atlas gave off pure moonlight. I could only stand back in awe at the effervescent shine in his pearly white scales and the silver ridges along his spine. A wingspan of nearly thirty feet rose up on either side of him, sharp talons protruding from the tips.

The dragon swept a wing into Theseus, sending him flying through the air with a clatter of swords. Icarus got to his feet and grinned at his brother. The dragon flicked him away and turned to the King and his daughter. He snarled, its vibration shooting right through me.

I'd never seen a king look so terrified. He fumbled with his sword and took several steps behind a wide-eyed Ariadne.

Icarus was beside me in a flash and I couldn't help giving him a gigantic hug. He returned it, smiling over my shoulder.

"We better get out of here, kid," he said into my shoulder, and tightened his grip on me.

I squirmed. “Why?”

“You probably don’t want to see this.” Icarus tensed, straightening. I gasped when large amber wings unfurled from his shoulders, just as impressive as those belonging to Atlas. A light lit them up from within in a warm golden color as the wings lifted, propelling us off the ground.

“Holy Zeus!” I held tight.

Icarus’s smoldering eyes gleamed. “Close your eyes.”

And we were off.

Jade Davis

Unseen Forces

The covers of the bed laid lightly upon me as I stared up at the ceiling. My thin pajamas felt flimsier than ever beneath the sheet that was meant to shelter me from the cold. My quaint bedroom and worn clothes weren't much, but they were mine. Through the small window I could see the setting sun lighting the sky with soft pinks, oranges, and faint traces of purple. I glanced at the skin of my wrist before watching the sunset yet again.

When the sun had set, leaving the sky with the last remnants of its light, I glanced at the inside of my wrist again.

It was time.

I closed my eyes and pressed my fingers to the now glowing crescent symbol on my skin.

The Hunt was on.

Opening my eyes, I glanced around, taking in my surroundings. The trees of the forest were more purple than they were last night, and frost dusted the shriveled blue and purple leaves. I shivered and pulled my dark green hunter's cloak tighter around my shoulders.

"Alycia."

I turned, looking toward the source of the voice before falling to my knees and bowing my head. "Lady Selene."

Lady Selene wore a pale blue dress with a silver cloak, white fur lining its edges. A soft glow emanated from her as the moon touched her skin. "It is good you arrived now and not later. They are restless and relentless."

"Have they all been turned?"

"They have."

My heart sunk. "Where have they gathered?"

"The Lake. You still have your Light Arrows?"

"No, Lady Selene. I used all of them last night."

"I see. And your bow?"

"It should be where I left it."

Lady Selene looked into the distance, toward the lake. She looked back at me. "I have restocked your arrows and left you a pair of moonskates. They should be useful when hunting on the frozen lake."

"Thank you, Lady Selene."

"Serve me well, Alycia."

"Yes, m'lady."

With a nod, Lady Selene shimmered and vanished into the night. I rose and began the walk to where I always left my supplies by the weeping willow by the lake.

With my bow and quiver in hand and the moonskates adorning my feet, I was ready to get to work. I made my way over to the frozen lake, careful to avoid any of the nightmares. I stepped onto the ice, the blades of moonlight stable beneath me. I began to glide around the ice, testing my balance before pulling out my bow.

I skated across the lake, glancing around. I nocked an arrow and waited. A black figure darted between the trees and I tracked it, waiting until there was a clear shot. I took a breath, and let loose the arrow, the fletching brushing my cheek as it flew past.

The arrow spun as it traveled, sinking into the flesh of the nightmare. As the arrowhead entered, there was a flash of white where it melted into the horse's coat. A spot of white formed, spreading in a spiral until it had covered the horse. The dreammare neighed and stood in its starry white glory, no longer trapped by the darkness. But I didn't have time to admire my work as another nightmare darted through the trees.

I spun on the skates, loading another arrow of light into the bow. As I continued to skate, I let the arrow fly, nailing the nightmare in the flank. It let out a whinny, transforming before it galloped to the other dreammare at the edge of the lake. The noise was all it took for the nightmares to descend upon them. I continued to shoot my Light Arrows into the hoard of darkness. One by one the remaining nightmares broke off from the group, recognizing that I was the real threat. I skidded to a stop.

"You want me? Come and get me."

As the nightmares charged toward me, the first few skittered and slipped on the ice. After that, the others circled the lake. I began to skate, readying my bow again. I let my arrow fly at the nightmare that had slipped while I glided backward, reloading my bow. I aimed at nightmare after nightmare, each turning to dreammares as the darkness was expelled.

Behind the nightmares, the leaves of the trees unfurled, becoming healthy and lush. The blues and purples faded to white before swirling with hues of green. The forest began to blossom, getting brighter with every nightmare vanquished.

I continued to skate, my arrows penetrating the darkness of the nightmares and replacing it with light. I could feel energy seeping away as I continued my barrage. My limbs trembled with each arrow I let loose. My hands began to shake, and a shot went wide. My feet screamed at me to rest, but I couldn't.

I wouldn't.

It was my responsibility to fight the nightmares. From sunset to sunrise, it was my job, and I refused to quit. I pulled my bow taunt again, my hands still shaking. I let the arrow fly, and again it went wide.

"Alycia."

I spun on the toe pick of my moonskates and respectfully nodded my head. "Lord Helios."

Lord Helios was adorned in a golden tunic and a wreath of laurels upon his brow. "It is nearly sunrise. You have done well."

"But nightmares still remain."

Lord Helios smiled. "Alycia, there will always be an endless amount of nightmares, since you're only one person. But look at the forest. It is much brighter than it was when you came at the beginning of night. The trees are green and lush, the bushes bear fruit once more, and if birds existed here, they would be singing. You have done well, Alycia. There will always be nightmares, and you will always be here to fight them during the night."

I smiled back, exhausted. "It's tiring work, Lord Helios, but I'm glad you and Lady Selene have chosen me to do it."

Lord Helios nodded. "You are one of the best hunters we've chosen for the job. Now hurry and return your bow and arrows to the weeping willow along with the skates, it's nearly sunrise."

When I skated to the edge of the lake, I noticed the nightmares huddling at the edges of the forest. They had moved that direction when Lord Helios appeared. I pulled off my skates and walked to the weeping willow. I gently set down my bow and arrows as well as the skates. I turned to Lord Helios again.

"I shall see you tomorrow night, Lord Helios." I knelt, bowing my head.

"Rise and travel safely, Alycia."

By the time I had risen, Lord Helios was gone. I looked at the glowing sun on the inside of my wrist, right below the pale, crescent moon.

I closed my eyes, took a deep breath, and pressed my fingers to the sun.

The Hunt was over. At least until sundown.

I opened my eyes, and found myself in bed, the chill of the morning seeping through my thin pajamas. The sun shone through my window, light splaying onto the floor of the small room.

"I'll be back tonight" I whispered to the shadows in the corner, "to chase away the darkness and bring back the light." I stretched, getting out of bed. As always, I felt strangely well rested when I rose. I stared out the window at the brightening sky outside and smiled.

Today was going to be a good day. I could feel it.

Kaitlyn Howes

White Capped Waves

The boat rocked on the starlit sea. Wood creaked against the swell of the tide. Everything ached from the base of his spine to the tips of his bone-thin fingers. His head lay balanced on the edge of a burlap sack, the only forgiving part of the rowboat. A moan creaked through his lips like a skeleton rattling in its grave. The only thing separating him from leagues of darkened waters was a thin layer of rotted planks. He let his body remain stiff and molded to the shape of the wood. Nothing could convince him to move, not the untrustworthy boat balancing inches away from pitch saltwater, not the untold monsters below, and not even the horrors he left behind.

The wind howled against the otherwise ghost-quiet night. Along the painted straight horizon a glimpse of flames danced, piercing into the charcoal of the night sky. He pinched his eyes shut to block it all out. Bile rose in the back of his mouth and his fingers twitched as he slowly came back to life. His eyes opened—though it made no difference in the darkness of the night—and he peeled himself from the deck to sit against the small hull of the boat. The waters below were thick and murky. Wind danced along his spine, leaving a trail of goosebumps. A howl called out in the night. His eyebrows drew in close. His head swung back and forth, checking the seas, and the sky. Empty. Nothing was there but again the screams drew out in the air. His pulse spiked. His hands grew clammy with sweat when they reached for the sides of the boat like it was a vise. The heart beat rattled in his head, banging against the sides of his skull like a ticking clock. The water rippled. It was small, just a little bubble disturbing the serene glassy surface.

The image of his reflection returned. The image was him with the onyx hair and sun weathered skin but it was crooked, slanted among the waves like the picture of himself he'd become so well acquainted with in the mirror through the years but replaced by something else. Something new. Someone else.

His breathing grew shorter and more rapid. It was like a cold bucket of ice water poured over his head and over his shoulders. It ran down his back like frozen tendrils of smoke puckering and digging into his skin.

The darkness seeped around him and again the water rippled. His fingers hung suspended over the waves and again there was a movement. It was almost like a flash of a ghostly white pale stretch of skin.

Twisted and curved it was almost like animal claws cutting through the water. It was a brief flash that shot in and out of view before once more, gone. He jerked his fingers away from surface and clutched his hands tightly against his chest. His boat slid over small waves and he shook his head again. There hadn't been anything in the water; there couldn't possibly be anything this close to the surface this close to his boat just after the fires. Nothing that looked like that. It must have been his imagination.

He placed his hands on the rim of the boat and leaned over the edge. His face wavered inches over the water. It lapped at the boat and sprayed his face with a mist. His fists were iron clamps on the boat. He stared into the waters where there was nothing, absolutely nothing, but cold pitch. Another scream let loose in the darkness, it came from the water but there wasn't anything there. It was only him sitting alone on the long expanse of the ocean.

He moved closer to where his nose nearly brushed the water. There was something.

Something white. But again it was flashing in and out of view. It could have been anything, a fish or some kind foreign white kelp pushed to this side of the world by a current. But something told him it wasn't anything like that. It was whiter than any sea animal he'd ever caught in his lifetime as a sailor and it was something about the way it moved with clunky oddness not the gracefulness of any carp or trout he'd seen. If he knew anything about the sea he would have guessed that it wasn't anything that belonged in the sea.

He was still puzzling over it when it shot into view again. This time it didn't stop. The hand wrapped around his throat. It was slimy with a steely grip. The fingers dug into his throat and pulled him down closer into the water until his face was submerged. He closed his eyes and pulled back against the grip. He dug his own fingernails into the white bloated hands until they let him free.

He choked down oxygen into his lungs. Water sprayed all around him as he shook it from his hair and eyes. The frigid waters sent him shivering. He spun around wildly, grabbing a box of matches he'd packed in his sack before jumping overboard along with one of the old cracked lanterns already packed inside of the row boat.

He ripped out a match and struck it. Nothing happened. The match was soaked. He dug through the box until he could find the driest one. His heart was pounding, thudding in his chest knowing that whatever it was, whatever was hiding in the water would come for him, it was just a matter of where and when it would attack.

Again, he struck the match. It lit. He shielded it with his cupped hand and placed it to light the wick of the lantern. The night burst with illumination. He lifted the old rusted thing and turned in every direction, looking and searching for the monster. In his other hand he held one of the ores. His feet were planted along the base of the ship and he refused to budge against the whipping winds and the ever growing tide below the boat. The boat creaked.

The nose of the rowboat dipped under the water. Cobalt waters flooded, churning inside the boat. He backed up against the far end clutching onto the lantern and oar. He glanced to the other end of the boat where hands held it up. His heart stuttered, there were dozens of hands, not just the one from before.

All he could do was watch as one of the hands whipped around from the back end to the side and shoved it. He tumbled from the boat and into the icy tar.

The lantern plunged into darkness and the oar fell from his grasp. He tried, struggled all he could to reach the surface for that single reliving breath of air but he only sunk farther and farther down. The white hands followed him.

They circled around him and then there was more than just the fingers. There were faces too. Every face ranged in ethnicity, shape, and age. But if there was one thing they all had in common it was that they all were drained of any flush on their cheeks and they had skin peeling away from their bones.

The skin that remained was bloated and puckered with a blue-gray tint. Their eyes were drained of color, unseeing and listless in their skulls. Some wore scowls and twisted expressions while others were sad. The worst ones were those with no expressions at all. His lungs burned with the strain of fighting back against their grip on his legs and feet, pulling him down even farther.

They howled, screamed with perfect clarity. There was one other thing that each and every face had in common: he knew them all.

You. The voices clanged in his head, accusatory. *You. This is your fault. This is your retribution. You know the tales, and the captain must always go down with the ship.* He struggled even harder, he kicked and spun. It wasn't his fault. He hadn't meant to do it. Darkness encompassed him and the pressure on his body only grew as he sunk lower and lower like a shackle and ball were holding his foot.

The faces swirled around him growing faster and faster with speed like they were making sure he could see each and every one of them. Some even grinned with feral teeth bared at him. His lungs ran out of air and the water seeped in. His body hacked and jerked in every direction. His legs twisted and his fingers clawed at his throat. He'd do anything for that last breath, the last breath he hadn't offered his crew. It had been his fault. He had lit the fire and he had been the one to send his crew to their deaths. He hadn't even offered them any form of rescue because he was gone on the only rowboat long before anyone else had known about the fire.

He gave one last look to the ghosts around him before they attacked like a pack of sharks with their phantom fingers gouging into his flesh and tearing apart his clothes, they ripped at his hair and nipped at his ankles and his body twisted and squirmed as the water filled into his lungs though it was almost instantaneous once his lungs were full everything became serene. He couldn't feel the tearing at his body any longer and he closed his eyes while the ghosts still tore apart chunks of his skin like it was chum for the fish. Finally, his eyes closed and he let go to join his crew.

Michaela Watters

The Guardians of Time

Morgan ran. That was the only option left. She had never been caught before, and she didn't want that to change.

"There she is!" someone called from behind.

She didn't dare look back. She knew who was pursuing her. She ran down a crowded street in hopes of losing them.

"Stop! Police!" someone shouted.

Yeah right! She was not going to give up now. Clutching her bag tighter, she darted into an alleyway before slipping into a basement through its window. She heard the cops run by in confusion, paying no mind to the alley. She smirked, knowing she had succeeded.

"Did you get it?"

She turned around. Her black hair stuck to the back of her neck. She was hot, sweaty, and tired. She nodded, still out of breath.

"Give it to me!" the man demanded. He stretched out his hands to her. She frowned at him. "Payment first. That's what we agreed on, Oswald," she told him.

"Listen here," he said. "I need to make sure you got the right one." His voice was laced with excitement

"Fine," Morgan said. She shuffled through her bag to retrieve a small box. "Take it."

"Thank you," Oswald said softly. Morgan frowned at the sudden change of emotion, not that she was surprised; he was as variable as the wind.

She crossed her arms and huffed. "Okay, I got you your box. Now pay up," Morgan said. Working with Oswald was like trying to figure out a complicated riddle. She never knew how he was going to act. Morgan just wanted to be done with him.

"Now, Morgan, is that any way to treat a client?" he said as he fiddled with his money bag. She ignored him.

That was another thing that bugged her about the man. He looked like he belonged in a renaissance fair. He wore a tall pointy hat and a long robe. He had a long white beard that was cut unevenly, some pieces coming down to his waist while others were clipped a short distance away from his chin. Morgan snapped out of her thoughts as Oswald pulled out a single coin and handed it to her. "What is this?" She asked, "Some kinda joke? I want my full payment!"

"That is your payment."

"What? A coin?"

He gave her a sympathetic smile. "It is all that you need."

She inspected the coin in her hand. One side was smooth while the other was rough with writing carved in it. The gold color reflected onto the ceiling above her. "What am I…" She trailed off as she noticed that Oswald was gone.

Typical. Morgan threw her head back and growled at the ceiling. "Why?" She took a deep breath and bent her attention back to the coin. The smooth side was so smooth that she could see her reflection in it. She flipped the coin over to try to read what was carved on it. Squinting, she tried to see by the dying sunlight from outside.

Never daring to turn a light on in fear that someone would notice, she lived in the dark basement. It had been abandoned during World War Three, so it was run down and still ran off electricity. It did have a solar panel that she had rigged into operation. She needed the juice if she wanted power for heat and cooling, the ancient Macbook, and other stuff like that. The power companies were fifteen years gone. She survived by her own sweat and smarts, or nothing. Not that she wasn't grateful to have a place of her own, but it would make life easier to have something new to use for a change. Holopads, for instance were untraceable and versatile, instead of the all-too trackable Wifi signal of the laptop. It would have made hunting things for Oswald much less dangerous. Maybe Oswald secretly wanted her to get caught. If that were true, he wouldn't take such obviously genuine pleasure in the things she brought back.

She used the sleeve of her shirt to wipe the dirt out of the carved words and held it up to the last shaft of the setting sun.

"Paint me red, and I will show you,
Leave me gold, and you will never know.
Let me rust, and your past will be as dust.
Get me wet, and you can help protect. ~2249"

"Red?" she asked to herself. She rubbed her thumb over the side of the coin. "Paint me, red." As she moved her thumb around and around, she thought about what it meant.

"Ow!" she yelped. She dropped the coin to inspect her thumb. The coin's old edges had nicked her skin, enough to draw blood. Morgan picked the coin back up, looking at the small sides of the coin. Turning to angle it into the light, she noticed an edge that had become sharp over time. The coin's golden color was becoming more of a copper red, which sparked an idea. She pressed her cut against the words on the coin. Though the wound wasn't large enough to cover the whole coin, the dark red liquid seemed to spread across the surface. Soon the coin began to feel warmer, and the red began to glow slightly. She dropped the coin again, and it clinked to the floor.

"Jason, I already told you that it's suicide!" she heard a male voice say. She turned around to see her father standing behind her. Somehow, she was no longer in the basement, but a small bedroom. Her father was packing a bag full of clothing, while another man stood behind him. She recognized the other man as Oswald.

"Oswald, you know I have to go," her dad said. "I'm not worried about my own safety—yours and the world's. And most importantly, Morgan's."

"Jason," Oswald said.

"No, it's okay," Jason said, putting a hand on Oswald's shoulder. He lifted a coin that was the same one that Oswald had given her. "If I don't come back, make sure Morgan gets this because she has to continue the work. The Time Scavengers must be stopped, and if I don't succeed…"

Oswald looked like he wanted to argue, but didn't. "Of course, brother," Oswald said, taking the coin. "I pray for you and for her that you can stop them."

"Me too, brother. Me too."

Morgan rubbed her eyes with her knuckles. When she opened her eyes again, she was back in her basement. She searched the floor for the coin she had dropped.

"Looking for this?"

Morgan jumped. Oswald was standing there, holding the coin in one hand and a cane in the other.

Oswald. *Her uncle.* She couldn't decide if she was happy or not. "You're my *uncle*? My dad's brother! Where's my dad?"

Oswald smiled sadly. "Yes, Morgan. I am your uncle. But dear, your father is gone."

Morgan looked at him. "Gone? What do you mean?"

"He died fourteen years ago."

"Died?"

"There is much you don't know."

"I've been living on the streets since I was five, and you didn't help me?" She breathed heavily, balling up her fists.

"Let me explain," Oswald said, hands outstretched, trying to calm her.

"Fine," she sat down in her chair. Oswald sat on the old dusty couch against the wall.

"Since the beginning of time, there have been people called Time Guardians. Their job is to protect the flow of time. Interruptions could be fatal to our very existence."

"So, time travelers?" Morgan interrupted, causing Oswald to glare at her.

"Ahem. In a way. They don't go gallivanting across time for fun. Instead, they travel to protect the fabric of the universe. So many people through the years have tried to invent a time machine, but they always fail because of the Time Guardians."

"What exactly do they do?"

"Sometimes they will go undercover to sabotage the machine or scientists' notes or tools will suddenly go missing. There have been a couple of cases when someone was successful, and then the Time Guardians fix the resulting mess."

Morgan gave him a confused look. "What does this have to do with my dad?"

"He was one of the last Guardians. It's not a job you choose. It's a job that chooses you. And just like your father and I, you are a Time Guardian."

"You're crazy. I don't believe you," she told him

"No. I am definitely sane."

"Really?" she asked. "Then show me how this time travel thing works."

"I can't."

Morgan mocked surprise. "Really?"

"I can't because I've been cursed since the night your father died. I was doomed to know all realities."

"What do you mean by that?"

"I've been granted the ability to know what happens in all possible realities. The Time Guardians protect one specific timeline, and my job is to fix any tampering."

"Do people live in a timeline that is wrong?"

"They can. In fact, that's why I'm here. I need your help to fix a timeline."

Morgan laughed. "This is a bad dream. Next you're going to tell me the screwed-up timeline is this one."

Uncle Oswald just looked at her.

"You have to be kidding me," she said. This would turn out to be one of his weird jokes.

"The people who killed your father were once Guardians, but they went rogue and altered time rather than protecting it."

Morgan remembered what her father had said in the vision. "He went to stop the Time Scavengers that night, didn't he?"

"Yes."

"How do I know that you're not confused about this being the wrong reality?"

"You don't know that. At least not yet. Give me time and I can prove it."

Morgan breathed deeply. She ran a finger over the bulging seam of her broken chair. Dusty sofa, hotplate, tins of beans. A whiff of brimstone from the jury-rigged electricity intermittently powering her decrepit laptop. High up on the empty gray cinderblock walls, grimy windows faded to black at the end of another long, lonely day. "What the heck," she said. "No timeline could be worse than this one. I'm in."

"We need to fix time," Oswald said, handing her the coin. "This coin is the key to being part of the Guardians of Time." He walked back over to the couch and grabbed the box that she had stolen for him. "This," he told her, shaking the box as he walked back, "will help us know what is the best time to travel to, down to the second." He set the box down on Morgan's rickety table.

Oswald opened the small box that would only fit a few pieces of jewelry. "Put the coin in there."

She dropped it in, expecting to hear it hit the flat bottom of the box, but the sound never came. Leaning over the table, she looked inside. Before she got too close, the coin came flying out into the open air. She took a step back and caught it. It landed in her hand with a soft 'thump.' "What just happened?" she said.

He smiled. "This box contains time and space or things as they are and things as they should be."

"So, it's magic?"

"*Magic*? No," Oswald scoffed. "Think of it like a black hole that's full of the knowledge of all possible realities. At the center of the black hole is the reality that we need to repair. When we put the coin in there, it searches for tears in the realities and ways to mend them back into the one true reality."

She let that statement sit there a moment. "So, it's magic, then."

They glared at each other. Oswald closed his eyes. "Fine. It's magic."

Morgan smiled triumphantly. "How many realities are there?"

"One."

"But you said—"

Oswald sighed loudly. "Let me finish. There is supposed to be only one reality. When something happens that wasn't supposed to happen, a whole new reality branches off. If something else changes, whether in the original or new reality, it creates another branch. And the cycle continues over and over."

"Are any of our choices actually ours?" Morgan said.

"What do you mean?"

"If making a choice violates what 'should' happen, and that choice creates a new reality, then how do we know what choice to make? Is freedom even a thing?"

"No. What is supposed to happen is what does happen. We create the one true reality, all of us, by being ourselves. We have complete freedom to act. But if someone goes back in time and changes something that has already happened, then we get a fork or an alternate time. That fork is the one that has to be rejoined to the true line." He rubbed his hands together. "Now, what are the numbers on the coin?"

She lifted the coin and showed it to Oswald. "The numbers match this year, 2249."

Oswald raised an eyebrow. "You sure?"

Morgan looked at the coin. "The numbers have changed to 1831."

"I suspected as much. Morgan, who was your sixteenth president of the United States?"

"John Breckinridge. Why?"

Oswald ignored her comment. "And who won the Civil War?"

"The South! Everyone knows that! Why?"

He once again ignored her. "When the South seceded, what was the name of that new country?"

"The United States of Confederacy!" She paused. "Well, until World War II, then they became part of Germany, which doesn't make sense geographically, but…"

Oswald rubbed his chin. "This is worse than I thought."

"What is?"

Oswald groaned. "You will know soon enough." He rubbed his eye, then looked at Morgan. "Flip the coin into the air, then let it drop to the floor."

She rolled her eyes, then flicked the coin up into the open air and stepped back to let it hit the floor.

The next thing she knew, she was lying in the open with the bright sun beating down on her. She blinked rapidly and sat up. They were in a field of grass just outside a small old fashioned town. Morgan breathed deeply. The air smelled so fresh. She pulled a handful of grass out, the dirt sticking under her fingernails. She relished in the experience. In the year 2249, things like the grass were rarities.

"Beautiful, isn't it?"

Morgan looked up at Oswald, who was standing a few feet away. "Yes, it is," she replied, looking down at the clump of grass and dirt in her hand. "Where are we?"

He smiled. "I think the correct question is, *when* are we?" His misty gray eyes looked serious, his smile was one of excitement but also determination.

She stood up, brushing her dirty hands on her jeans. "Okay, when are we?"

"Before I answer that, I am going to ask you again. Who was the 16th president of the United States?"

"Abraham Lincoln," Morgan said automatically. She gave a nervous laugh. "Wait, what is going on?"

"We are in the year 1831, the same time as the numbers on the coin. Something went wrong in time, and we need to fix it. In the reality that we just came from, Abe Lincoln was never president. My guess is he never became a legislator either. In the correct timeline, the town's schoolteacher, Mentor Graham, suggested that he should run as a legislator. That town," he said, pointing to the town by the field, "must be New Salem."

Morgan looked at the small town. "What exactly are we supposed to do?"

"I'm guessing someone did something to Graham before he could suggest to Abe that he run as a legislator. I think we need to find Graham before the Scavengers do."

"Looking like this, we won't last five minutes."

Oswald looked down at himself and then back to Morgan. "Good point."

"Are you wearing pants under that dress of yours?"

"Excuse you, missy," he said. "But this is a *robe*, not a dress."

She rolled her eyes. "Fine. Is there anything under your *robe*?"

"Yes," he said, raising his chin to make himself look taller.

"How about a shirt?"

"I'm fully clothed under here."

"Perfect," she said. "Give it here." She put out her hands, ready to accept the robe.

Oswald looked reluctant. "Merlin gifted this to me when I healed King Arthur's fever with a Tylenol. He said that he was proud to be acquainted with a powerful mage and hoped I would stay in Camelot."

"Well, that explains why you never take it off." She examined the robe with awe. "I thought you didn't believe in magic." She put her hands on her hips.

"I said time-travel wasn't magic, but I never said I didn't *believe* in magic."

"Fine!" she said. "Now that I know why you are so attached to it, I'll be careful. But give it here anyway."

Oswald groaned as he pulled the robe over his head. He thrust it into her hand before folding his arms in a pout. Taking the robe from him, she sat on the grass. She pulled a pocket knife out of her pocket.

"What are you doing?" he yelped, "Don't cut my robe!"

"Chill, I'm cutting your hat." Before he could say anything else, she had grabbed his hat from where it had fallen when he had taken the robe off and started cutting it into a long strip of fabric.

Oswald groaned and mumbled under his breath, "Do you even know what you're doing, creating costumes?"

"Sure," she said. "I'm going to fix this robe so it will fit into *Pride and Prejudice*, only it won't be as classy."

"*Pride and Prejudice*? You know that book?"

She stared at him. "It's Jane Austen. Everyone knows Jane Austen." She stood and pulled the robe over her head. It was big on her, but it was all they had. She grabbed the used-to-be hat and tied it around her waist like a sash. She then stood up and looked at her uncle. "Well, how do I look?" She spun in a circle.

Oswald sighed. "Do I get the robe back when we're done?"

"No, I want to burn it in a bonfire while singing *Kumbaya*." She paused, waiting for a reaction. It didn't come. "Yes, you can have the robe back."

"In that case, you look lovely, miss." He bowed.

"Good. Your turn." She picked her knife back up and marched over to him. "Hold still." She grabbed a chunk of his beard and drove the knife through it.

"Hey! Stop!" Oswald protested.

"Hold still, or you might get cut." He stopped fidgeting and let her work. She cut until his beard was neatly trimmed above the neck. "There!" she said, stepping back. "Now you don't look like a crazy old man."

He huffed while rolling his sleeves up.

They walked through the town, trying to blend in. Even with their new looks, they stood out. Some stared at them while others avoided them altogether.

"We need to find Graham," Oswald whispered.

She nodded, her black curls bouncing. She hated wearing her hair down, but Oswald told her, "It will make you fit in better."

"Where do we even start?" she asked.

"You stay right here. I'm going check that store and ask about him. Someone will know." Before she could protest, he walked off toward one of the nearby stores. She huffed and crossed her arms.

"You look bored."

Morgan looked behind her. Leaning against the side of a brick building was a man. He was tall, skinny, and slightly familiar-looking. Wearing a suit that looked about two sizes too small, his pant bottoms came up to his ankles and his sleeves past his wrists. He smiled at her, his top hat casting shadows over his face.

He pushed himself off the wall and walked closer to her. She smiled at him, not wanting to be rude.

"Just waiting for my uncle," she replied.

"I see." He looked down at her dress. "I like your dress. I've never seen anything quite like it." He paused. "That was supposed to be a compliment, but I'm not sure if it came out that way." He sighed, pinching the bridge of his nose. "Sorry."

She looked at him in confusion. "Why are you sorry?"

He laughed. The sound of his happy laughter made Morgan's heart do cartwheels. It was the warmest laugh she had ever heard, deep and embracing. "Well, for someone who loves to tell stories and jokes, I have a tough time talking with women."

She smiled at him. "You're doing fine, sir."

"Well, look at me, I haven't introduced myself yet." He shifted his book from his right hand to his left. He grabbed his hat, brought it to his chest, and bowed. "My name is Abraham Lincoln."

Morgan fought to keep the shock off her face. She knew that she had seen him somewhere. "Oops," he said as a couple of letters fell out of his hat when he went to put it back on. This snapped Morgan out of her daze, and she bent down to retrieve the letter that fell at the hem of her dress. "Oops," he said again. "It's just a force of habit. You see, I used to deliver mail, but I also love to read. Walking from house to house would take time, so I would read, but I needed to put the letters somewhere." He rubbed his forehead. "Sorry, I'm rambling, aren't I? I don't know why I'm like this. I do fine in crowds, and with men, but…" He stopped talking and rubbing his forehead when Morgan began to laugh.

"It's fine," she told him. "It's natural to be nervous."

He blushed and smiled, his long legs shuffling in the dirt. Morgan cleared her throat, not wanting to embarrass him anymore. "Anyway. I'm Morgan." She handed him his letter. He took it silently. "And I think your stories are great. You are going to do big things one day."

He laughed lightly. "I'm not sure about that, but thank you."

"Mr. Lincoln, I'm serious. You never know what lies ahead; go and find the impossible, and then do it."

He smiled. "I like that. Thank you, Miss Morgan." He tipped his hat to her. "Well, I best be off. See you around?"

Her smile wavered. "Maybe. My uncle and I are just passing through."

He smiled sadly; a smile Morgan had seen often. It was the smile he always had in his pictures. It was hard to believe that the man before her was a man that had such influence on the future.

"Well, in that case, it was great meeting you, Miss Morgan." He tipped his hat again.

"You too, Mr. Lincoln.

"Please, miss, call me Abe."

She smiled. "All right, good day to you, Abe."

He smiled at her again, turned, and walked away.

Almost as if on cue, Oswald came out of the store. "All right. He's at the church in the center of town. They use it as a schoolhouse during the week."

"Okay, then let's go."

"Who was that you were talking to?"

Suddenly the dirt at her feet became very interesting.

"Morgan?" Oswald said. "Who did you talk to?"

"Abraham Lincoln."

"*What*? What were you thinking? The timeline is at risk as it is, and you could have made it worse!"

Heat burned in Morgan's cheeks. "You don't get to scold me since you are *not* my father. You may be his brother, but you never stuck around when I needed you most."

Oswald's frown changed to shock.

"All you do is speak in riddles and tell me what to do. You showed up in my life, pretending to be something you weren't."

"Morgan, I—"

"You're what? Sorry?"

"Yes," he said firmly. It caught Morgan off guard. He then turned on his heels and walked away.

Morgan followed in silence. She hadn't realized how angry she was at her uncle. Morgan knew nothing of her mother, and her memory of her father was limited since he died when she was very young. She had been an orphan for most of her life, and yet she had an uncle who could have helped her. He could have taken her in and she wouldn't have had to be alone. Hating to blame her uncle for how she felt, she decided that she deserved answers. More than anything, she wanted to know why her uncle had waited so long to be a part of her life. Just this morning, she had thought him to be a crazy, old man, but now he felt like family. And to her surprise, his neatly trimmed beard and change in clothing made him look much younger. If someone had told her this morning that he was in his mid-fifties, she would have laughed. Also, she noticed that he no longer used a cane, which straightened his back, making him taller than before. He looked completely different.

"Wait!" she yelled, "Oswald, I'm sorry." Oswald stopped walking but didn't turn around. She came up beside him. "I'm sorry. I was upset, and I shouldn't have lashed out."

She looked around her at the shops lining both sides of the street and the horses pulling buggies down the dirt roads. "This is all just so much to take in," she said gesturing with her hands to their surroundings. "I know that shouldn't be an excuse. Earlier this morning, the only interesting thing in my life was making sure I didn't get caught stealing a box from a museum."

She waited for a response and was met with silence. "I just…" Her voice cracked. "Why? Why did you leave me alone? I was scared, and I spent years assuming Dad didn't love me anymore. It seemed like the only explanation." A sob escaped her lips. "Dad was an amazing salesman, and I assumed he was on the road following jobs. I never knew about the Time Guardians, and I never knew he was dead until today. I always fantasized him coming back for me, whether he had to fight pirates or evil knights to get way back to me. Part of me always knew he was never coming back, but I still dreamed." Tears were now flowing down her cheeks. "Uncle, why did you leave me?"

When he turned to her, he had tears in his eyes. "I wanted to tell you, but that night I was cursed. That night, I got sent through dozens of realities. You can make someone know something." He sighed. "There have been realities where I have come to you sooner, and together we try to mend the riffles in time. Each of those paths never turn out. You died almost every time." Tears were now flowing freely for both of them. "When your father asked me to protect you and to make sure you got the coin, I've been doing it the only way I know how. But I keep failing. And I don't think I can watch you die again."

Her breath caught in her throat. She never considered that he might have wanted to come to her sooner but couldn't. She threw her arms around him and cried. From the way he was holding her, she could tell that he was crying too. They stood like that for a long time before they separated and wiped their eyes and continued to the church.

As they walked up to the church, Oswald began talking. "In every other reality, I kept you in the dark. I told you exactly what to do without explaining why, even if it meant putting you in danger. This time I want you to have a choice. Things could get messy, and you can walk away if you want."

Morgan's eyebrows drew together. "Can you can do it on your own? I thought the curse…"

"The curse prevents me from traveling on my own, but in-between travels and reality changes I can do what I wish." He tried to make it sound not so bad, but Morgan saw right through it. The message she got was, 'Help me. I want to go home. I'm tired of running. I want to spend more than a day with you."

"Uncle," she began, using the title more and more. She loved that it meant family, and she was afraid that if she didn't say it, he would disappear. "I'm with you till the end, and we are both going home." They approached the steps to the church. Morgan threaded her finger through her uncle's, and squeezed. "Let's hurry up so we can get home. Together."

He smiled at her and together they walked to the doors of the church. Oswald pushed it open and they walked in. "Can I help you?" someone asked from the front of the room. "If you are looking for the children, I sent them home early today."

They walked closer to the man. "No, we are looking for Mentor Graham," Oswald said.

The man at the desk looked up from what he was working on. "That would be me." He stood up. Suddenly Morgan felt like something bad was about to happen but she wasn't sure what.

"Mr. Graham," she began, trying to keep her voice from wavering, "we came to talk to you about something. Do you have the time?"

"I'm a busy man. Come back tomorrow."

She started to approach him. That was a mistake. She heard the gunshot before she felt it. Looking down at her upper arm, she saw that her clothes where turning slightly red with blood. Gulping, she realized that the bullet had grazed her arm. Another gunshot echoed through the church, and she dove behind a bench to protect herself from any more bullets. She briefly wondered who was firing at whom when more shots sounded. Suddenly the schoolteacher was next to her. Morgan realized that he must have crawled over.

"Miss, are you okay? You're bleeding," he said, pointing to her arm.

"I'm fine; it only grazed me." She had never been shot before but she knew that she was in no serious danger. While it hurt, it was hardly bleeding.

He nodded. They both looked up when Oswald began to talk.

"Todd, you know what you are doing is wrong. Time is something we should treasure and protect, not manipulate," Oswald said to someone. Morgan couldn't see her uncle or the person he was talking to from her hiding place.

"And what has time ever done for us? I'll tell you what, all time ever does is run out! Why let time control your life when you can use your life to control time? To mold and create the perfect world," the other man said.

"That's crazy and you know it," Oswald said.

"Maybe, but it's better than living like you."

"A Time Scavenger? No thanks," Morgan blurted from where she hid.

There was a dark laugh that filled her with fear. "Time Scavengers? Really Oswald?" The man's voice got louder. "Princess, where are you? Come join the Time Gods; we aren't scavengers. Why would we have to scavenge something that we already own?"

"No one can own time," she replied, hoping that she was creating enough of a distraction for Oswald to come up with a plan. The steps got closer. She forced herself to her feet, Graham following suit. The man turned to her from where he stood at the front of the church. He was tall with curly brown hair and green eyes. He smiled when he saw her.

"Hello, my name is Todd." He bowed his head to her in mock respect. "I bet Oswald hasn't shown you all the marvelous things you could accomplish."

There was a loud bang and Todd hit the ground with a thud. Morgan searched the vast room for her uncle, and her eyes settled on him in the opposite corner as he lowered his pistol.

"Wow," Graham said. "I've never seen a musket like that!" His amazement fell when Oswald sent him a glare.

Oswald then looked at her. "Are you all right?"

"I'll live."

He came over and hugged her. "Oh, Morgan we did it."

She nodded, and then looked at Graham. He fidgeted under her gaze. "I'm sorry he shot you. I should have warned you he was there, but he threatened my family," he said.

"It's all right. I would have done the same thing for my family," she said looking back at her uncle. He grabbed her hand and smiled, not needing to say anything else.

Graham cleared his throat. "So, time travel? I'm guessing you guys aren't from this time?" Before Oswald could protest Graham added, "Please, I'm a smart man. And besides your clothes definitely give it away. And those guns you guys were firing," he said, "are something else."

Morgan snorted, while Oswald grimaced. "All right, you caught us," he said, putting his hands up in surrender. "We came back to make sure you stayed on your true time path. That guy was trying to stop you from your destiny."

"Which is?"

"You need to tell Abraham Lincoln to run for legislator."

Graham smiled. "I was planning on doing that anyway."

Morgan grimaced as Oswald fished the bullet out of her arm with a pair of tweezers. "Almost there," he mumbled.

"I have a question," she said, wanting to distract herself from her arm. "How come such a decision like Graham being killed caused such a ripple effect? How did everything after this like the loss of World War II or America splitting into two countries hinge on one small act?"

"Well," Oswald pulled the piece of metal out of her skin, "when John Breckinridge became president instead of Abraham Lincoln, the war was an easy win for the south. John was very much in favor of slavery. Since so many other people and states were against the idea, he decided it would be best for the south to succeed. When that happened, America never grew into a powerhouse. As World War II broke out, the south was an easy take for Germany, which then made the north an easy take. As a result, America lost the war." Oswald started cleaning up his supplies.

"Wow," Morgan replied. "It's crazy how much effect one person has."

Oswald nodded. "And there are more of the scavengers out there. They need to be stopped."

Morgan jumped down from the table. They were back in their own time now for about an hour. Morgan looked around her new home. It was an apartment belonging to Oswald that was time locked. When she asked Oswald what that meant, he told her that no matter what happened in time this would stay the same, like a safe house. Oswald wasn't sure if fixing reality had messed with the abandoned basement where she had previously lived. It would take some reconnaissance to find out. Honestly, she liked this new place better with its a real bed, working lights she could turn on and off as she pleased, and many other amazing things she had lived without. Her gaze fell on her uncle's robe. The sleeve now had a hole in it and was stained with blood. "I'm sorry about your robe."

He smiled. "It's fine; I have something better." He pulled her into a hug, resting his chin on top of her head. They stayed like that for a long time before they pulled away from each other. "Morgan, you freed me. You broke the curse the moment time was fixed and I was freed. And I am sorry that I was never there for you before, but I'm here now." He hugged her again. "I know I'm not your father, but I hope you know that I love you."

"I love you, too," she replied. She pulled away and wiped the tears from her eyes. "Now," she said, taking a deep breath, "how do we stop the rest of the Time Scavengers?"

Joseph Rogers

The Republic of Briariia

Raas

"Raas! Come here!" Cody called from the deck.

Shab it, Cody! The last time he hollered for me was just for his own sick entertainment. When he claimed land was mere minutes away, I hobbled away from my refuge to take a look. I was severely seasick and holed up in my small cabin in the back holding on to my hammock for dear life.

I refused to move from my room and to give that oaf the pleasure of seeing me squirm.

My thoughts were interrupted by a level voice that reminded me of the crumbling landslides back in Havtrospa. "The Republic of Briariia is a few leagues out," Cloud quietly but firmly intoned. No one recalled his true name, and everyone refused to ask after his last reaction to someone stupid enough to try. "Prepare to disembark."

Finally! I gathered my assortment of blades, strapping some on and putting the rest in a rough sack. I double checked to make sure Rolfe, my favorite knife, was firmly attached to my belt. As I stepped onto the wind worn deck, sunlight assaulted my eyes, reflecting off the imposing waves that make me so nauseated. Sound beset me from every direction as the ship hands made landing preparations. Other travelers like me crowded in the fore of the boat, ready to glimpse the famed Republic of Briariia.

I was distracted from my thoughts as two young men approached. The one on the left stalked toward me with the quiet grace of a predator cat. He was of average height with wired muscle and a shock of white hair. Across his broad shoulders was slung a massive longbow and a crowded quiver of arrows.

"There you are, Raas. We thought we'd lost you there for a second!" Cody teased me. My tormentor was tall and well-muscled. He carried a large battle-ax at his hip and a standard issue campaign backpack on his brawny shoulders cutting a very imposing figure.

"Not quite. You aren't that lucky, Cody," I responded. Shorter than both and slimmer at the shoulders, I could kill either with relative ease.

Cloud interrupted our small showdown, "We'll be landing shortly, so don't go anywhere." His voice carried the slightest hint of humor I learned to pick up on years ago. He found it amusing to tell us to stay put when we have nowhere to go.

Finding a comfortable seat among a pile of excess rope, I waited for landfall and inspected Rolfe. Its small elegant blade was forged by Ellizon the Strong centuries ago. Ellizon was one of the finest smiths to ever live and was of both elven and dwarven descent. Due to their craftmanship, his blades never lost their edge and never broke. As a warrior, he ended the ten-thousand-year civil war by the edge of his blade, dying in the process.

I found myself thinking about my approaching destiny. As the knife passed between my hands, it caught the glaring rays of sunlight, appearing to be in wonderous flames. I wondered if Briariia would have the organized crime of Havtrospa or the grand, sprawling markets of New Cretad. Either way, there would always be a job for a skilled assassin, no matter how noble or innocent the country seemed.

Hidden in my nest among the ropes, the radiant sun was suddenly blocked by wreaths of shadow. Passing by gargantuan trade ships, I knew we had pulled into the massive harbor in the large, bustling port town of Cape Ralmsley. Catching a view of the sheer grandeur of the city, I became spell bound. Buildings made of local stones and wood sprawled in every direction. Unlike the buildings in the country that served as my home, these buildings extended several stories in the air. The largest, with a massive central tower, appeared as a giant to the surrounding city. The city extended in every direction as far as the eye could see.

As we pulled into a dock, I sheathed my knife and moved to join the others. Ropes were thrown to the numerous port workers and the boat was firmly lashed in place. A gangplank was shoved over the side for the forty odd travelers to disembark.

I was stopped by the port official looking for a weapon license. "You got rights to carry those, son?"

I sighed. "Of course, give me a minute." I rummaged in my small sack for the weapons license I forged on the long, tedious trip here.

"Ah, here it is," I proclaimed as I located the forged document.

I held my breath as he examined my credentials. It wasn't my best job, since it had been hard to keep a steady hand on the ever-moving ship. He seemed to hesitate during his examination of the signature, and I worried that the mark wasn't sufficient since I didn't have spare parchment to practice it beforehand.

"Very well. Welcome to the Republic of Briariia," he drawled in a flat voice.

I jogged to catch up with Cody and Cloud. Cloud appraised me with one of his rare smiles. "Very good, Raas. Your papers stood up to inspection."

Feigning indifference, I beamed with joy on the inside. Cloud's quiet praise was equivalent to blaring bugles and three shouts for joy.

"Thank you. It was a close thing though. Only made it through 'cause the guard was half asleep."

Cody decided this was a great opportunity to jibe me. "Wouldn't have been so bad if you'd gotten left behind. Then I wouldn't always have to look after you."

Sometimes I wondered why Cloud decided to hire the extra muscle. We could pull any job better without this lump of flesh blundering around behind us.

Cloud broke the long silence that followed, "Cody, find a suitable inn and rent a room please. Raas, listen around and find any potential jobs. We'll meet in the town center at sundown."

"What will you be doing?" I asked.

"I have a debt to collect."

I decided not to pursue the issue. If Cloud didn't want to disclose something, he wouldn't. Ever. He never ceased to surprise me with his extensive journeying, and he seemed to have contacts everywhere we went. Cloud seemed to know everyone there was to know, and yet he remained a mystery to the world. He had no jail record or warrants for his arrest. None of his clients ever saw Cloud or knew who he was. Cloud always worked through middlemen, usually someone like me or Cody.

Hitting the main road, we split off to complete our various jobs. Each of us was supplied with fifteen skikes and a day's worth of cold rations in case of separation. I headed west toward the homes of the upper class and walked past decrepit inns and garish taverns vying for my attention. As I passed the waterfront, the buildings became larger and more respectable. The primary building resource used here was a light gray stone roughly cut into large blocks and sealed together with mortar of a similar color. It was completely alien to me, and nothing like the stone used in Havtrospa. In my hometown, the stone was dark gray shot through with the shadows of deepest black and was naturally rough but polished enough to see your own distorted reflection in its glassy surface.

As I stepped into the Bored Stag, a large bustling tavern that catered to the rich and powerful, a few heads turned in my direction, but most were too involved with their cups to notice me. Building a tavern in an upscale community such as this seemed odd, but it evidently did quite well. I strode quickly to the bar stretched across the back wall and sat down at a corner stool. The bartender, a large brawny fellow who was evidently overly fond of the drink he served, greeted me. His cheeks were flushed, and it appeared that he'd been working too hard for too long.

"And what can I do for you today, my good sir?" he asked. "Perhaps a pint of ale or a flagon of beer?"

I shook my head. "Actually, I'm here for information." As I said this, I slid one of my golden skikes across the bar. "I was hoping you could help?"

The man made a furtive glance around the establishment and then ushered me through a side door. He led me down a long, winding staircase made of sandstone that I recognized from New Cretad. The floor was made of gray flagstones that reflected orange rays in the flickering light. The stairs were well kept and lit by blazing lanterns placed every three meters. At the bottom of the descent was a large oak door enforced with steel strips and a heavy deadbolt. There were no windows and no visible knobs on the outside. Someone went to a lot of trouble to put up this kind of door. *I wonder what's inside.*

The now sweating bartender firmly knocked four times, rap-rap… rap…rap. As he finished, the door swung open on flawlessly balanced hinges without the slightest squeak. My eyes took a second to adjust to the dim firelight inside, and I blinked away the lingering spots. The sight that greeted me made my hand drop to Rolfe's ivory hilt.

Cloud

I headed toward the castle at the center of town. The fortress was a massive, nineteen story tower built during the old empire by the dwarves that once lived there. It cast an imposing shadow over the colorful splash of the markets to the east, throwing them into an early dusk. I entered through its only entrance on the north side. The large brawny guards flanking the door didn't so much as blink as I passed them. Inside I found a large clerk's desk made of stone with an equally large clerk behind it. With graying hair, he had two spare feather pens stuck behind his ears that gave him the appearance of horns. His long, wrinkled fingers were stained in dark ink because of his profession. There were four windows in the circular chamber facing toward each of the four points of the compass. Each window was stained to depict some saint or knight.

The clerk looked up from his paper. "Do you have an appointment?"

"No."

The clerk seemed flustered, since it was not often someone visited without an appointment. Most of the citizens steered clear of the tower if possible and the rest made appointments far in the future to postpone the inevitable.

"If you do not have an appointment then you cannot see the baron," he explained as if I were a child.

"Tell him that Cloud is here," I said, fingering my massive longbow. "If he does not wish to see me, I will kill him." *I'm going to kill him anyway.*

The clerk's face turned into a mask of horror. "R-r-r-right away, sir."

I smiled to myself, thrilled that threats always worked in my favor. Seven minutes later, the clerk came waddling back down the stairs panting.

"The baron will see you now. Right this way, sir."

I followed the man up the rambling spiral staircase to a large door made of thick oak. The hefty man knocked once and then entered the office, and I found myself in the top floor of the castle. One half of the tower was a large window overlooking the expansive harbor, while the other half was taken up by a massive curved bookshelf. In the center of the room was a large wooden table that the baron used as a desk. Piles of official looking papers were stacked on and around the desk, threatening to fall with the slightest provocation. The office had little in the way of adornments, making it seem quite plain. The baron himself sat at a large straight-backed wooden chair. When his dark green eyes found mine as I walked in the room, he seemed to sink further into his chair. The pudgy clerk sensed the tension hanging in the air and hurriedly backed out of the office.

As the door closed with a soft click, the baron's handsome face sunk in despair. There were no witnesses for whatever I was about to do. No one was going to save him from my wrath.

"What do you want? I've done nothing wrong!" The baron whined.

I simply unslung my glistening bow and nocked an arrow to its taught string. When the baron saw the graceful weapon, he cringed even further back.

"Please! Don't hurt me, I'll give you whatever you want!"

"A life for a life, Alrick." I grinned. "That's what you always said, no?"

As I said this, I pulled back the string until the feathers brushed my cheek. Before Alrick could make another futile protest, I released the string. The arrow hit him straight in the heart with a wet 'thunk.'

"That was for Carmen," I whispered.

I turned away from his lifeless body and began the lengthy trek back down the stairs. *I've finally avenged you, Carmen. Now go, rest.*

Cody

The tall, swarthy man had been following me for some time, keeping a safe distance but always present. Out of place in his forester garb, his immense spadone sword attached to his leather baldric attracted many side glances. He made no move to hide himself or blend in, simply striding down the middle of the road. I stepped into a small side alley and waited for him to follow. As he entered, I got a good look at him for the first time. He was powerfully built and possibly stronger than me. He carried two other swords on his left hip. This guy was a walking arsenal!

Without saying a word, he drew both of his swords, holding the left in a reverse grip that was foreign to me. In his callused right hand, he carried a shimmering broadsword that he swung in small circles like it weighed nothing. His left hand boasted an elven short sword. It seemed to give off a silver radiance as it swung gracefully back and forth through the air. His advance was slow and measured, and every stride was perfectly balanced. I drew my axe and unslung the large buckler from my back. If this man wanted to kill me, he had another thing coming.

He lunged at me with a large overhead swing from the broad sword. I caught it on my axe and barely put my shield up in time to block the darting elven blade from entering my ribs. As we stood there locked in combat, he looked at me *and smiled!* It was not the smile of a maniac who enjoyed war and violence, but that of an older brother filled with pride. The thought perplexed me, as he almost cleaved off my head. I countered with my shield and made a massive overhead stroke that would have cut him from head to sternum if it had connected. In a flash, the strange warrior appeared behind me.

How did he do that? He just disappeared!

I swung just in time to block a low slash from the right. Possibly, he was the best swordsman I'd ever fought in single combat. Resting my sweat soaked body, I took a step back to recover and catch my breath. The mental strain of being toyed with was more exhausting than the combat. The lean warrior sheathed both swords and silently watched me.

Oh good! It's over!

He smirked at me and then drew the biggest sword I had ever seen from his back.

Oh shab.

As he attacked with a two-handed left swing, I raised my round shield to block the powerful blow. The stroke simply took off the top third of my shield. I tried to get in close enough to defeat his superior reach, but each time he masterfully deflected my increasingly desperate attempts.

Giving up, I yelled, "Yield! I yield!"

The tall man nodded as if he had foreseen this very moment and was patiently waiting for it to happen.

"Well done, Cody!" he said as I blinked. "Aren't you just the perfect opponent? That was a close one. You gave me a run for my money there, you know."

Wondering how he knew my name, I nearly laughed at this comment. "You were toying with me and you know it." I growled, "What do you want and who are you?"

The swarthy swordsman sighed. "My name is Rush. I was hired by a mutual friend, I think. It's always hard to tell with him, but the style is familiar."

This was starting to sound familiar and my stomach dropped. *It couldn't be him; he wouldn't do that.* "W-what's your employer's name?"

"Well if my hunch is correct…"

"Just tell me!" I yelled.

The powerful man dropped into a guard position. "I have been led to believe it's Cloud."

No, no, no, no, no! I refused to believe Cloud wanted me dead. I was knocked out of my explosive fit of rage by a gleaming sword making a perfect arc toward my head.

Shalin Hale

Raven

Warning: This story contains explicit depictions of violence, gore, and abuse that may be upsetting to some readers.

I tiptoed quietly into the house and set my package of goods on the table. I couldn't see any signs of my mother and assumed she was still intoxicated and most likely unconscious. I breathed a quiet sigh of relief as I opened the package and set the vegetables, bread, and meat on the counter. I had just begun slicing the pork into bite sized pieces when my pointed ears picked up on the sound of footsteps approaching the kitchen. I held my breath and braced myself for the worst as I turned around to face my mother.

To my surprise, I found before me a tall human with a long blond beard and blue eyes. He recoiled upon seeing my face, making no attempt to hide his disgust at the scarred skin and gaping eye socket. I quickly turned away to face the food on the counter again.

"I apologize," I said. "I thought you were my mother."

The man was silent for a moment, contemplating. Then he called, "Ylladove!"

I heard my mother's soft footsteps approaching from her bedroom. I squeezed my eyes shut and offered a silent prayer.

"I thought you said your… daughter—" I flinched at the repulsion in his voice. "—wasn't going to be here for another hour."

I didn't have to see my mother's face to know she was glaring at me. I quickly spun around to apologize.

"I didn't know you had a guest," I started.

"Ravarie, where is your mask?" my mother seethed.

I bit my lip. "Stolen."

I heard the slap before I felt it. She had hit the undamaged side of my face, and I knew she'd done it on purpose. The nerves on that side of my face were still intact and active, and a searing pain raged through them like a blazing forest fire. A whimper slipped through my lips and I felt tears emerge from the corner of my eye. I trained my teary gaze on my feet.

"I'm sorry, darling," I heard my mother whisper to the man, her voice suddenly kind and gentle. "I didn't mean for you to see her."

"I'm sorry," I whispered.

My mother grabbed my chin and forced me to look at her. I winced as her long nails dug into my skin. I could feel my skin break and blood began dripping down my neck.

"I don't think he heard you," my mother hissed, ignoring the wounds she had inflicted.

"I'm sorry," I said, a little louder this time.

My mother threw me onto the ground. I gasped and felt the wounds on my neck. They were still bleeding, but I'd had worse.

"You're pitiful," she snarled at me.

"I'm sorry," I repeated.

"No you're not."

"I am. I'm sorry."

Her foot found my stomach. I grunted and doubled over in pain, unable to breathe. I heard the man chuckle.

"How pathetic. I've known most elves to be strong. This one is a weakling." He spit on me and laughed, a great deep chortle that filled the room and bounced around in my head until I felt sick. I would have thrown up had I eaten recently, but it had been two days since my last meal.

"I'll be in the bedroom," the man told my mom. I heard his footsteps retreat.

"Get up," my mom demanded. My muscles screamed in pain as I rose to my feet. I held back the tears that were fighting to slip out. I couldn't cry. That would only make it worse. I took a deep breath and forced myself to meet my mother's glaring eyes.

I hated her eyes. They were gray and stormy, as if the summer sky lay behind their shining irises. They looked just like my sister's, and I hated that reminder.

As if she had read my mind, my mother said, "Why can't you be like your sister? Why can't you be more like Miarelei?"

I gasped as panic rose in my throat. My chest felt tight. I couldn't breathe.

"Why didn't you save her?" Mother was yelling now. I couldn't see through my tears.

"I tried," I managed to gasp. "I tried. I'm sorry!"

"I don't care! Your sister *died* because you couldn't save her!"

She slapped me again. The pain was all I needed for the anger in my stomach to boil over. I had been scared before, but now I was too furious to let fear stop me.

"You didn't even try to save her," I whispered.

My mom paused, her hand poised to hit me again. "What did you say?"

I could feel the rage burning in my eyes. She couldn't keep doing this to me. I wouldn't let her.

"I risked my life for Miarelei!" I screamed. "And you sat back and you did *nothing*!"

Silence fell like an executioner's axe. My mother's eyes widened and her mouth fell open. She looked as surprised as I felt. I had never yelled at my mother. But now that I'd started, I couldn't stop.

"You did *nothing* for her, and you've done *nothing* for me! Ever since father died—"

"Don't mention him," my mother hissed.

"Why not? You don't care about him! If you did you wouldn't go around having sex with every handsome man you meet!"

"I don't—" my mother started.

"Then who is *that*?" I pointed an accusing finger at the door to her bedroom.

"He isn't—" she tried.

"Don't pretend," I seethed. "Don't pretend you still care about my father, or Miarelei, or me. You *don't. You never did.*"

"I do love you."

"No you don't! Every day you do nothing but mock and abuse me! I'm sick of it! I'm sick of you! *I hate you!*"

My mother's eyes were wide. But she wasn't looking at me. She was looking at my hand. I followed her gaze and gasped.

I didn't know when it had happened, but I had a tight grasp on the handle of the steak knife I had been using to cut the meat. My knuckles were white from holding it so tightly.

My mind told me to let go, but my hand wouldn't move. I looked at the knife, then back at my mom. The color drained from her face. She offered a small shake of her head. The storm in her eyes was raging. She looked just like Miarelei, right before the fire consumed her.

Afraid.

I couldn't take it anymore.

I plunged the knife into her right eye socket.

Blood was everywhere, and my pointed ears were ringing with the sound of screams. Most of them were from my mother, but I could also hear myself screaming, over and over again, every time I brought the knife forward for another blow. I heard a man's scream. I looked up from my mother's mutilated face to find the source of the shout. The blond man was standing in the doorway to the kitchen. His skin was tinged a sickly green and his mouth was agape. His wide eyes met mine, and I saw fear and revulsion pooling in their depths. I could see the gears in his head turning as he made a fight or flight decision.

I didn't think about it. Before he had time to run, I threw my knife as hard as I could. It rammed into his right calf and he collapsed. I smirked as he shrieked and clutched his leg. I couldn't help it. He was so weak and helpless.

I turned back to my mother. Her eyes that had once been filled with stormy life were now two terrifying voids that were overflowing with severed nerves and dark, red blood. Her mouth was hanging open in a perpetual scream that pierced the air around her. Several bloody gouges were scattered around her eyes from when my knife had missed its mark. A large chunk of her nose was missing.

I realized I was gripping my mother's shirt collar with my left hand. I dropped her and she immediately crumpled into a bloody heap on the ground. A second later, her scream stopped. She was dead.

I turned my attention from her to the man who was slowly and painfully inching toward the door. I slid across the bloody kitchen floor and stepped in front of his pitiful frame.

"Please don't kill me!" he pleaded.

"I don't even know your name," I said. "Why would I?"

I reached down and tore the knife from the man's leg. He screamed and grabbed his bleeding calf. I wiped the bloody knife on his tunic, staining the beautiful yellow fabric a deep scarlet. A glint on the man's belt caught my attention. A glittering sword hilt was protruding from his beautiful maroon scabbard.

"This is pretty," I said as I removed the sword from its sheath.

The man watched me examine the sharp blade of the sword. In all honesty, I didn't much care for the sword's design. I was contemplating whether or not I should use it to kill him.

I'd never seen the man before today. By the looks of his clothes, he was a wealthy noble. The engraving on his sword hilt told me he was from a different kingdom, although I wasn't sure which one. Besides this, I knew nothing about him. As far as I knew, he had done nothing wrong. I had no reason to kill him.

"If I spare you," I reasoned, "Will you promise not to tell anyone what you saw tonight?"

The man hesitated. I shoved him to the ground and pressed my foot into his chest. He gasped for breath as I pushed harder. I heard a small crack come from beneath my heel.

"I promise!" the man begged.

"You will tell the townsfolk that a man broke into the house and attacked my mother. You will say he stabbed and beat you, but that you managed to survive. You will say he abducted me and that you don't know who he was or where he went."

The man nodded furiously.

"And if you don't," I continued. "If I hear any whisperings or rumors that it was I who killed my mother, I will kill you."

"I don't doubt you will," the man almost laughed, which became a pained cough. I released him and watched as he gently rubbed his sore ribs.

"How pathetic," I said, repeating his very words from earlier. "I've known most noblemen to be strong. This one is a weakling. Now if you don't mind, I'll be keeping this sword."

"And if I do?" he asked.

"Then I might be using it on you," I said.

He didn't answer. I pulled off his belt and fastened it around my own waist. It fit surprisingly well, and I couldn't help but notice the gold embroidery that adorned the leather. I was certain I could sell it for a great deal of money.

"You're rich, are you not?" I asked.

"Yes," the man said.

"How much gold do you have on you?"

"Look, girl—"

"My name is Ravarie."

"Ravarie, I've already offered you so much. My sword, my belt, my promise to keep your secret… surely that is enough."

"And I've offered to spare your life. Don't I deserve a little kindness?"

The man sighed and reached into a hidden pocket. He regretfully dropped a pile of gold and platinum coins into my hand. I didn't bother to ask if he had more. I knew this much could last me a year.

"Thank you."

I stepped over him and made my way toward the door. Quietly, I slunk into the night and to the horse stables. I picked out the strongest horse, a stallion named Farnorin. I leapt onto his back and dug my heels into his sides. Without hesitation, Farnorin galloped into the darkness, away from the stable. Away from home.

I could hear noises behind me as I bounded past the final house in the village, but I didn't look back. I pressed Farnorin to go faster. Trees sped past my vision, smudging together into a blur of browns and greens, almost black in the night's darkness. I urged Farnorin off the path and into the woods. When I couldn't hear anyone following us, I assumed any pursuers had continued down the road. Still, I refused to stop. We ran for hours, out of the forest and through nearly a dozen villages. Finally, when the moon had started its downward journey, I allowed Farnorin to come to a stop. I dismounted and led him to a nearby stream. We both drank, and I cleaned splattered blood off my hands and face. I would have to worry about my clothes later.

When I had finished, I trekked into the woods, taking care not to leave any footprints behind. If the villagers managed to follow my trail, it would end with Farnorin by the stream. I was light on my feet and knew to tread lightly on hard packed soil. Besides, if my mom's lover stayed true to his word, the townspeople would be looking for a large man capable of violent murder and kidnapping. I doubted they would suspect me. And if they did, no one knew what I really looked like. I made sure I was rarely seen by other people, and I almost always wore a mask that covered my entire face. It was all coming together perfectly. My escape was flawless.

After about an hour of walking, I decided to rest my weary legs. I found a thicket and slipped into the dense underbrush. I cleared branches out of a small area and collected soft moss for a makeshift bed. As I laid down, I felt my stomach grumble unhappily, and I remembered I hadn't eaten in nearly three days. I searched the area around me and was delighted to find a plant with beautiful orange and red buds. I dug around its stem and pulled a clump of young white tubers out of the ground. I brushed the dirt off the best I could and took a bite. It wasn't as sweet as I had hoped, but I had never liked dusk lilies anyway. But when you're alone in a forest and haven't eaten for an unhealthy while, you take what you can get. I ate five or six until I couldn't keep my eyes open anymore. Within moments, I had fallen asleep amid the moss and grass.

I dreamed that I was in my old house. No, my old home. I was looking for something, but I didn't know what. I searched the wardrobe and behind every curtain. I was becoming frantic. Where was it? I needed it. I could die without it.

A scream sliced through the air like a hot knife through butter. I tried to cover my ears, but I could still hear it. Where was it coming from? I spun around to find the source of the shriek, but it was all around me, and inside me. I couldn't find it. I couldn't make it stop.

I curled up in a corner, my hands pressed flat against my pointed ears. I was screaming now too, trying to drown out the agonizing shrieks that threatened to tear me apart.

"*STOP!*" I screeched.

I looked up and saw smoke pouring through the doorway and billowing toward me. It filled my lungs and cut off my scream, squeezing my throat tight.

The realization hit me like a pound of bricks. This wasn't just a nightmare. It was a memory.

Panic rose and boiled inside me. It mixed with the smoke, making it nearly impossible to breathe. I was shaking uncontrollably and my stomach had twisted itself into all sorts of intricate knots. My head was pounding and my ears rang from the screams that still had not been silenced.

I felt myself rise slowly to my feet. Don't do it, I told myself. Run away. Leave through the back door. Escape while you can. But my body wouldn't listen. My legs moved toward the smoke, and in a moment I found myself surrounded by flames.

In the dream, I couldn't feel the fire. It licked at my exposed skin but I ran onward, unaffected by the heat. I followed the screams around a corner and into a hallway that stretched ahead of me for what seemed like miles.

"Miarelei!" I shouted. There was no response but the screams. I kept running as their volume mounted. My head felt ready to explode from the noise, smoke, and panic, but I kept going. I had to save her. I had to save her. *I had to save her.*

I burst through a doorway into a small room. In the corner, flames licking at her feet, a girl. Miarelei. The storm in her eyes was raging with mindless fear.

"Ravarie!" she shrieked. "Ravarie, help me!"

That was when the ceiling caved in.

I was still in the doorway, safe from the falling wood, but I stumbled backward and fell. A beam landed on my legs, pinning me to the ground. The left side of my face landed directly in a patch of flames.

Suddenly, my nerves came alive.

I screamed as the fire tore at my skin. The pain was indescribable, like the very gates of hell had opened to receive me. My hair sizzled and broke and my skin boiled. I felt my eyelids melt away, exposing my precious eyes to the scorching heat.

My screams tore through the smoke and fire. Only then did I find the strength to pull my legs from under the beam. Still, I couldn't fathom the idea of standing, let alone running away. I crept away from the fire. My arm screamed in pain as I used it to push myself against the wall. I gaped down at it. The skin had peeled away from my fingers, revealing muscle and bone. Blisters and burns covered the rest of my arm, painting my honey-colored skin shades of pink, red, yellow, and black. I didn't want to see what my face looked like.

I tore my gaze away from my arm and noticed a bucket sitting in the middle of the hallway. That was strange. I didn't remember this. But, of course, dreams had a way of twisting the truth. I approached the bucket carefully and found it filled to the brim with ice cold water. I nearly cried out from joy as I picked up the bucket and rushed toward the room Miarelei was in.

"I'm coming!" I cried. "I'll save you!"

There was no response besides the crackling of the fire as it ate away at the rubble. I couldn't see Miarelei. I realized I couldn't hear her either. Her screams had stopped when the ceiling collapsed.

"No," I said, more to myself than to anyone who might be listening. "No, she's still in there! She's still alive!"

I swung the bucket of water, but nothing came out. I looked again at it. Not even a ripple disturbed the water's surface. I screamed in frustration as I swung the bucket again. Still nothing. I dropped the water and attempted to cup some of it in my hands. Nothing. It was like a stubborn child, refusing to leave its home.

"Stupid water!" I screeched. "Stupid dream!"

I glared into the bucket. The water was dark and cloudy, reflecting the smoke around it. But as I stared at it, I saw clarity break through, turning the surface into a perfect mirror.

"No," I said. "I don't want to see it."

I tried to look away, but I couldn't so much as blink as my reflection came into view. The burns covering the left side of my face put those on my arm to shame. Black patches hung off my cheeks. Crimson and yellow scars blanketed my forehead and scalp. The skin by the corner of my mouth was all but gone, revealing teeth and gums. I could see bone peeking out from below a flap of charred skin on my chin. Blood was everywhere, running in rivers down my disfigured face.

Most of it was coming from my empty eye socket.

I almost wished I'd lost both eyes. Then I wouldn't have to see the gaping hole where a beautiful green iris should have been. I wouldn't have to stare into its deep abyss and see the blood and fluids draining out. I may not have to know that fire, in fact, can melt eyes.

Still unable to tear my gaze away from the horror in the mirror, I saw my other eye disappear and watched nearly perfect, albeit slightly wrinkled skin cover the scars, shifting my reflection into my mother's face. At least, what her face looked like now. Sans eyes and complete with several stab wounds. Shock flooded me. I had done that to her. Me, Ravarie, with only a steak knife. I had killed my own mother. In a fit of mindless rage, I brutally murdered the woman who birthed and raised me. I was a monster.

The reflection changed again, this time restoring my mother's eyes and pure, unblemished skin. But a moment later I realized it wasn't my mother. She had the same stormy eyes, but she was smiling. She was Miarelei. And suddenly I was in my kitchen again, and instead of my mom I was stabbing her, again and again and again, but she was still smiling, and I heard her say, "I love you."

I woke up drenched in sweat, despite my lack of a blanket and the cold breeze that was blowing against my bare arms. I couldn't breathe. I couldn't think.

I rolled over and threw up my small meal from the night before. It made me feel surprisingly better, albeit a little hungry. I pushed the dream deep into my mind and got up. I wouldn't let a silly illusion distract me. I ate a small breakfast of roots and set out again through the woods. I had slept longer than I meant to. The sun was already up and birds were singing. I guessed it was almost noon.

I soon emerged from the trees and found myself outside of a small village. Several houses and a three-story inn were scattered on the outskirts. I tentatively approached the town, lifting a hood over my head and carefully placing my hair over my face to cover my scars. Some shopkeepers and townspeople were milling about, but it was rather quiet. No one paid much attention to me as I made my way to the middle of town. A central square opened up before me. There was a fountain in the middle, surrounded by trees and shops. I walked past the buildings until I came to a window through which I could see a beautiful mask.

Perfect, I thought as I opened the door. A small bell rang and a fat, bearded dwarf came running out from behind a rack of tunics.

"Hello, welcome!" The dwarf greeted me with a nearly toothless smile. His voice boasted a thick accent, and I could tell by the pin cushion he was holding that he was a tailor.

"I need a mask," I said. "And maybe some new clothes."

"Right away!"

I followed the dwarf to a row of shelves that were full of different types of masks in all colors of the rainbow and decorated with feathers, jewels, or paint. I skimmed over the decorative masks and found a shelf of plain white ones. I was admiring a full-face mask when the dwarf came up to me holding a pile of clothes.

"You're rather petite, but I think these might fit you. There's a room in the back if you want to try them on."

I set the mask down and took the clothes from the dwarf.

"You're not really considering *that* boring thing!" The dwarf wandered back to the more elegant masks.

"I don't need something too fancy," I reasoned. "I'm just trying to cover up a few scars."

The dwarf peered closely at me and I quickly checked my hair to make sure my empty eye socket was covered. Finally, he walked past me and toward the simple masks.

"At least consider something with a little more style," he said. "How about this one?"

He held up a white half mask that I estimated would cover most of my scars, including my left eye socket and cheek. I gratefully took the mask and tried it on. The dwarf led me to a mirror. I smiled at my reflection for the first time in a long while. The mask fit perfectly. It looked almost like I had painted the left side of my face white. Barely any scars were visible, and the worst were hidden.

"How much is it?" I asked.

"25 gold."

"And for the clothes?" I said, picking out a red tunic and black fitted pants.

"Ten."

I fished in my pocket and pulled out a handful of coins. I counted out 35 and handed them to the dwarf. After thanking him and changing into my new, bloodless clothes, I followed the dwarf's directions to a nearby tavern so I could eat something besides dusk lily tubers.

The tavern already looked old and dilapidated on the outside, but the inside was even worse. Paint was peeling off the walls, which were covered in stains and scratches. A fresh pool of vomit was on the floor next to an unconscious man who had clearly drunk too much. Every floorboard creaked as I made my way to the rotting wooden counter that I assumed was the bar, judging by the orc standing behind it. As I walked, I heard fragments of customers' conversations.

"Did you hear about what happened in Halaverin?"

I stopped dead in my tracks. Halaverin was my hometown. Surely news of my mother's murder hadn't spread that fast. I hurried over to the table.

"Pardon me," I said. "But I couldn't help but overhear your conversation. You said something about Halaverin?"

I could tell the man was a storyteller by the way his eyes lit up as he took a drink and prepared to speak.

"I did," he started. "It seems there was a murder and a kidnapping."

The people around me gasped. I held my breath.

"Not in Halaverin," a woman said. "It's such a peaceful village."

"It's true," the storyteller said. "Yesterday night, the townsfolk heard screaming comin' from a house, so they got some guards and went to check it out. When they got there, they found a man in the entryway. You folks know Edward Delmon from Iaburg?"

A few of the people nodded. One said, "'e wasn't the murderer, was 'e?"

"No, the townsfolk didn't know there'd been a murder yet. But Edward was hurt real bad. He said he'd been stabbed in the leg and robbed. Then he pointed to the kitchen. The townsfolk headed on over and do you know what they found?"

The people leaned forward, their eyes brimming with curiosity.

"They found Ylladove, dead on the floor."

"Who?" someone asked.

"You know, Ylladove. The war hero Elwind's wife. She was lying in a pool of her own blood. Someone had stabbed her to death. And if that isn't bad enough, they got 'er right in the face. She didn't have eyes no more and there was blood and all sorts of stuff draining out."

The people gasped. I shuddered at the memory.

"And that's not all. The guards searched the house, but they couldn't find Ylladove's daughter. Edward said she'd been kidnapped by the murderer."

"I thought Ylladove's daughter died," the woman said.

"One of them did, but she had another one. There's rumors that she was badly burned in the fire and hasn't been seen since without her face covered."

A man piped in. "I hear she lost both her eyes in the fire!"

Someone else added, "My friend told me that he saw her once, and he said half her nose was missing and she was completely bald."

"I hear she has a stump for a hand."

"Someone told me that all the skin on her face burned off, so now she's just got a skull for a head."

I laughed. "Don't be stupid. You couldn't survive if you were burned *that* badly."

The people looked at me as if they hadn't yet noticed I was there.

"I should know," I said, lifting up my mask. "I've been burned too."

Normally their shocked expressions would have offended me, but now I just laughed as the woman fainted and one man threw up. I readjusted the mask and sauntered away from the table, feeling unexpectedly confident. On my way to the bar, I accidentally bumped a table, knocking a glass mug to the floor. It shattered into a million pieces, surprisingly loud amid the din of people talking and laughing. The tavern fell silent and everyone turned to look at me.

"I'm so sorry," I said, turning toward the man whose drink I had spilled. He looked up at me with brown eyes that pointed daggers at me. I stepped backward as he got to his feet and approached me. A crowd started to gather around us.

"I didn't mean to," I said. "I'll buy you a new drink if you want."

The crowd started chanting at us to fight. I backed farther away. I couldn't take this guy. He was nearly a head taller than me and looked like he could squish me between his fingers. He glowered down at me and aimed his giant fist at my face. I ducked out of the way just in time. The crowd cheered. I tried to get through them, but someone pushed me back into the circle.

"Look, I don't want to fight," I said. The man tried to punch me again, but I dodged. My hand brushed against something on my belt and I remembered that I'd taken Edward's sword. I smiled and unsheathed it.

"All right; you're stubborn. Fine. If it's a fight you want, it's a fight you will get."

The crowd started cheering louder, and I heard the shouts of people placing bets on who would win. Most were for my opponent, but I heard at least two in my favor.

"Impressive," the man said, admiring my sword. "But do you know how to use it?"

"You'd be surprised."

The man cocked his head, shrugged, and reached behind his back. He pulled out two daggers and lunged toward me. I raised my sword, blocking his attack. I kicked forward, catching him in the stomach. He flinched and took a couple steps backward, but he quickly recovered and ran toward me again, this time aiming for my ankles. I jumped over his dagger easily, which sent him sprawling out across the floor.

"Just because I'm a girl doesn't mean I can't fight," I said. I jabbed my sword into his right hand and he dropped his dagger. I kicked it away, into the crowd.

"Come on," I urged. "Get up and fight. Or are you too hurt?"

The man growled and leapt to his feet. I dodged his next three attacks effortlessly. The fourth one caught my left ear, but I couldn't even feel it. The fire had left most of my face with damaged nerves, so blows to my left were almost always painless. I lunged forward with my sword, but he skillfully blocked my attack with his dagger. I pushed harder, knowing his blade wasn't strong enough to stop mine. Finally, he gave way. My sword found his left shoulder and he stumbled backward. I sliced just below his kneecap, sending him to the ground. He dropped his dagger and clutched his leg. He was completely helpless. I could kill him easily.

I brought my sword above my head, ready to strike. But then I remembered my mom's face as I stabbed her and the dream I'd had last night. I lowered my sword, spun it around, and brought the hilt down hard on the man's head. He stopped screaming and immediately went limp. The crowd cheered, and someone started to chant, "Kill him!" The orc from the bar stepped out from among them and grabbed my hand. He lifted it above my head and shouted, "And the winner is… Elf Girl!"

"I have a name," I said.

He looked at me expectantly. I opened my mouth to tell him my name, but shut it when I realized I couldn't reveal that. People knew I was missing. I couldn't let them catch me. I racked my brain, searching for something I could call myself. I looked down at my sword hilt. A bird was painted on the bottom, its inky black wings caught mid-flight. I smiled.

"Raven," I said. "Call me Raven."

Lexi Rogers

Side by Side

The sea breeze threatened to seep through the knit of my sweater and I almost shivered. I wrapped my arms tighter around myself and smiled. I still loved these foggy mornings when life seemed to stand still and thoughts hung low to the ground, moist with salty water. My whistle pierced through the cold, gray clouds like a knife. Paddy came loping out of the fog, his tongue hanging out happily.

"Hey buddy, let's go inside. It's going to rain soon," I said, scratching his ears. We raced each other down the rocky beach and all the way up the tall, spiral stairs to our small living space.

"Ha! I won again!" I said, joyfully. Paddy just looked at me with his big brown eyes and flopped down onto his pile of blankets in the corner. "What should we do today, bud? Watch the storm and pretend we're saving a lost ship or watch the storm and pretend we're useful? You're right. We should do both."

I made a cup of coffee and snuggled up to the windows with my sketchbook and started to paint the boiling sea. I didn't look up again until hours had passed and night had fallen. "Paddy! You forgot to remind me to turn on the lights!"

I winked at him and ran to the top of the lighthouse, whooping as the strong beams shot across the dark water. I loved feeling like those lights might someday save something. My lighthouse was located in a sparsely populated area and no boats ever came close enough to need my warning lights. Only the locals even remembered that my lighthouse was here. I opened the glass door and leaned on the railing, listening to the wind howl. I felt the first few heavy raindrops on my arms, but I didn't want to go inside just yet.

I watched the beam searching the sea and I thought I saw a dark shape bobbing in the water. I strained my eyes to make out any details. What if it was a boat? A boat that would get shipwrecked in a storm. What if it got shipwrecked and I had to nurse the crew back to health? What if they were transporting a great treasure like salvaged books from the lost Library of Alexandria, and I was a hero that saved them *and* the books? I shook my head to clear the thoughts from my rampant imagination. I looked back at the water and couldn't see anything anymore. I sighed. It must have been debris blown over by the wind. The rain continued to pick up, so I went inside and made myself another cup of coffee and fed Paddy.

I cuddled in bed and watched the waves crash against the rocks, spraying seafoam twenty feet in the air. I usually loved the sound of the storms and the feeling that came with being snuggled up safely inside while it raged on all sides. But tonight, I felt alone, and the storm seemed angry. I patted the blankets and Paddy jumped up.

"You can sleep with me tonight, buddy. I'm sure you don't want to be alone during a storm." He put his head on me and sighed, both of us knowing who really didn't want to be alone.

I listened to the whistling of the wind as I fell asleep. Wishing that I could be important, I dreamed of struggling captains on slippery decks saved by the strong beam of a nearby lighthouse.

I woke up to the storm still raging outside. "I guess we'll spend the day inside."

Paddy whined and ran to the top of the staircase. I smiled. "Fine. You always win." I put on my earmuffs and gloves, pulled on my raincoat, and tugged on my boots. "Look at all that I have to do for you."

As soon as I opened the door, the temperature dropped at least fifteen degrees. Paddy didn't seem bothered and he loped down the foggy beach. His running body drew attention to a dark shape on the shore. My heart skipped a beat. As I got closer, the shape became clearer and I realized it was a boat. Or rather, it had *been* a boat.

The wreck was bad. There were splinters of wood flung everywhere on the sand and dark fluid was leaking over everything. I heard Paddy bark and I ran toward him. "What is it, buddy? What did you find?"

A splintered chest lay on its side while the tide started to seep into its contents. I pulled it farther up the shore and knelt next to it. There didn't seem to be anything inside of it. I pulled my screwdriver out of my belt loops and plied the walls of the chest apart so that it lay flat. It was empty except for a small engraving on the inside. Looking closer, I realized that it was an address. An address carved into a chest with nothing else inside or even strewn around the beach. I broke off the piece of wood with the address and tucked it into my overalls. Paddy barked suddenly and I jumped, startled.

"Remi!" I heard a voice call. Anya, my friend from inland, was walking toward me. I waved at her and waited for her to approach. "What happened here?"

"We finally had a shipwreck!" I grinned.

"Hmm, that's not the reaction you should give to the warden." She said, laughing.

"Is he coming?"

"Yes, I called him when I saw the wreck at the top of the cliffs. I figured you could use some help moving this mess."

I smiled, glad that Anya always knew what to do. I wanted to tell her about the address I found, but something told me that I should keep it to myself. "I haven't seen any crew members, dead or alive, so maybe they were lucky."

Anya gave me a dubious look. "Maybe."

A few minutes later, the warden showed up with a few other people and we got to work moving the washed up ship up the cliffs to be used as firewood for the town. As I got ready for bed later that night, I set the piece of wood with the address on the table and looked at it every time I passed by.

"It probably doesn't mean anything right, Paddy?" He snorted and snuggled deeper in his sleep. "Maybe it does, though. What if the person who lives there is an escaped convict with a special treasure? At any rate, I should probably tell them that their boat has crashed and there's no sign of their crew. I'll write them tomorrow." After settling down in bed, I immediately realized that I wouldn't be able to sleep until I wrote the letter. I swung my legs back out of the blankets, grabbed a piece of parchment and began to write.

To whom it may concern,

My name is Remi Sanders and I am a lighthouse keeper on a forgotten coast.

Your boat washed ashore last night in a rather angry storm. I am afraid that it was wrecked badly and is now being used for firewood. I hope this is not a great inconvenience to you. I did not see any crew members. May God help them. However, I did see the only apparent piece of cargo, a small chest, and it seemed empty except for an address carved onto the inside. I am sending this letter to that address. I thought I ought to let you know what happened to your boat so you wouldn't have to worry. Please write me back to ease my curiosity on why a boat would only be carrying such obscure cargo.

Best wishes,
Remi Sanders

After sealing the envelope, I set the letter on the table and fell into a restless sleep. Waking up early, I bounced with an eagerness to send the letter out. I ran down the stairs and whistled three times in the direction of the cliffs. A few minutes later, a large raven flew out of the mist and settled on my arm.

"Hello, beautiful. It's been a while since I've needed you. Will you please take this letter to our new mysterious friend?" I knew the bird didn't understand me and was trained to take letters to the post office, but I wanted to believe that she was my messenger bird who could find anyone in the world. The raven took off and I wrung my hands. I did not want to wait for an answer to my letter. I walked back into my room and started a painting to keep my mind distracted.

Miss Sanders,

My name is Evan. It is a relief to write my own name on paper and send it out into the world. I was very shocked to receive your letter as I do not often get mail. As shocked as I was, I was overjoyed to learn about you. What is it like living in a lighthouse? It must be wonderful to live next to the sea. Are you alone in your lighthouse? How often do people's ships run up on your shore? I apologize for all the questions; I am always eager to learn about another corner of the world.

To answer your question, the boat crashing is of no importance to me, because I did not know that it existed. I do not know who might have sent that very cryptic piece of cargo on a seemingly empty ship, but I have my suspicions. I know why my address would be sent as a hard-to-find treasure, but I will not tell you until you write me back and reassure me that we can be friends.

Yours truly,
Evan

Evan,

Do you have a last name or is it only Evan? You talk as if you do not have contact with the outside world. What story have I stumbled upon?

I do not live alone, since I have an Irish Setter named Paddy and a raven who comes when I whistle to deliver my mail. However, I do not live next to any people. I love living in my lighthouse, because it is cozy inside and I can watch the storms rage around me as I paint and read. Your mystery boat was the first boat in ten years to wash up on these shores and I was very excited by it.

Of course, we can be friends, but I cannot believe you would hold trivial information over my head in exchange of friendship. Who are you really, Evan? You must tell me, or I'll never write you again.

Best,
Remi (you mustn't call me Miss Sanders ever again)

After two weeks, I hadn't received a reply to my letter, and I was worried that I had scared Evan off with my persistent questions and my teasing. Maybe he was an invalid that worried about interacting with people. With that thought, I realized that I didn't even know how old he was. He could be fourteen or eighty and I had no idea! I resolved to ask him when his letter came. *If* his letter came.

Suddenly I heard flapping wings and I tripped over Paddy in my rush to get down the stairs.

Remi,

My name is longer than Evan, but I cannot tell it to you even though we are friends. I can never predict whose hands these letters could fall into. Thank you for giving me such lovely details of life at your lighthouse. It seems perfect. I also love to read, but I am an abysmal artist. I have noticed your little sketches in the corners of the parchment you use, and I can tell that you are not an abysmal artist. I wish I could see some of your paintings.

You asked for a story, so I will give you one. Many years ago, a young prince was raised by two exhausted parents. The King and Queen didn't know what to do with their rebellious son and they often left him to the equally exhausted maids, where he would create as much mischief as possible. As he grew up, he became increasingly worse until he started fraternizing with the wrong crowds. He created a wild life for himself, full of adventure, plundering, and terrorizing the citizens instead of preparing for rule. His parents, finally tired of the public disgrace, banished him to a remote working camp where no one knew his face. The camp gave him a new identity and took away his freedom. The prince tried

and tried to escape, but he was trapped. The King and Queen told their citizens that their son had died in a tragic sea accident. They promised to visit him once a year, but that promise was quickly broken. The prince disappeared and no one has heard from him since. I sometimes wonder if he's matured in his imprisonment. I don't think he would want to be prince ever again, but I bet he's very ready for an adventure after all these years.
I can't tell you whose story this is, but since you sit and watch the stormy waters, I'm sure you understand someone's soul much more than a story can tell you.

Yours,
Evan

Evan,

Who sent the address? Why would someone be after a prince who had been forgotten? Is someone trying to break the prince out? Where would he go if he was given freedom? Please respond quickly, as I can no longer sleep for curiosity.

Forever,
Remi

P.S. I have enclosed a small painting of my lighthouse and the sea surrounding it. I hope you can picture what it's like to be me.

Remi,

I am so very sorry to have been the cause of you losing sleep. The prince had dangerous friends before he was banished. If they knew he was alive, they would come to claim old debts and settle old fights. The address could possibly have been sent by an enemy trying to let others know that the prince was still alive. I am grateful it fell into your hands instead. I do know what would have happened to him. I wish I knew where the prince would go if given freedom, but I bet it's somewhere quiet and peaceful with a lot of fresh air.

Thank you very much for the painting. You are incredibly talented and incredibly lucky to live in such a wonderful place. Do you mind me asking how you became a lighthouse keeper? And how you found a raven to deliver your mail? I am very curious and if you don't answer, I will threaten loss of sleep.

Yours ever curious,
Evan

Evan,

I am sorry for the prince. I wish I could meet him. He seems very gallant and very interesting. Too bad I met you instead.

I wish I could learn more about the prince, but I am worried about compromising his identity. Instead, I will answer your questions. My father was the lighthouse keeper before me. He was a single father and a gruff man, weathered by many storms. However, he taught me his trade. In the course of working together, I got to know him. I loved living in the lighthouse with its tall spiral staircases and cozy rooms from the beginning. We would chase each other up the stairs to see who could be the first to turn on the lights and we would watch the beams shoot across the waves. When he died, I adopted Paddy and he became my constant companion. He loves to bark at the lights as they search the waters.

My dad trained the ravens to go to the post office. He taught me how to call them, and they haven't failed me since. He simply didn't like the long trek inland and he didn't like to talk to people if he could help it. I simply adopted his habit. I wish you could see this place; I have a feeling you would love it.

Yours,
Remi

Anya narrowed her eyes at me over her mug. "You want to—what?"

"You heard me, Anya."

"But you don't know him at all!"

I didn't answer and sipped my tea instead. I wanted to find Evan and free him from his banishment. No one deserved to disappear like that, and I knew he couldn't get out on his own. He was relying on me, even if he didn't say it in his letters.

"Remi. Listen to me. If he *is* a banished prince, then how do you plan on getting him out? How would you even afford to go halfway across the world? You've been talking to him for months, but you still don't know what he looks like or if he even wants you to break him out."

"I have an idea to get him out. Using the money that I've saved from working here, I'll have just enough to travel. After reading his letters, I feel like I know him. I know he wants to get out of there."

Anya rolled her eyes but didn't say anything else. As I started to lay out my plan, I saw her hesitancy turn to interest. Her eyes shone bright with mischief. She held out her hand to shake and I pulled her into a hug. After wishing me luck, she headed back to the inland to run my errands and buy passage on a boat. I ran around the rooms, packing furiously while Paddy stared curiously at me.

"I'm going to have to leave for a few weeks, buddy. But don't worry, Anya's going to take care of you and the lighthouse. I'll be back as soon as I break a banished prince out of a labor camp," I said, grinning.

The refreshing, sea air felt good on my face. It was warmer here than it was on my shores. We would land in the port near Evan's labor camp in a few hours. I was fidgety with excitement. Heading down to my bunk, I checked my trunk one more time. Everything was ready and itching to be used. I fidgeted on my bed until I heard the ship's horn announcing arrival.

Walking off the dock, I saw green hills rolling into the distance and I took a deep breath. The fishy air smelled like adventure. I walked to a train station with a stop a few miles from the camp.

Green landscapes flew past me in a blur and I occasionally saw a clump of houses surrounded by lush farms. At every train stop, my heart started to pound. With a shaky breath, I stepped off the train at my stop to find myself in the middle of nowhere. As I walked about a mile toward the remote camp, I decided I should start phase one of my plan. I needed to change now while I could do so without being noticed.

I ducked behind a large tree trunk and stripped. I pulled out the things Anya had bought for me and started to put them on. Thick, cream stockings that went up to my knees, a heavy petticoat with tight laces, dainty shoes that were entirely impractical, strings of pearls, and a ball gown made of red velvet that fit me perfectly and draped along the ground. I pinned my hair on top of my head and twirled. When Anya said she could make me look like a noble, I didn't quite believe her. As I held my skirts up to avoid dragging them in the dirt, I felt like I owned the world. What would my father say to this crazy plan? I laughed out loud and continued the rest of the walk toward the camp, rehearsing what I would say in my mind.

I heard the camp before I could see it. Loud engines made grinding noises, and voices yelled over the noise. Thick plumes of smoke rose into the sky. As I approached the thick iron gate, I straightened my dress and lifted my chin higher. The two guards stationed at the entrance gave me quick, disbelieving glances but didn't address me.

"I demand entry, immediately," I said in the most commanding voice I could muster. No response. "Do you know who I am? I am Duchess Isabella of the Western Isles. If you do not let me in, your master will be greatly displeased."

The guards exchanged glances and reluctantly opened the gate for me. I waltzed through the gate and walked down a narrow pathway to a heavy door and knocked. It was immediately opened by a wizened man who looked like he might suffer a heart attack from seeing such a finely dressed woman standing in front of him. He looked around me, searching for servants of some kind. I captured his attention before he could question my arrival further.

"I have come to talk to the master of this place. Direct me to him at once."

Not as alert as the guards, the man jerked his head at me and opened the door wider. I stepped inside a large room with beautiful floors and large chandeliers. This was a surprise compared to the run-down appearance of the building from the outside. The man led me to a pair of tall, wooden doors and pushed me inside. As another man watched me approach his desk, his eyebrows shot up into his hairline.

"And who might you be, miss?" The few hairs he had were neatly combed back and he had a pinched look about him. If I was director of this horrible place, I would look like the joy was sucked out of my life, too.

"I am Duchess Isabella of the Western Isles. If you disrespect me and call me miss one more time, I will make sure the entire royal family hears about it." As I said this, the man's face went red and his jaw grew more pinched.

"Yes, Your Grace. I apologize. What can I do for you?"

"One of your men has stolen a prized painting of mine."

"Forgive me, but my men cannot leave this camp. They would have no way of stealing any art of yours."

"I did not ask for your opinion, sir. A few months ago, I stopped by this camp to show my children what will happen to them if they are disrespectful, and my trunk was raided."

"I do not remember seeing you here a few months ago, Your Grace."

"That is because I did not wish you to see me. I do not know how one of your men got their filthy hands on my property. I seek punishment for the thief and the safe return of my property."

"How will I know which man to search, ma'am?"

"I saw his profile in the shadows. Gather your men and take me to them immediately, so he can face my judgment."

The man looked uncomfortable but nodded at the old man who was standing at the door. "Follow me, Duchess."

He led me out of the office and back into the beautiful great hall. As we went through a small door on the wall, I found myself in a world of smoke, peeling paint, and exhausted workers. Squaring my shoulders, I searched for Evan. He needed to get out of here.

"Here they are, Your Grace." He stopped in front of a line of around seventy men with dirt streaked faces.

All the men looked unkempt and tired. I knew most of these men were convicted criminals, but I still didn't like to see their pain. Slowly walking down the line of men, I searched for a sign of Evan.

The third to last man held his chin a little higher and his eyes were a steely gray, instead of the blank, empty eyes on everyone else. The slight difference was enough to let me recognize him. I turned to the director of the camp.

"Search this man's belongings. He is the thief." I watched Evan's eyes widen in fear and I tightened my jaw to remain emotionless. Two guards emerged from the shadows and walked toward the bunk area. I tried to catch Evan's eye, but his face was turned away in fear. A few minutes later, the guards returned. One of them was holding a small piece of paper in his right hand.

"Sir, we found this painting under his mattress," a guard grunted to the director.

I suppressed a smile. He kept it under his mattress? "Sirs! That is my painting!" Out of the corner of my eye, I saw Evan's eyebrows furrow with confusion. "I cannot believe this loose operation that allowed these men the opportunity to steal thousands of dollars' worth of art! The King will hear of this, I assure you."

"Duchess, I am incredibly sorry. I assure you the prisoner will be heavily punished. How can we repay you for this grave mistake?"

I pretended to consider for a minute, then turned toward Evan. With a look of disgust, I surveyed his body as if judging his usefulness. He was lean with long, dark hair. My heart sped up and I didn't dare look much longer. "Show me your teeth, thief." Evan bared his teeth without making eye contact. My heart was beating faster and faster with every second. It was time to get out of here. "Sirs, there will be no need for you to punish him."

"Your Grace—"

I held up a silencing hand. "I will take him back to my residence with me. There, he will receive the punishment he deserves, and I will gain a valuable servant. This one thinks he is better than everyone else here. He behaves like a little prince. I will break that out of him, because you have not succeeded in doing so."

At the word prince, Evan narrowed his eyes and stared at me. I stared back, trying to communicate silently. The corners of his mouth twitched.

"He—" started the director.

"I will pay for his release. Have him gather his belongings and meet me at the entrance."

"How will you get him to your residence without a husband or a manservant?"

I cocked an eyebrow. "Are you questioning nobility?"

Evan swallowed hard in an effort not to laugh.

"No, ma'am. I'm sorry, Duchess Isabella. We'll send him out immediately."

"Quickly. I do not want to spend more time in this sad excuse for a labor camp."

I lifted my chin and pranced out, while the old man stayed hard on my heels. A few minutes later, guards led Evan out with his hands tied behind his back and I handed them a small purse of money.

"Are you sure you can handle him, Your Grace?"

I glared at the guard and grabbed Evan's ropes. Without saying a word, we walked out of the building and down the path. I could hear his shallow breath turn to a small chuckle.

"Shh, not yet," I warned.

"Yes, Your Grace," he whispered. I kicked him in the leg. Just in case they were still watching. "What was that for?"

"Security," I said sheepishly, tugging him along. Walking in silence, I led him to the tree where I had hidden my trunk. Once we got there, I ordered him to turn around and I changed back into my regular clothes: a knit sweater, pants, and boots. I felt like myself again. After I unpinned my hair, I carefully folded my costume back into my trunk. I lovingly stroked the gown and said goodbye to Duchess Isabella. Stepping out from behind the tree, I untied Evan's ropes. He turned around, grinning.

"I have one question before you answer the other half a million running through my head. You *are* Remi, right?" His voice was husky from disuse, but it sounded exactly like I had imagined. "Yes. I thought that was obvious," I said, laughing.

He scooped me into a tentative hug. "Thank you." He suddenly drew back. "How did you know which one I was? I never told you what I looked like."

"I told the director I would recognize your profile, and I didn't technically lie. You looked a little less broken than the rest of the men and I just knew it was you. It did, however, take you a while to realize who *I* was."

"How was I supposed to know who you were? I had my suspicions when you knew about the painting, but I was still confused. I had never heard of a Duchess Isabella."

"Of the Western Isles."

"That doesn't exist."

"Oh, I know. The camp director sure didn't know that though. And take a look around! You're free! Evan, you're free!"

He looked at me strangely. "That is the first time anyone's said my real name out loud in five years." Then his face broke out in a huge grin. I watched him slowly take in the green world around him. He was dirt streaked and looked like he had been worked too hard for too long, but he still had an air of nobility.

"Where do you want to go, prince?" I said. While he reveled in his newfound freedom, we walked to the train station. He looked surprised to find us there.

"Freedom was so close the whole time," he whispered. "I can't go home since I'm not a prince anymore. There is a new king and queen and I have no desire to go back to that life."

"I bet you'd love to go somewhere quiet and peaceful. Somewhere you can let your soul heal. Oh! Just off the top of my head. Maybe a lighthouse would work?"

Evan smiled. When he smiled, I noticed that his nose wrinkled up and it made me want to smile too. "A lighthouse? That's very random. Where would I find a lighthouse?"

"I have no idea. It was just a suggestion. Look there's our train!" I said, turning away from him.

"Remi!"

He chased me down the tracks as the train screeched to a halt. He grabbed my waist and spun me around. Our smiles faded as we stared at each other. His eyes were the color of the sea. I cleared my throat and we jumped apart. We boarded the train and shared stories as the landscape flew by us. His were much more exciting than mine, but he denied it.

Later, we were so involved in our conversation about the merits of classic authors, that we almost missed our boat. Laughing, we walked onto the deck. As we reached the open sea, I watched Evan grow very solemn.

"What's wrong?"

"This is the most beautiful thing I've ever seen."

"You've never been to sea before?"

"No, I have. That was before I knew how to appreciate things."

I smiled and leaned against the railing. I felt Evan's eyes on me, and I turned to look at him. He held my hand and smiled softly. My heart was about to pound right out of my chest.

"Remi, I cannot thank you enough for what you did for me. I don't want to be presumptuous and I know we've only been talking for a few months, but I feel like I've known you for a long time. I'm falling in love with you."

"You're not the only one falling in love, prince." I pulled him close and kissed him.

I sat on a boulder, letting the cold seep through my clothes. I watched Evan chase Paddy down the beach, fighting for a prized stick.

"Boys, stop fighting! The stick doesn't matter!"

Both Paddy and Evan stopped and looked at me and I laughed at their scowls. I turned back to my sketchbook. Since I was focused on my painting, I didn't hear Evan sneak up behind me. He grabbed my shoulders and I jumped, my sketchbook dropping to the ground.

"Evan!"

"It was Paddy's idea, I swear!" He said, already running away from me. I chased after him and tackled him to the sand, Paddy barking around us. "Remi..I swear...it wasn't my...idea," Evan panted.

I laughed at him and put sand down his shirt. I went back to my rock, but only to take off my wedding ring so I wouldn't lose it. I looked around for Evan. Slowly creeping forward, I saw a dark shadow out of the corner of my eye, and I ran toward the ocean.

He caught me and he spun me around. Laughing, we fell into the sand with our arms around each other and watched Paddy try to fight with a crab. The gray clouds weren't hanging low today and we could almost see the sunset. I laid my head on Evan's shoulder and sighed happily.

This would be my next painting. Soft colors peeked from the horizon, the lighthouse to my right sent its beams searching, and the shadows of two people who looked like they had always been there, side by side.

Ariana Harrison

Breaking Barriers

Cell walls, building walls, city walls and expanses of plains.

Nothing.

Edge of a field, hut, edge of a field.

Nothing.

Kingdoms laid out side by side by side, rolling hills and mountains. Oceans plunging down for miles. Caverns filled with deep treasure and dark secrets.

Nothing.

Snapping back, blocked by the giant barrier.

My eyes fly open as I hit the barrier again, yelping when it almost physically throws me back. In my startled jolt, my hand slips off the edge of the bed and I fall. I hiss through my teeth as I smack my back against the cold stone floor.

"Quiet!" the guard stationed outside my cell grumps, rapping his taser-like device against the bars in a very loud, irritating way.

"Calm down. I just fell off the bed," I growl in response, rubbing my sore back as I pull myself up. "No need to get nasty."

I lay on the cot again, staring at the ceiling, wondering about the worlds I'd seen. Wondering if my sight could be trusted.

My name is Kyra, and I wasn't born as much as created. I'm the first in a series of experiments to see if people can be imbued with electricity. The idea is nice in theory: everyone's a walking battery and provides clean electricity at no cost to themselves or anyone else. Ideally, one person would be enough to run air-conditioning, water, and various electronics for one home by themselves.

But that's all fun and games until *you're* the lab rat being run through hundreds of painful tests to see if they can increase your "battery" capacity. I can't tell you how many bruises I've sustained, how many shocks I've undergone, how many times I've had to recuperate from yet another terrible, invasive surgery. To be honest, I'd rather die than have them prod around my ribcage one more time.

Of course, they wouldn't use a *real* human for these tests. Laws and all that jazz. So, they grabbed some organic elements, a metal skeleton, and some science-y magic and whipped it all together with organs grown from stem cells to create little old me. The first synthetic human. I didn't even have to progress from a baby to a teenager; I woke up as a fifteen-year-old. How'd they accomplish this? They grew my brain from a stem cell as well, but artificially stimulated the neurons during growth to 'program' basic knowledge, motor skills, and standard education into me. Though I look and act like a teenager, I'm technically only eleven months old, which is weird to think about.

I can do everything a normal human girl can. Breathe, think, eat, all the basics of life. The scientists created me to be as close to human as possible, so they'd have an accurate base to test on. It ended up making things more difficult for them since they had to make sure I'd continue developing like a normal girl, so I don't go insane. I'm glad they put the extra effort in, though, since I'd only be a human-shaped meat sack with a circuit-board brain otherwise.

I only have normal human capacities, though; no cool superpowers for me. The only thing that's different about me is that I've been experimented on to the point of having some weird gift with electricity. I'm a walking generator too, sure, but not to the extent they want. I can barely charge a smartphone without falling over from exhaustion.

What they didn't intend to create, though, was my sight.

I see like a normal human, but I can also sense electricity. I can kind of see it; I feel things giving off or surrounded by even faint electrical currents. Think of it almost like an extra pair of binoculars that let you see around and through things.

That's how I see outside of my prison.

I've been looking out at my surroundings ever since I gained my electric sight. I took small steps that progressively got larger. First, I looked outside of my cell. That progressed to looking outside the lab, which progressed to looking outside the building, which progressed to looking outside the block.

I can now see *far* past the city, but it's what's beyond the city that puzzles me.

Once the city ends, the land extends for a few miles before it drops. Not out of sight, but out of existence. It just stops. It's like an island floating in an abyss of nothing. It's not water. It's not anything physical. It's just...nothing.

It goes against every bit of knowledge they programmed into my brain.

What's even odder is that if I push further, I come across other islands. Some are enormous and span for continents before they drop into nothing. Others are nothing more than a hut in a tiny field. All of them are floating in this abyss.

It was only last week when I found the barrier.

If I push far enough, eventually the islands stop and I find a giant barrier. I've never had problems pushing through a barrier, but this one always repels me and forces me to stop my sight when I hit it.

As far as I can tell, it's determined to not let me past, but I've never been known for listening. I keep getting this feeling that there's something beyond the barrier, something big. I need to know what it is.

But first, I need to get out.

I seize the keys from under my pillow and grin giddily. I snatched these from a guard last week and have been waiting for the perfect opportunity to escape. I activate my sight and wait for the security switch.

Right on cue, the guard at my cell starts walking away. I have mere moments before another will take his place.

I slip the key in and out with a practiced hand and push the cell door open, bolting around a corner. I hear an alarmed cry the instant I notice a large guard behind me. I was too slow. I bolt around a corner, making a mad dash for the air vent I'd scoped out, the guard hot on my heels.

At the last second, I leap, grabbing the edge of the open vent. Behind me, the guard jumps too, and I try to twist away, but he's too quick. A rough hand grabs me by the back of my shirt and hauls me down, causing me to yelp when the collar digs rather painfully into my neck.

"Where do you think you're going, Kyra?" The red-bearded guard sighs as I spit out a strand of my sandy hair that somehow made its way into my mouth.

"Nowhere, apparently," I huff, frustrated to already have been caught but determined to play it off. At least he caught me instead of one of the grumpier guards. "How are the wife and kids, Greg?"

"Melanie got in a fight at school again," Greg says conversationally as he pulls me back to my cell as casually as if he was walking to the store. "Something about a bully calling Lizzy a freckle-head. Of course, Jessica and I are a bit exasperated about the whole ordeal, but I'm honestly proud of Melanie for sticking up for Lizzy like that."

"Melanie sounds like a great kid," I reply as Greg confiscates my keys. This is a routine we're used to. I try to escape quite often, but someone typically catches me. Once, I almost made it out of the building, but then they sent it into lockdown mode and the doorway was barred just as I got there. Greg is a guard I am well-acquainted with by now.

"Kyra, you need to be more careful," Greg tells me, his voice quieting.

I blink. "What?"

"There's talk of something bad happening if you keep trying to escape," Greg whispers, his words hushed and rapid. "I don't know exactly what it is, I'm just a guard, but you're a good kid. Watch out for yourself, okay?"

Before I can respond, he pushes me into the cell, locks the heavy, metal door, and is gone, taking any answers he might have had with him.

Greg's cryptic warning rattles me. Sure, I try to escape often, and I get punished, most often in the form of less food or some chores, but nothing more severe than that.

I'm spooked enough that I don't even bother trying to set up another plan for three whole days. I spend that time desperately sending my electric vision as far as I can before the barrier shocks me out. I keep stupidly hoping that maybe, just maybe, I can find a way out, maybe even to one of those other islands. I feel like there's some possibility I'm missing, some inaudible voice that holds the answers.

It's when Gavin comes to visit that seals my resolve to get out.

I typically see Gavin on Thursdays—that's when he comes to interact with me for half an hour while supervised. Gavin is a couple of years older than me and started working for the lab in exchange for medicine for his sick mother. He couldn't get the medicine to her in time, and she ended up dying, but he still insists that working is better than living on the streets. It makes me a little sick to think about.

At least the scientists let him come in to talk to me. Apparently, they have to make sure my synthetic brain is still developing from social interactions like a normal fifteen-year-old's.

Gavin's pretending to teach me sign language. By this, I mean that our supervisor thinks I'm a beginner. I already know basic sign language and use it to secretly talk to Gavin so our supervisor doesn't get mad if I bring up an escape plan. I am not as fluent as he is, but what I do know suffices.

"Morning, Kyra," Gavin chirps cheerfully upon entering. I instantly notice that his curly red hair is uncharacteristically disheveled and that his smile doesn't reach his wide brown eyes.

What's up? I instantly fingerspell, trying to make it look like I'm greeting him in sign language.

"Ah, you've been practicing! Good!" Gavin grins, the emotion not quite reaching his eyes again. *Not now, Kyra*, he signs back, pretending to return my greeting. His eyes dart quickly to Eleanor, the scientist acting as our supervisor for this go-round.

We sit facing each other on the ground while Eleanor takes the chair in the corner, staring at something on her tablet.

"Today, we'll be going over signs for household objects," Gavin informs me, fingerspelling out another message next to his leg, just out of Eleanor's sight. *You're not planning another escape, right?*

"What are we starting with first?" I ask him, imitating his out-of-sight signing. *No. Greg said something that worried me.*

This is how we have our real conversations. We fill up our "lessons" with some sort of unnecessary nonsense or fluff so we can multitask with signing where our supervisors can't see.

"Computers," he replies. *Good. You're in trouble.*

He starts "teaching" me the signs and I slowly imitate them back with my left hand while signing to him mainly with my right. This skill took me quite a while to master, but it's extra hard to concentrate when I was just given my second cryptic message within a week.

What do you mean?

I mean, he says, imitating my different hand technique, *that there's talk of them shutting you down if you keep trying to escape. I was working on cleaning one of the labs where I overheard a conversation with some of the heads of department. They say that if you attempt another escape, they're going to put you in an artificial coma and try to reprogram your behavioral patterns and personality to make you cooperate.*

"What!?" I cry, the word slipping out of my mouth before I can stop it.

Uh-oh. Eleanor looks up, startled by my outburst. I have to play this off before she gets suspicious.

"Why would they make up so many signs just for 'computer'?" I demand. "There's, like, seven; you only need one!"

"I'm not the one who invented sign language. Don't ask me," Gavin replies, looking somewhat amused through his momentary panic. "Can we get back to the lesson?"

"Okay," I agree, trying to put some level of huffiness in my voice. My attempt to not set off Eleanor's alarm bells must have worked, because she just snorts in exasperation and looks back down at her tablet.

I can't go through that again, I sign frantically, trying to keep my expression calm while Gavin resumes teaching me yet another sign for 'computer'. *I hate their experiments and I don't want to lose who I am, too. My personality is the only thing I have that they didn't grow or manufacture. It's precious to me!*

Your personality is not something either of us wants to be reprogrammed, Gavin reassures me as he verbally moves on to kitchen utensils. *So, if we're going to escape, we're going to have to give it our all. There's only one more shot; it's all or nothing.*

What do you mean 'we'? I cock my head in the slightest of inquisitive gestures while he keeps talking about silverware.

I'm going to help you because I want to come too.

No, I sign back instantly. *They'll use you for an experiment too.* I try to suppress memories that rise to the surface of my mind. Images of needles, high levels of electricity, and sharp medical tools dance in the back of my head, and I barely resist the urge to shudder. I can't risk making Eleanor suspicious again.

I'm going to take that risk, he insists. *I'll be back tonight—we'll escape through the air ducts.*

I've tried that already; it won't work.

Because you didn't have me working with you. Gavin risks a wink with this message, and I have to stop myself from giving him an exasperated smile.

I swallow my nerves. *Okay. Tonight.*

I finish signing in the nick of time. As soon as I end my sentence, Eleanor stands, signaling that our time is up. Gavin leaves with another wink and a reminder to practice, and I am left alone in my cell.

As soon as I sit on the edge of my cot, a sharp pain stabs behind my eyes. I wince, closing them, and my electric sight instantly launches, sending me past all the islands and taking me straight to the barrier at top speed. Unable to stop, I ram into it. A shock that I swear is almost physical sends me flying back into the wall and I end up hitting my head. Eyes watering, I rub my head as I slowly sit back up.

"Ow," I mutter.

What in the world was that? I wonder, soothing my aching skull. *A stress-activated power trigger, maybe? It makes sense, I've never been this stressed before—this escape really is my last shot.*

"I'm thinking too much like one of those goshdang scientists," I growl, running a hand through my unruly sandy hair and standing up so that I can properly pace worriedly over tonight's escape.

Four o'clock. I've probably crossed the length of my cell a couple hundred times before I finally sit down, tired from so much pacing. I try using my electric sight multiple times, but it keeps taking me to the barrier.

Five o'clock. I eat my dinner quietly when it comes, and I don't bother complaining that they give me baked beans with my roll and chicken instead of fruit. I don't want to eat, but I do anyway, knowing I'll need the energy later.

Six, seven, eight, nine all come and go. Somewhere in the middle, a scientist comes in to take my vitals, thankfully refraining from drawing blood this time. He leaves and all is quiet once more. No more luck with my electric vision, I'm still getting taken back to the barrier.

Ten o'clock. The lights in my cell go off, signaling that it's time for me to sleep, but the hallway lights remain on so the guards can see. I lay on the cot and stare at the ceiling, going stir-crazy from lack of motion, but not daring to move for fear of getting caught.

Eleven, twelve, one. The regular soft talking and rustling of the lab have quieted. The only soul I can detect is the guard outside my cell reading some sort of romance novel on her tablet. I can tell it's a romance because she keeps chanting "kiss, kiss, kiss" under her breath and putting a hand over her heart with a sigh every time something good happens.

Under normal circumstances, I would sneak over and try to read it over her shoulder, but these are not normal circumstances. This is my last chance to escape.

I risk trying to send out my electric sight to scan for other individuals on my floor, but it doesn't work. My sight just sends me shooting back to the barrier and shocks me out again. Because I was already lying down, I manage not to jolt too much, but it's still alarming.

My vision has been doing that every time I try to activate it since my conversation with Gavin. I can't control it. It's worrisome and infuriating. And honestly, it makes me nervous. I've never lost the ability to control it before.

The guard outside my cell complains softly about some character being an idiot for giving another character up. I swear, I hear her say "go after her, you nitwit!" at some point, but I can't be sure.

It's two o'clock in the morning and just as I'm thinking that I can't sit still for another instant or I'll explode, I hear a soft *shh-shh-shh* of some sort coming from right above me. My ears perk up, but I don't move yet, even though my heart is hammering.

A moment later, a small section of the ceiling is lifted away, and Gavin's grinning face greets me from the hole.

I'll pull you up, he signs quickly, offering me a hand. I slowly raise a single finger in the universal just-a-moment gesture, glancing over to the cell door. The guard is still reading her romance novel and insulting one of the characters. I lift the thin sheets away from me as quickly as I dare without making too much noise and gently gather my legs under me.

Standing is a painfully slow process that takes much too long for my taste. I need to move with enough haste to get out of here quickly without moving fast enough to alert the guard. Luckily, I've had practice from my other escape attempts. I manage to stand without the cot creaking.

As soon as I'm up, I grab Gavin's hand and he helps lift me into the air duct, which is an impressive feat, especially since he manages to do it silently. As soon as I'm stable, Gavin quietly slides the chunk of ceiling back into place and what little light there was vanishes. We're left in total darkness.

I jump when I feel a hand on my arm.

Just me, Gavin signs into my palm.

He guides my hand to his ankle so I can hold on, and we proceed to crawl in a very odd caravan to wherever Gavin is leading me. It takes me a minute to figure out how to synchronize my crawling so I can keep hold of Gavin's foot without falling on my face, but the sailing is smooth once I get it down.

We travel for a few minutes in silence before I risk a whisper.

"Gavin," I say, lowering my voice as much as I can without resorting to a croak, "how did you get the ceiling open?"

"Handy cutting gadget I managed to engineer myself," Gavin replies with a murmur, pride evident in his voice. "Working around the lab has taught me a thing or two."

We reach some sort of elevator shaft and drop onto the top of the elevator. It trembles the barest bit when we make contact, but it holds, much to my relief.

"We need to climb up to the lobby floor," Gavin says softly, leaning in so I can hear what he's saying. "It's forty feet up. I'll go first so I can help pull you up. When I shake the rope three times, start ascending."

"Okay."

My eyes are adjusting to the darkness and I can see the faint outline of a thick rope hanging down. As I'm holding it steady for Gavin, I notice that there are large knots every few feet to make climbing easier. Smart.

It's a good few minutes before I feel Gavin shake the rope three times. I take a deep breath, steel myself, and start scaling it.

I'm about halfway up, arms shaking and sweat pouring down my back, when I feel a tremor rumble through the shaft.

Oh, no.

The elevator roars to life, soaring upward at what looks like a breakneck pace. I stifle a yelp at the initial movement, but I can't keep in a small scream that slips out when my grip fails.

The fall that was originally twenty feet shortens to five as the elevator rushes up to meet me. I grunt when I hit it, but quickly get back up, preparing to launch myself into the vent where Gavin is. I don't know if this elevator will smash me into a pancake against the ceiling, but I don't want to stick around to find out.

I watch how much length the rope has left as the distance grows shorter. When there's about three feet between the elevator and the vent, I jump, crashing into Gavin as the elevator rolls to a stop.

When I manage to untangle my limbs from Gavin's with a whispered apology, I turn back to see that the opening of the vent has been cut in half, blocked by the top of the elevator. A gap I never would have fit through.

I silently thank my lucky stars that I jumped when I did.

Gavin crushes me against him in a bear hug. "Don't do that again. I thought you were going to break your leg," he scolds me in a hushed voice.

"It wasn't my fault the elevator moved." I scowl, then pause, the blood draining from my face as I realize what that means. "The elevator…no one uses the elevators at this time unless there's a change in night shift security. That's still forty minutes away. Someone knows something's wrong."

He freezes, and I can see him frantically debating courses of action in his head. "Let's hurry. If necessary, we can fight our way out the door, but once we're on the street, we're basically home free. All we need is some distance, and we could get to another city."

I bite my lip, deciding to tell him about the weird island thing later. "Sounds like a good plan. Do we have any weapons available?"

"I have my cutting tool," he mutters, half to himself. "I can use that…I don't know about you, though."

"It's okay," I reassure him quickly, trying to calm both of us at once. "I'll just use my fingers and poke them in the eyes if they get too close."

He barks out a humorless laugh. "We should hurry before others are alerted."

We crawl forward, a hurry to our gaits that wasn't there before. Gavin pauses and pulls out his tool, quickly cutting away a chunk of the air vent floor.

"Stay here," he orders. "I'll check to see if the coast is clear."

"Fine, but hurry," I whisper frantically. "We need to get out of here."

Gavin swings his legs around and puts them through the hole, preparing to jump down, when a meaty hand shoots up and seizes his ankle. Gavin cries out in alarm and I scream as someone yanks him roughly through the opening. He hits the ground and gasps for breath, the wind knocked out of him.

I stifle a sob of hopelessness as he stares up at me, panic in his eyes. "Run, Kyra!" he screams hoarsely as soon as he can breathe again. "It's an ambush; they knew we were coming! Run—"

Gavin's cut off as the thug that yanked him down grabs him and wrestles him up, twisting his arms behind him so he can't fight his way free. A different hand comes back up into the vent again, and I know it's searching for me. I scramble backwards, out of reach, tears streaming down my cheeks.

They knew we were coming, and now Gavin's going to be tortured just like I was, and I'll lose my personality, the only thing that's truly mine, and I'll have to go through more experiments and I'll never get out—

Without warning, my electric vision is triggered again.

No! Not now! I mentally scream as I rocket past the islands again and approach the barrier. *If I jolt back from the barrier again, I could fall through the hole!*

I brace myself, preparing for the worst as I push back with my powers, desperately trying to backpedal. But this time, I don't shock back. This time, the barrier cracks as I approach and I break through, soaring right past. What I find is so enormous that I almost overload my brain trying to process what it is.

The islands.

The abyss.

The barrier.

It *all* makes sense now.

All those other islands I see are other worlds, just like my city is a separate world. These have all been *written* into existence.

The abyss isn't an abyss, but a dimension that is housed by a computer. The barrier is the computer confines, and I somehow managed to see through it with my electric vision.

Sitting at the computer keyboard past the barrier is the girl controlling all of this, writing these worlds and people into existence, and weaving them into stories.

That girl is the author writing about my adventure.

And I need to get her attention. If I want to save Gavin and make it out of here alive, I have to convince her to turn the outcome around.

What's the opposite of what she wants me to do? I brainstorm frantically as I turn off my electric sight. Every instinct is screaming at me to run and get away. I quickly realize that my instincts are probably a pretty good hint.

I take a deep breath, and before I can chicken out, I launch myself through the hole.

The crowd of guards and scientists that had been waiting to ambush us in the lobby all whirl to stare at me, shocked by my sudden appearance.

"Kyra, no!" Gavin screams from his confinement in the unforgiving grip of a guard.

My breathing hitches when I see no sign of the author paying attention. Maybe I played right into her hands.

Eight guards rush me as I shriek in dismay.

Then everything stops. I mean, it literally stops. The guards freeze mid-run and the commotion dies like its been shot. I feel like I've stepped into a portrait of chaos.

"*What in the world do you think you're doing!?*"

A flash fills the room, so bright that I'm forced to turn away. When I regain my vision, a tall girl with dark hair is standing in front of me, looking royally annoyed.

Oh, boy. It seems I got her attention.

"You're the author of this story?" I ask weakly, attempting a sheepish smile but ending up grimacing instead.

"This isn't the way this story is supposed to go!" she roars, her rage causing the entire city to shake. I yelp when I'm nearly knocked off my feet, but I somehow stand my ground.

"Yes, I know," I say hastily, trying to avoid having the entire world cave in on me. "And I'm sorry for inconveniencing you; it's just that I don't like the way this story is going."

"Nor are you supposed to," she snaps acidly, her eyes sparking with anger. "I put characters through all sorts of crap so that they can develop the way they need to. And *you* are supposed to lose Gavin, and you're *not* supposed to jump back into the hands of the scientists!"

"What do you mean I'm supposed to lose Gavin?" I demand, an edge of fear creeping into my voice.

"The plot is that Eleanor tipped off her superiors to the likelihood that you'd try one more time to escape, and the scientists were able to figure out when you'd most likely try to get out and how by watching Gavin's preparation. Then, when you get caught, you escape, Gavin gets experimented on and dies, then you go on to become corrupted and take over the city as a supervillain and keep tabs on everyone with your sight." The author counts off these plot points on her fingers and I feel myself getting paler with each reveal. She shoots me an icy glare. "At least, that's what's *going* to happen when you stop being stubborn and start following the plot of the story!"

"The problem is," I protest quietly, now realizing how much is on the line if I can't change her mind, "that I want a different ending to the story."

"You don't get one," she scowls. "That's not the way it works."

"Think about it!" I blurt, trying desperately to think like an author. "Not only does the plot of my story get extended and open up more possibilities that way, but readers get that close-call sensation with the dread and relief when the hero barely makes it out by the skin of their teeth!"

She tilts her head and I can tell I've gotten her attention. "Hmm. I'm listening."

"Uh," I stammer, floundering for something else convincing. "Romance! You keep my story running longer, and you can introduce a love interest!"

"Already done that," she replies off-handedly with a gesture in Gavin's direction, much to my embarrassment. "But keeping him alive would open another door in that area, yes. Anything else you want to argue?"

I'm out of logical reasons. I'm panicking under the pressure of talking to a girl who has the power to crush my entire world like a bug, and I'm desperate to save Gavin.

"Look," I beg, grabbing her hand pleadingly. "I just want to get out of here with Gavin *and* myself intact. Please. I'll take him and we'll get out of the city and we'll go on a different adventure and give you something better to write about. I don't know what yet, but it would be something you'd like."

She gently pulls her hand away, the anger finally fading from her eyes. "Okay. I'm willing to try this," she sighed. "On one condition."

"What?" I ask, a little afraid to find out.

"If I don't like your story, we start over from the beginning. And I mean you-getting-created beginning. And we do the story my way."

"Deal," I agree, nearly hysterical with relief at a chance for something better.

"Go give me something to write about." She smiles for the first time. "Make it count."

"I will," I say with no small amount of determination. When she starts to turn away, I remember something. "Wait! How are we supposed to get out of here?"

"You know the way already." She grins mischievously. "Think of when you made it past the barrier."

There's another bright flash, and then she vanishes.

The barrier… This may be a stupid idea, but maybe it'll work.

The author must have had some mercy on me, because everything starts moving again, but in slow motion. I dodge the guards, squeeze through a pair of scientists and reach out to Gavin, grabbing his arm.

I squeeze my eyes shut and turn on my electric sight again, throwing myself at the island with the little hut while backpedaling. This time, I feel it. The slight tear in the distance this contrast creates. Instead of just sending my sight through, though, I leap in, pulling Gavin with me.

The lab vanishes as Gavin and I tumble to the ground in a heap.

"Kyra?" Gavin sputters, looking utterly disoriented as he stares around wildly at the field, still in fight-or-flight mode. "How— What—?"

"I'll explain it in a moment," I wheeze, out of breath and dizzy, but my eyes shining with triumph. "All you need to know is that we're free."

Gavin stares at me, his jaw hanging open.

"Also," I smirk, bursting with pride. "I totally just teleported."

It's been eighty years since that day I first teleported. Since that day, I've teleported to almost all the other worlds the author has written and explored. Sometimes, I even helped those main characters on their journeys in one roundabout way or another.

The author was serious when she said she'd made Gavin my love interest. He traveled with me everywhere I went—of course we fell in love and got married!

Gavin died a few years ago, though. I suspect that one was the author's doing, but I haven't interfered with her on that one. It was his time to go. Besides, I'm not stupid enough to mess with death; that only ends in misery.

I put down my pen, staring down at the scrawled map of the places I've seen. My work here is finished.

There's a bright flash and a hand rests on my shoulder. I look up to find the author grinning down at me. Her hair is longer now, but other than that, she looks the same.

"Your work isn't done yet," she tells me with a smile as my eyelids drift closed with sudden exhaustion. "I have one last mission for you: give the man you love a hug from me."

When I open my eyes again, Gavin is standing in front of me, a tearful smile on his face. "I've been waiting for you, Kyra," he whispers.

I pull him into a hug with a joyful sob, officially completing my final mission.

This is the last page of my story.

I daresay I had a good ending.

Shion Cook

A Little Mermaid

I welcomed the pouring rain, letting it slowly numb me. Walking toward the churning ocean, void of feelings, I dared a glance back at the palace.

Was there any hope for the failure of a prince I am? Something small told me there was, but I walked straight into the frigid water, for the voice saying it was hopeless was louder.

Seconds after throwing myself to the waves, I realized I didn't want to die. Struggling to see the surface, salt burned my eyes. As the water gave way to oxygen, I gasped and scanned for any bearing before a wave drove me back under.

Please, I cried internally, *If there is any God out there. Anyone. Someone save me.*

Every time I found the surface, another wave thrust me below. Exhaustion and the icy water sent a throbbing ache throughout my body. Darkness set in as something warm wrapped around me. With my last bit of strength, I fought to surface one final time.

"Help!" I coughed weakly.

"Help!" I heard an unfamiliar voice call, and I could barely recollect what she sounded like. I heard a small whimper followed by heavy breathing. Blinking the water from my eyes, I looked over at the stranger. Her long white hair transitioned to blood-red tips. No, she had a large gash on her side, blood stained her hair following the water current down her tail. Her tail?

Squeezing my eyes shut, I coughed up more seawater, half laughing as I did so. *By the skies,* I thought, *I've caught a mermaid.* Looking at her again, the tail had vanished. Closing my eyes once more, exhaustion won.

"Prince Derek!" the guards called.

"The girl," I breathed. "Save her."

Sunlight? Am I in the human realm? Enemy territory.

Legs felt weird. I hadn't expected being a human would feel so strange. Stretching each limb under the soft covers, however, was a welcoming feeling. I propped myself up in the bed, scanning the room for any indication of where I was. This looked nothing like the small homes on our underwater scrolls. Sliding off the silk, I tried to maneuver on these two short stubs. Nevertheless, they were as controllable as kelp, and human realm gravity worked differently.

Doors swung open, revealing an enemy, a human.

"Careful," the boy called rushing to my side, stopping my trip toward the ground.

I pushed myself away the moment I realized he had touched me, I struggled to find my balance in this shape. Stumbling toward the bed, I looked where his bare skin met mine, there was no pain.

"My apologies. I didn't mean to startle you." He took a step backward but remained close.

Eyeing this boy, I examined him as my tribe inspected our troops: dark hair, blue eyes, good muscle, carried a sword at his waist, no other visible weapons. The sun caught something silver on his head, and I inspected it as well until I realized what it was.

Kelpfish, what have I gotten myself into? The royal palace. Instinct took over and I pushed myself back onto the bed, putting distance between us. I was no match for him in this form. There would be no fight, just my death.

"Here, have some water."

A cup was filled and extended to me. I slowly grasped the smooth wooden exterior and held it, never relinquishing my gaze on him. I dumped the water over my face, and the cool liquid eased the dryness the air caused my skin.

"You are a Sia…"

My slap met his cheek harder than intended. I clutched my now throbbing hand to my chest, anticipating some explosion or a hundred guards, this impulse would seal my fate, but instead, he started to laugh. "Don't like that name. Does Mermaid suffice?" He drew out the word, seemingly afraid of what I would do. "No one else knows your secret; I promise. Not even my younger sister, Vanessa."

This boy was the prince then, but why keep me a secret from everyone else? Was he not planning a public execution?

Opening my mouth, I went to say something, but after a moment, I closed it. I had never believed the story that humans could steal mermaid's voices. The rumor was that all it took was one word from us. Still, it was not something I wanted to test.

"Derek, you aren't supposed to be out of bed. You scared your mother half to death," the little Princess Vanessa, I assumed, chided him. She had jet-black hair like her brother, the long strands pulled into a high ponytail, no weapon either.

"Oh, you're awake," Vanessa offered a warm sweet smile. "Where are you from? What's your name?" I looked between the two humans, not sure what to expect.

"She can't talk," Derek lied, or did he really not know I could speak?

"Oh, what a pity. Anyway, Father has requested your presence at the council this morning, if you are not feeling ill. I can return and make sure…she…is taken care of." Vanessa smiled at me one last time before leaving, and the Prince, Derek, soon followed leaving the door wide open.

I was not going to stay here any longer than needed. Slipping onto the floor once more, I attempted to walk again.

The little mermaid never seemed to stay in her room. It worried me that she wandered around the palace. I found relief when I discovered her in the library again on the third day.

"You seem to like reading. Do you write as well?" As I sat in front of the girl, she startled closing the book. She did that thing again, where she just stared at me, almost confused, and I could feel my heart beat a little harder. "Do you write?" I asked again.

Her lips formed an 'o' and she nodded before giving me a questioning look.

"So we can communicate?" I offered, "Since you can't seem to speak." I couldn't tell if the smile on her face was genuine or a smirk, but she nodded all the same. "I shall return shortly then."

I was still bothered by the fact that she might wander the palace. Mermaids were considered an enemy to humans. She did, however, save my life.

"Guards," I called two toward me. "I have an assignment. There is a lady in the library. She is a guest, but as she is not royalty, I do not want her wandering, and or disrupting anything in the palace. Ensure two guards watch her at all times, and she does not leave this story of the building, without me as her escort."

"Of course your Highness. Anything else?"

"Just keep me updated if she does anything."

I returned to the library with a small journal, a quill, and deep-blue ink that reminded me of the ocean. "Here we are," I offered, sitting down. I slid the writing materials across the table to where she had set aside her book once again.

What do you want to know? she wrote, turning the book around so I could read it.

"What is your name? Where are you from?" Those were simple enough questions.

Ariya, and I am from the ocean. I am a daughter of the southern tribe.

"Ariya is a lovely name," I said, running it through my head over and over.

"Derek, Father wants you." Vanessa had a habit of sneaking around the palace

"Very well. I shall return later."

Getting up from my seat the guards nodded, confirming my orders from earlier.

"Lady Ariya, you are not allowed downstairs without the prince."

It had not taken long to realize the guards following me were to keep me from snooping around more than necessary. I had already searched most of the rooms, but there were only a few that weren't rooms with beds, shelves, paintings, and other strange items I had yet to see a use for.

Smiling, I turned and followed the guards to the library, where I spent all my time while the prince was away.

"Good morning Ariya." Vanessa was the first to find me this morning, after breakfast. I scrawled out *Good Morning* on a new sheet, and she started off on her usual conversations about books, or items she's collected over time. A quiet girl at times, but she had a vast understanding of the world, nature, and even the ocean. It never ceased to surprise me.

"I haven't found anything super interesting, mostly cloth or an occasional rusted weapon that washed up after a big storm," Vanessa explained.

"I've seen her collection once or twice. It's more impressive than she lets on," Derek called, walking into the library.

I love the ocean. It's amazing that you collect items that get washed ashore. I'd love to see this collection sometime.

"Maybe another time." Vanessa stood. "I have lessons now. I'll see you later." She waved before rushing out the door.

Derek made sure Vanessa was down the hall before taking her spot across from me, setting a book on the table.

"I found another myth about mermaids."

I laughed aloud, trying to smother the sound with my hand.

This had been going on for days where we asked myths and fables about each other and gave the other person a chance to tell their side of the story.

"Just hear me out. Did mermaids really sink Atlantis? This book claims that it was a paradise and mermaids attacked, sending a wave big enough to sink the entire island."

I shook my head, laughing some more. *Atlantis is a fable among mermaids as well. It's not real. No merfolk or human has ever found any proof it exists, so I refuse to believe anything about it.*

"Bold statement," Derek added, his lips curving up ever so slightly.

I stared at the table for a moment before looking up and catching his gaze still on me.

I'm starting to, I paused, pen half dipped in ink when I caught myself. No. I can't like it on land. Humans aren't...I can't stay on land, not when there's a war, not when I have a purpose here.

"You're starting to what?" Derek asked.

To get hungry. I decided. *When is lunch?*

My parents joined us in the grand dining hall for breakfast this morning. Their presence brought quiet and manners, which hadn't been seen around the palace much since Ariya had arrived. They didn't question her presence much, believing the story that I heard a scream for help and jumped into the ocean to save her. However, I knew any longer than a week here and they would start questioning why she didn't speak.

I finished breakfast faster than normal and spent the rest of the time bouncing my foot silently under the chair. I watched Ariya quietly finish the last of her breakfast as well then glanced at my parents who sat in a quiet conversation. My father's face hardened into the emotionless expression I had examined many times during war training.

"We will discuss this later, Kathrine," my father stated simply, making a grand exit.

For a moment I saw the dark circles under my mother's eyes and worry lines creased her brow, but momentarily, she collected her expression.

"You are dismissed." Her voice though soft and gentle was loud enough to be heard.

I stood and left solemnly, allowing Vanessa and Ariya through the doorway before me.

"Ready?" I asked, knowing Ariya would eagerly nod, letting her red-stained white hair bounce, the blood was long gone but she had explained that mermaid hair was slightly different, it took to dyes and stains very easy. I grabbed her hand and we ran down the empty halls, slowing occasionally when guards or other important court members were present, then running as soon as they were out of sight.

I showed Ariya one room of the palace after another, explaining fun facts or childhood memories. I skipped over empty rooms and guest rooms.

I felt a tug on my jacket, and saw Ariya pointing to a room.

"Oh, that's my father's study. He doesn't appreciate people coming in…"

However, Ariya had already swung the door open, her eyes scanning the room. I didn't understand what she was looking for. When she had decided nothing was there, she closed it and looked at me to lead the way again.

"Are you trying to find something?" I asked, leading her to the next room.

She seemed to look ahead, but I noticed she started to bite at a piece of dry skin on her lip.

"Ariya?"

Another moment of silence.

"If I show you some secret passages will you talk to me?"

Finally a reaction. Her green eyes met mine and held my gaze for a moment. I was afraid she wouldn't agree, but her hair bounced in the light again as she nodded.

Behind a tapestry near the library was a crack in the wall. I found it when I was twelve. It branched off connecting to other passages all over the castle. Pride swelled in my chest as I finished showing my favorite secret tunnels and rooms. I caught Ariyas eye, she was motioning for something, but it was too dark to see what she needed. I felt for what she was holding, and instantly recognized the leatherbound book.

"It's too dark in here." I grabbed her hand, gently leading her through tunnels and outside into the flower garden overlooking the ocean. "What were you trying to say?"

I watched her grab the pen and ink from the small bag I gave her, and start writing in the nice curly handwriting I admired.

Can I tell you something?

"Of course you can,"

I mean really tell *you something?*

She seemed adamant to tell me, so I nodded.

"I need your help. Maybe as a land dweller, you know where it is better than I do." Ariya's voice was soft and gentle and melodic, unlike I had imagined and I was taken aback that she could speak after such silence. "Will you help me?"

"Of course," I nodded, "What are you looking for?"

"The trident."

←→

I could not stay focused on the book I was trying to read. Glancing at the glass doors after rereading the same passage did nothing to help. Still, there was no sign of either of the royal siblings. They should be here soon. I had been away from home for over a week, and with the possibility of the trident being so close…

"I found her," Derek said, Vanessa trailing behind him.

"What is this about, that you had to hunt me down like that?" Vanessa asked, sitting down across from me. I was happy to set the book down for once. I looked at Derek for reassurance and he offered the half-smile I was starting to love.

"I need to ask you if it is all right for me to see your collection, from the ocean." Vanessa frowned, taking it in for a moment.

"You want to see my collection?" she clarified, "Why?"

"I lost something important at sea, and I'm hoping it washed ashore and you might have found it," I offered.

"All right, let's go," Vanessa said, standing up. "I've been wanting to show you some of my new finds anyway. One of them is some strange golden pitchfork which doesn't make much sense, but you never know. Maybe some pirate wanted a fancy weapon or something."

I glanced at Derek, standing up to follow. Unsure of what a pitchfork was, I could assume that it might look something like the trident.

Vanessa talked all the way down the beach, listing other items, but all I could think of was the trident. Derek bumped my hand gently and I looked at him.

"Don't look so worried. I think Vanessa has it." He offered that grin that made me want to smile back, yet something in my heart clenched and I looked at the sand, watching my steps.

"Here you go. My collection."

Trimming a lamp, I looked around to see more items than Vanessa had ever let on. Tribe items, human treasures, rusted swords, coins of all kinds, and…the trident. Shimmering gold, it lay against the back wall as powerful as I remembered.

Vanessa started off about different items as I began to relive the night the trident went missing.

←→

I had been sleeping in my bed when noises outside started me awake.

"Ariyana, get up!" My older sister burst into my room dressed in full armor. She threw my sheets off, and helped me up.

"What's going on?" I muttered, shivering in the cold water.

"The trident is missing. The tribes are in full out war against each other."

"We cannot just stand down! We can't surrender. We didn't take the trident, and if we did we would have used it by now!"

"Ariyana! This is no place to voice your thoughts." My mother's words were swift and concise, shutting down any argument.

"If any of the other tribes took it, they would have used it by now as well. Especially if their motive is power, as many accuse. I'm afraid it's gone from our waters." My father wasn't a soft-spoken man, yet his quiet words silenced the chatty twins, barely a year older than me, and the challenging trio of older sisters.

"You're suggesting it could be lost at sea?" my oldest sister challenged.

The silence was enough for me to have another thought: *It could be on land.*

"Ariya?" I cradled her head in my arms, as Vanessa knelt next to me.

"Is she okay? Should I call the court physician? What could have caused her to collapse?" Vanessa's tendency to ramble was not helping.

Checking her vitals I slipped my arms under her small frame. "She's breathing and her heartbeat isn't irregular. We can take her back to her room and if she isn't feeling better in the morning, we can take her to the physician." I lifted her. "Let's go."

"But—"

"Can we talk about this later? I will answer your questions, I promise." The comment silenced Vanessa, but I knew she would be on me later with even more questions and theories of what might have actually happened, and who Ariya was. If I told her, maybe she would understand? Vanessa and Ariya had bonded right away, plus the stories we hear about mermaids are just stories. No one can prove they are true.

I managed to get Ariya under the covers and set a glass of water on the nightstand before finding two guards on duty.

"Prince Derek," they greeted, saluting briefly.

"Gentlemen, I need you to ensure that there are two guards keeping watch of Lady Ariya at all times today. You may be relieved of this post once she has gone to bed," I ordered.

"Are you expecting something to happen?" Vanessa was right around the corner as I started down the hall, ready with her new volley of questions.

The unusual clammar of guards rushing down the hall awoke me, I was long out of my bed by the time they reached my room.

"What's wrong?" I asked.

"Lady Ariya has…"

I didn't let them finish. I knew what was happening. I ran down halls and tunnels as fast as my legs would take me. She couldn't go, not yet.

"Ariya!" I called, reaching the sand. It was so dark. I couldn't see far. I bit back the sharp pounding in my head, "Ariya!" I called louder.

"Derek?" The quiet melodic voice was Ariya's, and it wasn't long before I could see her slender outline coming closer under the light of the moon, her white hair shimmering.

Desperation, panic, and a twinge of pain squeezed in my chest, I had to say something to get her to stay; instead I helplessly spouted, "Please don't go, Ariya. I love you!"

"Derek, I have to go."

I stepped closer to try and hold her, to keep her close, to never let her go, but I was met with a golden tip. I did not realize she was holding the trident until it was the only thing between me and her.

"You don't understand."

I tried to push it away only for it to come right back between us as Ariya took a step back, closer to the sea. "Then help me understand." I stopped advancing. "I want to understand. Skies, Ariya, I love you. I want to be with you. You saved my life, and every day since, have proven that you are not like anything anyone said. You're the most special and beautiful girl I've ever met.

Please don't go." Every ounce of effort I possessed held me back from visibly trembling.

She looked down momentarily before our eyes met one more time. I barely noticed the shimmer of a tear before she lowered the trident.

"I love you, too," she whispered, then she darted to the ocean.

"No!" I called rushing after her, throwing myself into the waters, but the more I tried to swim out the more the tide pushed me back to shore. Tears and ocean water stung my eyes. I could hear voices and mumbling. I attempted to fight the arms that tried to embrace me.

"Derek, stop it!" I turned to see my little sister grabbing my shoulders, wide-eyed and a furrowed brow.

"Ariya," I muttered.

"What about her? Where is she?" Vanessa clutched me harder. "Derek, talk. What happened? Why are you crying?"

I couldn't tell if the trembling was my own body, or my sister's hands. I could see the concern on her face.

"Ariya went home," I said looking down at my hands; they failed to hold onto her.

"She's a mermaid, isn't she?" Vanessa's expression changed into one of pity. "She's no different than any of the stories."

"You're wrong. She is different, and you know it!" I had no doubt she was different, and those last words, though barely a whisper, proved it. *I love you too.*

Vanessa didn't argue, just pulled me close. "Let's get you inside and changed. You will feel better in the morning." She gently led me back toward the palace.

I did not have time to think about him, but his words kept ringing in my ears. The trident shot me forward faster than I would have been able to swim on my own. As we reached tribe lands, I could feel the emptiness. Everything looked abandoned, but there were no bodies I could see.

"Where is everyone?" I asked the trident. It led me to the center of the four tribes, where the city was. The council hall and colosseum stood in part ruins. "What is going on?" I muttered to no one in particular. Swimming toward the ruins, I could hear voices, shouting. I swam faster, feeling no fatigue from the swim before.

"This is your last chance to give up the trident!" I recognized Chief Regonda's voice of the north tribe.

"For the last time Hakira, we don't have it." Father!

"You sent your daughter away with it, didn't you?"

"If we knew where Ariyana was, she would be here with us!" my mother snapped.

"Enough!" I called swimming into the middle of their arguing.

"Ariya!" my sister called.

"The trident!" My mother gasped. Mention of the heart of the tribe, other merfolk dared to see what happened, echoing the words as a question.

"The trident?" "She has the trident," "The trident has been found."

"You stole the trident?" Chief Mattia of Tribe West asked.

"No," I started.

"Ariyana, where have you been?" my father asked, rushing toward me.

"Where was the trident?" Chief Regonda questioned.

Too many questions and voices, and accusations.

"Silence!" I bellowed. The trident released a wave of energy adding to my command. I dared anyone to speak before me. "I've been on land these past weeks. I left in search of the trident because I knew it was no longer in our waters, and assumed it washed ashore during the storm. I was held by a human prince," I couldn't bring myself to say his name, not yet, "and, soon I learned the trident had washed ashore and the princess had stored it in a cave, not knowing what it was. I took it and made my way back here to end this fighting," I explained, casting my glance toward the four tribe leaders and their spouses.

"You were on land?" my mother gasped in shock.

"What's it like?"

"Are humans really gross?" the twins asked.

"That doesn't solve the matter of who took the trident, and how it ended up on human land!" Chief Geroan of the East tribe exclaimed, cutting off the side chatter.

"No one took me."

The look on everyone's faces told me I wasn't the only one that heard the strange voice. "I was created by merfolk and humans alike. This slander you throw at them is enough. I won't stand to see two brilliant species die out because of rumors and lies. You can't blame this young one for what happened. I simply pushed her to do what no one else would, and now we have a bridge between worlds."

I stared at the trident in my hands. "How did you know De…the human and I would get along?"

"I did not. I only picked someone pure of heart, a natural-born leader, who didn't quite know what to think of humans, and guided you to a prince who wanted someone to save him from the loneliness of his own mind."

I knew the voice was only speaking to me at that point as the merfold around me began to chatter, and I smiled imagining Derek.

"Ariyana! Explain what is going on." my mother snapped, pulling me from my thoughts.

"The Trident spoke the truth, and Humans are not bad." I relinquished my grasp of the trident letting it guide itself to where it belonged, before the tribe leaders issued a council meeting asking for my presence as well.

The days did not get shorter. All I managed the first day was to lay in bed, stare at the palace ceiling, and feel hopeless. I found the strength to walk the beach often, multiple times a day, replaying the last night, wishing I had done something different, if I had even just let her know, she saved me from more than just drowning, she saved me from my own thoughts and pain.

"You really loved her, didn't you?" Vanessa found me sitting against a stray log staring at the clear sky. The dark clouds in the distance left not long after Ariya did.

"I still do," I admitted, not moving an inch.

"Why? Why do you still hold onto her when you know she won't come back?" Vanessa asked, sitting next to me. "She's a mermaid. Our kinds don't get along, even if she is different from others."

"That's the funny thing about love. When you really care, even if they leave you, nothing can take away the feeling they gave you every time you saw them smile." If I closed my eyes, I could pretend, if only for a moment, she was here before my heart felt like it was being pulled apart again.

Vanessa was silent beside me gently rubbing her thumb across my hand, a calming gesture mother used when we were children. "I'm going inside, if you're up for it. I'll make you some of my chicken soup." Vanessa was trying hard to make everything all right. I loved her for that.

Closing my eyes, I took deep breaths to calm my emotions. The sound of the tide grew quiet, then the ocean started to churn. Startled, I stood up and watched as the water split to allow a goddess to walk to shore. I said nothing as I ran with everything I had into the waves, if only to hold her in my arms.

"Derek!" Ariya gasped as I threw my arms around her. Before she wrapped her own arms around me as well. The water seemed to move us to land as I held her in a tight embrace.

"Ariya," I breathed her name. I couldn't hold her close enough. Tears blurred my vision as I tried to make up for the lost days she had been gone.

"Derek, you're squeezing me," Ariya muttered, and I loosened my grip just enough to look at her face. "You're crying," she pointed out, wiping a tear off my cheek as her eyes started to glisten drops sliding down her own cheeks.

"No, you're crying," I laughed. My vision remained blurred no matter how many times I blinked the water away. Laughing and crying we held each other for so many magical moments.

Ariya pulled away first but I didn't let go, not fully, not yet.

"I missed you," she said looking down before meeting my gaze. "I love you," she stated, another tear escaping.

"I love you too," I said before leaning in, her lips meeting mine. It was not a short kiss, but it was not long enough.

"Derek!" Vanessa's voice startled both of us and we pulled apart a blush creeping up my cheek. "Ariya?"

"Hello, Vanessa." She took a step forward, arms outstretched, and I was surprised that my young sister ran into them hugging her.

"You came back!" She looked at me and smiled. "You brought Derek back." Tears filled her eyes.

"I never meant to leave, but I had to fix things at home first and I needed the trident too." That was when I realized she had the trident with her. "If you two don't mind, I need to have a word with the king and queen, and you two."

"My parents know you're a mermaid. They don't trust you," I quickly explained.

Ariya smiled, a little bit of a challenge in her eyes. "I know very well. That is why I'm here," she said, taking a moment to look at the trident.

"This is all true?" the queen asked. The things the trident spoke were many, explaining the nature of tragedies, ships crashing, sirens, and storms.

"I can't honestly say, your Highness, I had no clue half of these occurrences existed. I come from the largest tribe in these waters, yet never have I heard of merfolk bragging of sinking ships, or using any sort of siren ability. For years, we believed you to be monsters set to murder us, so we never came to shore," I explained.

"It seems we are both in the wrong. You have proved your kind are," the king paused thinking carefully, "not as we expected."

"This trident was made years ago between merkind and humankind to bring balance to the sea and skies. Let us do that again." I looked at Derek and smiled. "If I may be so bold as to say, I wish to do this with Prince Derek, to be the bridge between our kind, and try to mend old wounds."

"Are the merfolk all in agreeance?"

"It took much convincing, but the four mertribes voted unanimously that a bridge bringing the two worlds together is a good start."

"We shall discuss it. In the meantime, you three are dismissed." The king nodded. I bowed in respect before leaving with the siblings.

"How do you do that?" Derek eventually asked.

"Do what?" I asked.

"Lead, command, respect, and negotiate. You got my father to earnestly consider your suggestion." His gaze caught me off guard, and I smiled shyly.

"I just explained what I believed to be true."

"How are you so perfect?" he whispered, wrapping an arm around my waist and pulling me close.

It caught me off guard and my smile grew.

"Court her elsewhere please," Vanessa laughed, punching her big brother's arm. Derek let go of me only to pick Vanessa up and start running around the halls with her.

"Stop it!" She laughed. "Put me down!"

I laughed too as I watched them run, then turned my gaze down the hall we came from, and then to the trident still secure in my hand. It wouldn't be easy, bringing peace between the worlds, but I had faith.

Derek looked back and smiled at me.

We could do it. Together.

Ken Mears

MINDSCAPERS

"You can still back out of this Hugh!" Erwin pleaded desperately. "You don't have to battle him!"

"You know I can't back down now, Erwin!" Hugh said exasperated.

Deep down he knew his friend was right. It was far too risky to engage in a mental lock with Widald, the school bully. Few Mindscapers ever returned from a mental lock with another Mindscaper.

Erwin and Hugh rounded a corner and entered the common room.

Widald sat there waiting for them, a broad, cheeky grin on his face. "Well look who showed up. I was beginning to think you wimped out."

"I've put up with your crap long enough Widald. Besides, it's not like I'd pass up an opportunity to kick your butt," Hugh snapped back.

"Are we gonna keep talking or are we going to actually lock-in?" Widald said impatiently.

"Let's lock-in," Hugh said, taking a seat across from Widald.

The two of them touched hands, glaring into each other's eyes. Both lowered their heads, their foreheads touching in the middle. Their world went black as they each entered the other's mind.

Hugh felt nauseous as he entered Widald's mind, as though he got sick just from getting close to it. The darkness slowly transitioned to light as he fully entered the world of the mind.

Hugh slowly stood up as the world came into focus around him. A strange jumble of oddities surrounded him. A huge mountain of glass rose in the distance, a lake of living wood writhed nearby. Random shapes and animals floated through the dark purple sky. Bright pink fields spread in every direction. He was in the Mindscape. Hugh had only ever read about it. The Mindscape terrified him, there was a reason it was forbidden to enter. It was a world between minds, where you could do anything you wanted. The only limit was your imagination. Which made it the perfect place for Mindscapers to battle.

Hugh searched around for Widald, wondering where the bully ended up. He didn't have to wait long for his answer. A mountain shot up beneath him, sending him skyrocketing into the air. As Hugh flew through the air, he pictured himself floating, slowing to a stop. The world around him obeyed, and suddenly he hovered in midair. Searching for Widald, Hugh spotted him nearby, laughing at Hugh. Refocusing all the imagination he could, Hugh summoned two giant fists from the ground and started pounding Widald into the ground. The bully only laughed as he bounced around like a bouncy ball.

"Why are you laughing?" Hugh cried out, frustrated by the bully's delight.

"Because this is way funny. You can't hurt me punk! I'm invincible here!" Widald called back.

"Do you not realize the severity of our mental lock?" Hugh shouted. "We could be trapped in here forever, never able to leave!"

"Who would ever want to leave this place?" Widald asked. "You can do whatever you want here." Widald waved his hand and the whole world started to fold over. Hugh looked up just as the pink ground hurtled onto his head. Being shoved underground was not a fun experience. Dirt flew into Hugh's mouth as he traveled deep underground, not entirely sure which way was up. Hugh created a bubble around himself, protecting himself from the moving dirt. Gathering his focus, he pictured himself reappearing at the surface by Widald. The world disintegrated around him as he teleported above ground.

"Woah. Who are you?" Widald asked as Hugh appeared in front of him.

"You know who I am you, thick-skulled bully!" Hugh said irritated.

"No, really, who are you?" Widald asked. It dawned on Hugh that Widald was sincere in his question.

"I-I'm... I'm not sure who I am," Hugh said. He realized he didn't really know who he was. All he knew was that he needed to destroy Widald. "I think I am your enemy."

"Then I am yours too," Widald said. And the battle resumed.

Erwin ran as fast as he could to find Waldek. The old teacher must be hobbling around the halls somewhere. He screamed as loud as he could. "Help! Waldek, help!"

Erwin came to a halting stop as Waldek came hobbling quickly around the corner. "What is it, Erwin?" The kindly old mentor asked.

Erwin caught his breath as he tried to explain the situation. "Hugh... and Widald... mental lock... need you NOW!"

Waldek nodded in understanding. "Take me to them immediately."

The battle inside the Mindscape continued for years within the realm. Over time Hugh and Widald lost track of who they were before entering the Mindscape. All they could remember was their names.

One day, Hugh finally asked a question. "Widald, why do we fight each other?"

"I can't remember," Widald said.

"What is the point of our continued conflict if we do not know why we fight? How about we call a truce," Hugh said.

"I think that would be good," Widald said. "Let us make peace from here."

"Now what do we do?" Hugh asked.

"Look around us. This is a wonderful place, our world of the Mindscape. I say we explore it," Widald said.

"That sounds fantastic," Hugh said, pointing to the east. "Lead on, my new friend."

Erwin and Waldek burst into the common area, causing several students to jump back in surprise. Erwin pointed at where Hugh and Widald's bodies were still connected. Waldek hurried over to the two boys, evaluating the situation.

"How long ago did they engage in the mental lock?" Waldek asked.

"Maybe twenty minutes ago. I came to find you as soon as they locked in," Erwin said as he gasped for breath.

"Well done, my boy. Clear the rest of the students out and come back. I need you to ensure no connections are broken," Waldek commanded.

"Yes, sir," Erwin said as he started to herd everyone out of the common room.

Waldek knelt down beside Hugh and Widald. "Oh, you foolish boys. Couldn't you listen to our warnings?"

The old Mindscaper put his hands on the boy's heads, entering the Mindscape. It was time to bring them home.

Hugh and Widald strolled through the woods together. The blue trees around them glowed dimly in the late dawn light. Ahead of them, they could barely make out what looked like a small encampment. Deciding to investigate, the two of them forged ahead.

Strange creatures wandered around a big bonfire, setting up camp. Many were conglomerates of odd animal parts, and still, others were tall glowing humanoids. They didn't look terribly friendly.

"What do you think they are?" Hugh whispered.

"Nothing good," Widald said. "What do you say we attack them?"

"Are we sure they aren't friendly?" Hugh asked. "We shouldn't judge them by the way they look."

"Fine," Widald relented. "Let's try talking to them. If they attack, we destroy them. Agreed?"

"Deal," Hugh said.

The two boys stepped out of the woods and into the encampment. All eyes turned on them instantly. A particularly tall glowing person stepped toward the boys. Its voice echoed in their heads.

"Who are you and what business do you have?"

"My name is Hugh and this is my friend, Widald. We are just two adventurers, passing through," Hugh said, stepping up. "We mean no harm."

"You claim to mean no harm, yet you hold immense power within yourselves," the Being said. "How could you have such power and not wish harm upon others?"

"Why would we want to hurt you?" Hugh said. "You've done no harm to us."

"But you are of the Mindscaper race, are you not?" the being asked.

"Yes... I think..." Hugh said. "Honestly, we can't remember much about before we came here."

"Do you work for the high emperor?" the glowing being asked.

"Who?" Widald asked.

"The high emperor of the Mindscape," the being said. "Ruler of all and commander of the elements."

"Doesn't ring a bell," Hugh said.

"You wield the same power as him," the being said, an expression of hope spreading across its face. "Perhaps you could defeat him."

"Woah, why would we want to defeat some high emperor?" Widald asked. "We just want to explore."

"Please," the being pleaded. "Defeat the emperor and free the Mindscape."

The Mindscape materialized around Waldek, revealing a burning battlefield. Rainbow flames leaped into the air all around him, and debris scattered everywhere. The sky shifted to neon green above Waldek.

"The boys must have been here," Waldek muttered to himself.

Using his mind, Waldek created a compass to lead him to Hugh and Widald. The pointer led directly into a glowing blue forest. Bracing himself, Waldek set out.

"I'm coming, boys," he muttered

Widald and Hugh stood in front of a massive fortress. Having followed the glowing blue being's instructions, they were ready to end the high emperor's reign. Flames made of darkness blasted into the air around the castle, seeming to shake the ground with its roar.

"Are you ready?" Hugh asked.

"Ready as I'll ever be," Widald said.

The two of them stepped up to the castle and opened the doors. A single hallway led to a long staircase upward. They floated through the hall and up the stairs to the throne room. The castle gave off a very creepy vibe, with gothic paintings and architecture plastered with cobwebs.

As the boys reached the top of the staircase, they emerged into a large throne room. There, sitting on a throne of gold, sat the high emperor himself. His eyes were sunken into his narrow face, and a dark gray goatee covered his face. He looked dead inside, as though being inside the Mindscape for so long had drained his life force.

"What have we here, two more Mindscapers who think they can destroy me?" The high emperor's voice was raspy and hollow. "It's a pity I'll have to kill you. It's gotten so boring after all these years."

"We've come to end your reign!" Widald shouted across the room. "There's two of us and one of you. You stand no chance."

"We shall see about that," the high emperor said as he calmly floated up and toward them.

The ground suddenly felt squishy, and Hugh realized they were sinking into the stonework. The boys struggled against it, but couldn't move. Using their imagination, both boys slammed the walls into the high emperor as hard as they possibly could. It didn't even phase him.

"You didn't really think brute force would work on me, did you?" The high emperor chuckled. "Nothing can physically harm you here in the Mindscape."

Hugh and Widald shared a knowing glance.

"Since you're going to destroy us anyway, you may as well tell us," Widald asked. "What brought you here? Who are you?"

The high emperor seemed surprised. "You mean you don't know who I am?"

The boys shook their heads. "Nope."

"My name is Bragi. I am the first Mindscaper to ever enter the Mindscape," he said, his hands dropping to his sides. "I have ruled over this realm for thousands of years."

"Well, why haven't you left?" Hugh asked.

"Because there is nothing for me outside of the Mindscape," Bragi lamented.

"Are you sure? Isn't there someone or something you care about outside of the Mindscape?" Widald asked.

A sad expression came over Bragi's face. "Why yes, there was one thing. My darling Aina."

"Why haven't you returned to her?" Hugh asked.

"She is long gone," Bragi said.

"Are you sure?" Hugh asked. "Because I think there's a possibility she is still alive."

"Impossible." Bragi's face bent in sorrow. "She would have died a long time ago."

"Have you ever had any real confirmation of that?" Hugh asked.

"Well, no," Bragi said, pacing.

"So how can you be sure unless you check?" Widald added.

"You know what, I will check!" Bragi said. "Thank you. Perhaps I shall find my darling, Aina."

Bragi began to glow and shift as he excited the Mindscape. He disappeared in a flash, leaving Hugh and Widald alone. The two boys manipulated the stone to release them.

"Well, what now?" Hugh asked.

"Now we continue to explore." Widald smiled.

Waldek slowly hobbled toward the stone fortress, following the arrow of his magic compass. The two boys emerged from the structure, chatting as they went along. They stopped when they saw the old man.

"Hello, boys," Waldek said.

"Hello," Hugh replied. "Do I know you? You look familiar."

"Yeah, you do look familiar," Widald said. "How do we know you?"

"You know me from a time you have now forgotten," Waldek said. "Now come; it's time I take you home."

Amanda K. Grant

THE TRIALS OF PSYCHE

"I am part or parcel of God."
Ralph Waldo Emerson

I rub my eyes, pulling myself from my afternoon reverie, full of daydreams of people I have never met. The sun is beginning to set and I stand up, going to my school desk from my window seat. My eyes wander before falling on the screen of my laptop. I stare at the background, a lagoon in Greece. I don't know how long I stare, how long I wonder why that place has always been so familiar. I felt like I had been there before, even though I had never left Minnesota. But something told me I *needed* to go again.

"Parys! Phone call for you!" my mom shouts up the stairs.

I run down the stairs, more curious than anything since it's very rare for me to get phone calls. I'm not terribly involved at my school or with the people in it, though I do try. She smiles, or more like grins, and hands me the phone, which I anxiously grab.

I put the phone to my ear and a heavily accented voice begins to talk. "Parys Cliff! You have been accepted for the Foreign Exchange Program of the Grecian Islands! We have received your application and blood results and discovered you're the perfect candidate, based on your direct ancestry from the Grecian Isles. We expect you at the Minneapolis Airport on the thirtieth of May. We have mailed a packing list that will arrive shortly, with more instructions. The only cost is the flight here."

The caller hangs up without waiting for any kind of response from me. I had taken one blood test in my life, and it was to check for disease susceptibility. I never knew I was a single bit Grecian; I was fostered and then adopted at a very young age. The kitchen reeled.

"Mom? Did you do the application?"

She shakes her head and the kitchen fades from my eyes. My eyes close and a vision fills my mind. I'm in Greece, the buildings are bright white in marble and quartz, the sky overcast. I am walking with a gentleman, a friend, and I am leaning on him as we walk down a crowded street. I am powerful and I know it. And then I am back in my too still kitchen, compared to the bustle I was just feeling moments before.

"I'm going anyway," I whisper, running up to my room.

31 days had passed. I'm at the airport in the bathroom, staring at the mirror. My flight has been delayed and there are several hours before I need to board. I stared at the bathroom mirror, and my simple brown hair, makeup, felt off. My reflection had always felt off, no matter the styles I tried or the way I tried to force myself to smile or look serious. Some days it was bad enough I hid from the mirrors in general. Today was one of those days. My body felt like something entirely separate from me. My mom said that happened with adopted kids a lot, but it seemed different than an eating or mood disorder. I sigh and look down, breaking eye contact with my reflection. Then I quickly tuck my mustard jacket around me and walk out into the crowded airport. I walk to the check-in and hand the worker my passport at one of the seemingly millions of kiosks.

"Name?" The worker seems incredibly bored.

My mouth opens to state my name, but the words aren't on my tongue. I wrack my brain. *I should know my own name!*

"Name?" Now she is irritated instead of bored.

"I don't… know…" I whisper. Several names float through my head, but I know none are correct. *"Cordelia… Sera…*

Anne..." Vague memories come with each name. Rustling gowns, a carriage tipping over in the snow, an angry ocean.

"Well, miss... I can't help you if you don't remember your own name. Go get some medical help." She hands me back my passport, which in obvious print says, "Parys Cliff." I laugh softly. Of course, that was my name. I had known that all along. I reenter the line while repeating my name over and over to myself in my head and get through without a hitch.

The flight was long. I dreamed while we flew. It seemed the closer I got to Greece the worse the daydreams were. They had plagued me my whole life, but this time it wasn't just in Greece, it was London, somewhere in Asia, and just about everywhere else. As I deboard at the Galway Airport I look at the ticket that has been clenched in my fist ever since I got on the plane. I was no longer in the same country I was born in.... A slight shiver runs through my body and down my spine as I look around, trying to find the next terminal for my transfer. There were so many languages and people. I got caught up in the crowds while looking for the terminal, and I start to feel hazy. *Another daydream? Now?* I fight it away but my brain fogs up and all I can think of is me smiling and sitting right against someone, a crush of people around us. But I am at home in this crowd. I shake my head and realize I've still walked with the crowd and lost my terminal. Panic tears through me and I rush to the gate but by the time I get there, the gates are closing.

"No!" I run right up to the doors to my flight but the security shakes their head.

"Sorry, the flight is already preparing to leave."

"There's no other way to get me on?"

She shakes her head again

"No other flights to Greece soon?"

"Definitely not." She chuckles

I nod numbly and walk away, clutching my small luggage case. Where was I supposed to go?

My feet take me back to the ticketing desks and my mouth starts to talk. " I am so sorry, ma'am. I missed my flight."

"I'm sorry, but there is no Parys listed for the flight to Greece." The woman at the kiosk looks at her computer. "We can't change a flight you never had. I'm sorry."

I nod and wander to the front of the airport and call my mom.

"Hey, Parys!"

"Mom, I missed my flight. And the airport says it never existed," I huff.

"Oh… Well, you need to buy another ticket then, don't you?"

I shrug and then remember she can't see me. "Suppose."

"Well… You know your Aunt June lives in Galway. I haven't seen her in a long time, she and I are estranged…of sorts. Why don't you stop by her house… I haven't talked to her in a while, but I bet she will be happy to see you! Stay with her until I can find another flight for you."

She ends the call, and I sigh, heading out to the cabs and the baggage claim with no other choice. I get into a cab and my phone pings with the address. I show the cab driver the address and he speeds off down the street. Forty minutes later we stop at a small house seemingly in the middle of nowhere. I grab my bags and walk to the front door.

"I'm praying to every holy thing that this works," I whisper before knocking on the door.

A lady that looks exactly like my mother, down to the tired expression on her face, opens the door.

"Hi… Who are you? Can I help you?" She tilts her head a little. It is unnerving how much she looks like my mom.

I stammer for a second "My mom…is your twin sister… She should have called letting you know I missed my flight and that she would send me here."

She nods and smiles "Yes. I am June. It was nice to talk to your mom again." Her accent is thick and beautiful, but her sentences are always simple. "Though I am afraid I can't help you much. I can't pay for another flight, and I don't even have the money to lodge you. Get some money then maybe I can help. You can sleep on my floor. I have no blankets to spare though. I am so sorry." She shakes her head, frowning.

"But…"

"Look in the town a mile or two from here for work maybe? Even if your mom and I aren't close I want you taken care of." She points down the street.

"Thank you anyway." I smile and walk off, not seeing another option, but internally I am near tears. Some adventure this was, I think as I walked into the town and basically into the only motel I can see. The man greets me and I walk up to him "Sir? I missed my flight at the airport… I need some quick money so I can get another ticket or lodgings."

He chuckles softly. "Girlie, the only job I can think of is Crazy Don's file projects."

"Would I get paid quickly?

"As soon as you finish the project."

"That's perfect." I nod

"All right." He looks dubious and leads me out of the small motel down the road another half a mile to a very shabby and large house. "Ey, Don!"

An old man pops his head out of one of the windows "What?" he says gruffly.

I smile up at him. "I want your job!"

He chuckles. "This is a joke!"

"Sir, I missed my flight and I need this, I am trying to get to Greece! I have to!"

He smiles slightly. "Ah, youth," he says sarcastically. "Come on in and we will get you started."

I walk in and he walks silently to a back room with me. There are stacks and stacks of manila folders. "Once you start, it won't pause easily. This is old town genealogy; sort by family and then date."

I nod and force a small smile. "Thank you, sir."

He leaves and I get the strongest sense of déjà vu again. In my head the stacks of folders become piles and piles of seeds to sort. I shake my head. When had I ever sorted seeds? Never. What a useless task. I sigh and try to shake the feeling lingering in my head and creeping down my spine and into my ribcage. I need a therapist. I start sorting the piles but quickly become discouraged and grouchy. Yet another pile tips over and I growl then almost dissolve into tears when suddenly I hear a knock at the door.

"What?" I snap, expecting reprimands from *someone* on what just happened.

"It's your Aunt June. One of my friends told me someone took Don's job." She chuckles. "I could only assume it was you. Wanna let me help?"

I just silently nod, thankfulness welling up in my heart.

"Let's get this sorted out and have you on your way, shall we?" She smiles and sits down next to me.

Eventually, we clean out the whole thing and present our work to Don, who pays us and sends us on our way.

A few days later, I finally get another flight and this time I board immediately, spending the flight daydreaming. This dream was about ants and more seeds, and at the very end a very silky and angry female voice, rattling me from my fog. The flight lands and I grab my directions to the address where I am supposed to meet to find my new place and get settled into Greece. A thrill ran through me. Greece!

I quickly get in another cab and show the small woman in the front seat the address. She drives off and I get to enjoy the view. There was green everywhere, but also buildings and people and *life* everywhere, an odd contradiction. I feel completely at home, and for once there isn't the nagging feeling in my neck and rib cage. But the cab, instead of taking me to a business building, house, or anything else, takes me to a beach.

"This is the address!" she says with a chipper voice.

That can't be right… I check the address over and over again, putting it into my phone and everything but it takes me basically to the spot I am at. This trip couldn't get any worse!

"Go on, miss," the cab driver says softly.

I drag my things out and just walk onto the beach, flopping down on the sand, again, running out of options. Just then, it starts to rain. I shiver and look to see the cab drive off, and I kick the sand with a pout, letting it take some of my frustration. The rain turns into a deluge and I jump up and run for some of the only trees in sight.

"What have I done to deserve this?" I shout up at the sky.

I could have sworn I heard the same female chuckle that I heard in my dreams on the plane.

"Even just a blanket would be nice!"

I sit down and grab a stick from the tree and break it, trying to calm down. Some of my anger dissipates at the sharp crack it gives off, but I hear a whisper of wind come from it as it cracks. I shake my head and laugh. "Therapy when I get back…," I mutter, clenching the stick. The whisper comes back, and the previously dead branch becomes supple in my hands, the green color it once had returning and even a few buds popping out from the tip of it. I shriek and drop it.

I back away slowly, with panicked laughter. "I'm going crazy." I grab it again, checking to make sure it is indeed still green, which it is.

So I find another branch and break it. Again I hear the small whisper coming out of it, like the sigh of the last breath. I let it go and grab the pieces again, and I hear the second sigh, like a person gasping for breath after coming out of a pool. "This…is a joke…I sure hope this is a dream…" I close my eyes, trying to force myself to wake up. Instead, I fall into a deep sleep, but again it is full of dreams. There is a golden sheep chasing me, there is a choir of flutes, a flap of wings, but a tender one, brushing my face. This beach again, with more wing flapping and tender touches. That is the last thing I remember of my dreams.

I start awake as the sun rises, and realize a golden blanket has been carefully wrapped around me.

"Hm?" I look around for anyone in sight, but it is still misty and too early for tourist beachgoers.

I stand and hold the blanket, feeling its soft but very tight weave. I am hit with even more déjà vu. I am holding a yellow rug, at least I think, before a stunning lady, but she is scowling as I hand it to her. The moment she snatches the rug away from me the thought dissipates and I am left on the beach with a yellow blanket. I sigh and pick up my damp luggage and haul it across the beach to a bus stop nearby. I must have had enough money for the bus fare at least, but I was lucky I didn't try for a hotel last night. I pay the bus the last of what I have in cash and coin, I had spent all of it on food and cabs. Though I don't exactly know where I am headed in Greece. It is a lot bigger than I thought but still familiar. The bus drives through several stops before beginning to drive up a steep hill. I look up to where it is going and see the famous Roman Parthenon. A familiar tugging rises in my chest.

The bus stops at the very front of the Parthenon and I grin and run out of the bus, but stumble. I gasp for air as the ground spins below my feet. My feet find the stairs and I basically collapse on them. The déjà vu feeling I had been experiencing so much of had become overpowering. I search desperately for a drinking fountain but find none in sight.

"Miss?" An older gentleman approaches me quickly, very overdressed for tourism. "Are you okay!?"

"Water," I gasp.

He nods and grabs my hand, guiding me to a drinking fountain, but I can barely bow my head to reach it.

"Drink," he urges, but I shake my head, just grabbing the drinking fountain. He sighs and from somewhere, I can't figure out where he pulls out a crystal tumbler. He fills it for me at the decrepit looking drinking fountain. Taking a drink I spill onto my hands and face. I close my eyes and the world stops spinning quite as much. I turn around to say thank you, but the man is gone. I stare at the glass cup in my hands, expecting it to disappear too.

"I don't like this…" I whisper to myself. The Parthenon has opened by this time and I walk in to find it completely empty. "Oh." I look around as I walk in, feeling right at home. My memories flicked back to what I had felt like back in my kitchen. Powerful, strong, beautiful. I felt that again.

"Ah, about time." I hear a soft female voice. I whip around and see the small dark-skinned lady from the cab, but this time her hair is long and full, with flowers woven through it. She looked like a goddess. She walks directly up to me and places a soft hand on my cheek "Look at all this potential you have, little goddess…"

My head whirls and I close my eyes, trying to still the world. I remember being a little girl in Greece praised for my beauty. I remember being left for dead on a crag because I was too beautiful. I remembered Cupid, my soulmate, my husband. The trials I went through to be with him…I remember drinking ambrosia and the burning that overtook me.

My eyes snap open and I see the woman standing in front of me in a new light. She glows faintly, and you can feel both power and kindness radiating off of her. She and I are now both dressed in the traditional togas of our ancient hometown.

I smile and curtsy. "Persephone. Thank you again. I know this is not the first time you have helped me."

She smiles and inclines her head a little "Do you know who you are?" She looks serious.

I shake my head "I do not know my true name, and I cannot remember my powers. But I remember…" I get choked up "The many, many lives I have lived. I remember Aphrodite's anger, but I also remember Eros, whom I did it all. I do not know who he is, though."

"Let me tell you a story, Parys."

I nod and sit on the ground of the Parthenon, and she sits next to me. My name sounds wrong on her tongue, and as I try to form my name in my mouth it feels unfamiliar.

"There once was a beautiful girl, and her name was Psyche."

The name causes a rush of joy through me, and I nod.

"And Aphrodite became so jealous of this beauty that she demanded that her son trick the beautiful girl into marrying a demon. Her son, Eros, or as most of us know, Cupid, was sent to shoot her with an arrow to force her to fall in love with the demon. But Cupid fell in love with the girl on sight."

I gasp and nod, some memories filling into my head.

"Eros had her taken to his castle, where they grew closer, meeting only at night. She was never allowed to see him. One night, concerned, and feeling lonely, she snuck into Eros's room, and saw his wings, realizing he was the god of love between lovers. She startles him awake, and he tells her that love between a mortal and a god is impossible, then flies away."

The tender caress of wings I had felt in my dreams all of a sudden felt more real, and an overwhelming sadness overtakes me. My other half, I had always known he existed, had said our love couldn't be possible.

She looks me right in the eyes as she finishes. "Psyche went through three tasks to be reunited with Eros. One that connected her with the people around her, and taught her to accept help."

"Sorting seeds." I nod, "Or in this case…files." I chuckle softly.

"The next one connected her with nature."

"Collecting the golden fleece!"

She nods. "And you have never been able to do this before, but you were able to discover some of your godly power during that trial." There is true respect in her voice. "And the last trial is obtaining the water of the River Styx. Which connected you with yourself."

"There's one more." I stop her.

"Ah, that is true to a certain extent. The fourth task was getting beauty cream from me, which represents knowledge. Which I have been able to give you, here in the temple. So welcome home, Psyche, Goddess of the Soul."

"Thank you." I smile. "Can I go find a mirror? I want to know what my true form looks like if I have changed as you did."

She nods and guides me to a bathroom nearby. I walk in and study myself in the mirror. Physically, I haven't changed much at all.

"What? Why do I still look the same? I thought I was supposed to be beautiful."

Persephone chuckles. "Beauty comes from our thoughts and actions, our soul if you will. And in that, everyone can tell you are truly beautiful."

I nod and walk out into the central hall of the Parthenon. "Can you explain the stick to me?"

She smiles brightly "In ancient times my husband and I," she looks sad for a second, "ran the underworld together. You were gifted the ability to bring things that have died, within reason, of course, their souls back, so that they might continue this life should you see fit. It frustrated my poor husband to no end sometimes…" She chuckles softly.

"That's amazing!"

Persephone nods. "You and your husband," I blush, "represent the two parts of a successful relationship, along with your daughter, Pleasure. You will have to find her like you have to find Eros, or there is a small chance you and him will have her together, though I have never witnessed that before."

I smile, yet feel fiercely determined at the same time. Hope and memories rise within me. "I have to go find Eros."

Diérdre Keppner

Taking Flight

Arian awoke to the warm sunlight pouring in through the window. Her bed begged her to not leave as it tempted her with its warmth and comfort. Reluctantly, she stretched and rose, mind still clearing. She looked out the window of the hut at the small village she lived in. Mieru was a quaint little village full of families who had known each other for generations; everyone helped and included each other. Seeing as how most other races looked down upon them, it was the only support they experienced in life. Anax Sapiens were rare, but they had been mistreated and hunted in the past. There had even been times when some had been sold into slavery. Secluded in the far reaches of Tasane, the Anax Sapiens were safe.

Suddenly Arian remembered what the day held. This would be her last day in Mieru before undertaking the journey to Situs, the capital of the country, to confront the Council about the state of Mieru. Over the past few weeks bandits had come and stolen some of their harvest of lacusweed, a rare plant that the Anax Sapiens were best at harvesting due to their dragonfly ancestry. The Council had done nothing about the thievery and none of the villagers were trained in fighting. They had attempted to hide or protect their harvest, but to no avail. It seemed that the bandits were well versed in finding that which they sought. The Wise Circle had decided they needed to directly contact the Council instead of sending pointless letters, and Arian had been the one elected to do so.

Arian dressed quickly and braided her hair, careful of her wings and antennae. When she grabbed her satchel of tools for harvesting lacusweed and headed out the door, she was enveloped by warm sunlight and the sound of a bustling village. Children ran around playing and giggling with their wings uncovered, adults taught young adults the correct techniques of extracting lacusweed, and the sounds of sloshing water filled the air. Arian hurried to where her aunt Lydis stood pulling lacusweed from the lake.

"You're up later than usual," Lydis commented with a smile.

"I'm sorry, I don't know how. Why did no one wake me?"

Her aunt handed her a woven basket. "We decided you needed the rest for tomorrow's journey."

Arian wasn't sure how to respond, so she continued to silently organize the plants into different baskets. Her thoughts wandered to a memory of her mother teaching her this skill. She had been six years old and her mother had patiently taught her while Arian whined. Arian smiled sadly at the memory. Now, Arian lived with her aunt, Lydis, due to her parents' death. Her father had died when she was young in a building accident. He had been building a hut for his family when the structure collapsed and gave him a puncture wound, leaving him only a few days to live. Arian and her mother were taken in by her mother's sister, Lydis, but soon her mother became ill. By the age of eleven Arian had become an orphan, but at least she still had her extended family to care for her.

The day's harvest went smoothly, other than the reminder that they were short of their usual amount of lacusweed due to the bandits. As the sky darkened, everyone gathered everything up and headed home. As Arian made her way toward her family's hut, Vermot of the Wise Circle called after her. Obeying his gesture to follow him, Arian entered into the Wise Circle's tent where she was met by the most esteemed and wise of the Anax Sapiens. Orange firelight lit their faces, and Arian noticed that their silk wings were exposed.

"Please, sit," Vermot offered as he joined the other members of the Wise Circle.

"Arian, you know that we have chosen you to represent our village of Anax Sapiens. We have already made it clear to you why we have done so," Lyra, the head of the Wise Circle said, glancing at the other members.

Arian nodded, remembering. Her uncle had been the steward of their people, but he was too sick now to take on the journey. Aunt Lydis had to remain behind to take care of him and her children, which placed the burden of the trip on Arian's shoulders. But Arian wondered why the Wise Circle was repeating things they had already told her a few days ago.

"As you know, this meeting with the Council is a very pressing matter," Lyra continued. "We fear that the portion missing from the harvest will increase soon if these attacks continue and we will not have enough to pay our taxes. That is why you must make haste tomorrow and rise before the sun. And…"

"We want you to use your wings to get there," Vermot finished. Arian blinked. Use her dragonfly wings beyond the village? That was suicide!

"Wise Circle, I respect you all. But…is it not forbidden to use our wings beyond our land because it is so dangerous?" Arian asked, questions rising within her.

"We realize this, and we still believe in the importance of the rule to keep our wings hidden. Under the circumstances, we cannot find any other way for you to get there fast enough."

Arian left the tent in a daze after a few more words were spoken. It had been generations since the Anax Sapiens had shown their wings to any outside their village. Rumor had spread that they no longer were born with wings, and the Wise Circle saw it as an opportunity for others to underestimate them. Arian wondered how she would survive the next few weeks as she tried to fall asleep.

At the break of dawn, Lydis was gearing Arian up for the journey. Arian kept her wings tucked away for now. The Wise Circle had come to the conclusion that it would be wiser to not let the other villagers in on the secret of using her wings after generations of not doing so beyond Mieru. Which, to be fair, would probably arouse a lot of questions, but Arian hated to keep it from her family. Her little cousins slept peacefully in the family bed, and Arian realized how long it would be before she saw them again. Situs was a long way off and who knew how long she would have to stay there to figure things out with the Council.

"You look so grown up," Lydis said softly, tightening the belt around Arian's waist. "Do you have the gown packed?"

Arian nodded, showing her satchel.

"Folded all nicely as to not wrinkle it," Arian replied.

Lydis nodded approvingly, then pulled Arian into a hug. "Stay strong, Arian."

Soon Arian was hugging goodbye to most of the villagers and waving as she trudged away. After a few hours the village was nothing more than a miniature in the distance. Arian realized with a shudder that she was truly alone, and a daunting task lay ahead of her. But the Wise Circle had chosen her, and it was a great honor to represent the Anax Sapiens.

When she no longer saw the village, Arian removed her coat to stretch and spread her wings. It was an odd yet invigorating sensation. It felt so… natural. Of course, that made sense because they were a part of her, but it had been a long time since she had flown. Anax Sapiens were trained from infancy how to fly, but they rarely used the technique the older they got. Occasionally, they stretched their wings to remember how to do so.

With a small giggle, Arian warmed her wings up and began running. The ground beneath her blurred and became distant as she rose into the air. The wind brushing against her silk wings tickled and her senses heightened with the help of her antennae. Though Arian wanted to twist about and experiment while flying, she stayed focused on her mission. She just enjoyed the feel of speeding through the air. There were times Arian became so sore and tired that she continued on foot for a few hours. When her feet became sore, she continued to fly. So far, the road stayed empty, and she encountered no one, but she kept an eye out in case of danger.

At nightfall Arian slept under the open sky since the woods thinned to rolling prairie. She was a bit uneasy about it but there were no other options. Since she hadn't seen anyone, it would have to do. She was exhausted and the thought of doing it all again in the morning made her groan. Snuggling under her blanket, Arian heard a strange noise. A creature, perhaps? Arian lifted her head, and sure enough, she spotted a little slender creature. It danced toward her, tilting its head.

"Hullo there." As Arian reached for it, she felt a sharp bite on her hand. "Ow!"

Startled, Arian scrambled out of her bed and backed away from the creature. It made a high-pitched gargling noise, snatched her blanket, and ran off. Arian attempted to catch it, but it was long gone, and she was too tired to look further. After an unpleasant sleep that night, she felt slightly rested the next morning.

The next day was even worse. The flat, grassy landscape stayed the same, and she was sore from the day before. After not getting enough sleep and flying the day before, Arian was exhausted. She could barely put one foot in front of the other.

Over the next few days Arian passed by only a few people and saw only a few towns off in the distance. She had already gone through four different lands over the course of seven days, and it would be another five days until she arrived in Situs.

The air grew frigid as Arian passed into Ifran, a land well known for its towering mountain ranges and cold air. Far ahead, she saw dark mountain ranges reaching toward the sky. A strong wind blew Arian off course and tossed her about. She screamed and tried to get back on track, but the wind was too strong and too cold. The air howled around her and she felt herself being lifted higher. In an attempt to land, she folded her wings. Instantly she dropped, plummeting toward the ground. A few yards before crashing she unfurled her wings and stumbled to the ground. Shivering, she dug her coat out and put it on, blowing hot air onto her hands. As Arian walked on, her thoughts wandered, and she stared blankly at her feet. She wondered if she would ever meet someone while out here. Sure, she had seen a few people, but they had not noticed her because of how high up she had been in the sky. Perhaps being on foot would bring up the opportunity.

As if on cue, footsteps sounded not far off. Arian looked up, her antennae perking. A man was walking toward the path from the treeline, and he was staring at her. Arian stiffened and continued onward, making sure to glance back every now and then. He did not say anything, and his expression didn't look angry or dangerous, but neither did it look kind or friendly. Just... curious. As Arian continued on, she got the chilling impression that the man who walked a few yards behind continued to watch her. Unsettled, Arian quickened her pace. She had an uneasy feeling about him and did not want to find out what he was capable of.

Arian eventually outdistanced the man, but his figure was still in sight when she looked behind her shoulder. In an attempt to forget about him, Arian began singing. She sang of Mieru's traditions, the wind, and the way of the Anax Sapiens. The louder she sang, the more she became caught up in the moment. Soon, she did not realize she had slowed down and the man had gotten closer. Glancing back, she nearly shrieked at the sight of him, stumbling forward. Hot embarrassment burned at Arian's cheeks and up her neck. She turned quickly, beginning to run. She kept running until she was panting hard enough that she could hardly breathe, so she leaned against a tree, closing her eyes for a moment. When she caught her breath, Arian opened her eyes and looked back. The man had disappeared.

The next several days passed by uneventfully, but soon she was entering the city of Situs. Large, intricate buildings with detailed and differing stonework came into view. Arian gaped at the buildings, the cobblestone roads, and the crowds of many different people. Fair folk, Jinlee, humans, hobstones, and many different races walked the streets. But no Anax Sapiens. Arian appeared to be the only one of her kind here in Situs. Weaving her way through the crowds, Arian asked for directions from a soldier. He reluctantly gave them, eyeing her suspiciously as he did so. Trying not to be discouraged, she made her way toward the courthouse and found a gruff shopkeeper to direct her to a place to change her clothes. Once dressed in her gown with her red hair tamed, Arian entered the bustling lobby. Detailed marble arches hovered high above her, palm trees lined the halls, and a giant water fountain spouted in the middle of the room. An attendant asked her business and Arian informed her that her tribe had sent her to the Council. They told her that she would have an entrance with them the next day.

With nothing to do except wait, Arian decided to explore the city a bit. She was overwhelmed by the sights and sounds of the city: carriages and carts, the yell of merchants, the clucking of chickens, and the smell of soot and different foods. Arian wandered the streets into the market and became intrigued by the sparkle of a bright blue jewel. The seller instantly noticed and shoved it toward her.

"400 jevn! It would look very lovely on you, no?"

Arian staggered as he began to put it around her neck.

"No, please, I was just lo—"

"Do not worry, you are getting a very good price! Now hand me the money please so you can be on your way."

"But sir, I don't have enough for this and I wasn't looking to buy it..."

The man's look became dark. "You put on my necklace and then say you will not pay?"

"What? No, I didn't! Please sir, I..."

"You better watch yourself maggot, or I will call the guard."

Arian's brain scrambled as she frantically tried to think of a way to get out of this situation when a voice interrupted the cries of the seller.

"Now sir, I believe you're being very unfair to this little bug."

A smiling man walked out of the shadows with a dangerous look in his eyes. The merchant glared, standing taller.

"It's none of your business."

"Ah, yes, well this little bug happens to be a friend of mine. Now take the necklace off her before *I* call over the guard."

Arian stared speechless at the man while the merchant grudgingly took off the chain. The stranger took her by the hand and led her away.

"Don't think too much of it, dearie," he said with a wink before Arian could say anything. Without another word, he slipped into the crowd and disappeared. Shaken and confused, Arian decided it was time to find an inn. Soon she was paying double the amount for a regular room and dinner, but she was too frightened and too tired to fight for a better price.

The next morning after Arian's bath, she tried to braid her hair to make her antennae less obvious. She took great care to hide her wings. Upon arriving at the courthouse, she was admitted an audience with the Council. Sitting upon their thrones, the Council members were dressed finely with their trademark matching pendants around their throats. Each was a different species, notably the most populated and well-known ones. Arian curtsied.

"Arian of the Anax Sapien. We were informed of your visit yesterday. What could the Anax Sapiens possibly want?" a Jinlee councilor said with a small smirk. Arian rose.

"If you would, sire, we seek aid and protection in my village."

"Protection?" a human woman asked.

"As you may know, we harvest and trade lacusweed. By doing so, we are able to pay our taxes in full with savings leftover for the spring planting. As of late, some disguised men have raided our harvest night after night. If this thievery continues, we will not be able to pay our tax and we will run low on food."

"Have you tried defending your crops?" a bulky woman asked. A few chuckles sounded. Arian prickled.

"We have, but we are not strong enough. My people are not warriors, only mere farmers!"

The Councilors shared glances.

"What other measures have you taken?"

"We have tried to hide the harvest as well..."

"Enough of this. We do not send soldiers to guard a small village of farmers, Anax Sapiens, nonetheless. Since it is your problem, you must fix it."

"But we cannot pa—"

"I am sorry, but Councilor Marrot is right. We have bigger problems to deal with, and it is not our obligation to protect you. Your people must fend for themselves," Councilor Viren, the Jinlee, stated.

Arian walked numbly out of the courthouse and into the streets now covered in shadows. After all she had gone through to get here, after all the time and effort, after *everything*—

"I know the feeling."

Arian whipped around to find the same man who had saved her from the merchant earlier that day. Now that she was no longer living in a blur, she could make out his features; he had curly black hair, facial hair, and dark eyes. He must be a human.

"Excuse me. I saw the look in your eyes—that frustration that the Council never does anything—and I understand," he said as Arian began to back up. He stuck out his hand. "I'm Calif."

Arian hesitantly took it. "Arian."

He glanced at her antennae, and she stiffened, quickly releasing his hand.

"So... You're an Anax Sapien?" he asked. "Don't see many of those these days."

"And for good reason," she responded.

Calif raised an eyebrow. "Look, kid—" Arian glared at his use of the name. "I know what it's like to be rejected by the Council. But I also know what it's like to figure stuff out without their help." Calif paused, studying her. "I can take you to someone who can help your people."

Arian furrowed her brow. "How do you know about my people?"

Calif laughed a little awkwardly. "Lucky guess? Point is, I have what you want."

"No thanks." Arian began to walk away, but Calif was faster.

"What, you're just gonna go back empty handed? After all the journeying and time and effort? You know that won't be worth it."

He certainly knew how to get to her.

"And what would be in it for you?" Arian asked skeptically.

Calif grinned. "Can't a person just be charitable and giving?"

Arian walked on, ignoring him as he trailed her.

"Admit it! You need me," Calif called.

Arian turned around in time to witness his smirk. She charged back toward him, which seemed to mostly amuse him.

"Fine, but this better be worth my time. I've already got a long journey ahead of me," Arian threatened, holding a finger to his face. Calif held up his hands, laughing.

"Don't worry. It's not that far out of the city. Just a few days toward Adustus."

Coincidentally they were staying at the same inn, so it wasn't a problem finding each other the next morning. Arian didn't trust Calif even though he had saved her, but she knew he was a better option than going back without any help. Plus, it was on the way back. Still, she would have to be careful.

They didn't talk much as they headed out of Situs, but it wasn't long before Calif began a discussion while they trudged through the desert.

"Not to be rude or anything but… I imagined Anax Sapiens to have big… ger eyes," he hastily finished after Arian's glare.

"We may not have big eyes, but our sight is far better than yours could ever be."

"Oh, I see, you're not afraid to brag. Ha, *see*."

"Do you always act like a child?"

"It makes life more exciting, something I doubt you know anything about." Calif's eyes twinkled with mischief. Arian shot another death glare.

"Is that all you ever do, bugaboo?" He laughed at the timing of her next glare. "Glare?"

"I am not an object that causes fear, Calif," she said, referring to the nickname he had given.

"Ohh, using my name now. You must be awfully mad. And you're right, you don't scare me, so you can stop glaring."

As Arian angrily stomped on, something suddenly clicked. She spun around to face Calif. "You're the man who followed me on the trail, aren't you?" she accused.

Calif's smile widened. "Finally figure it out, my ladybug? You have always had the habit of walking away from me when we are together, haven't you?"

"That was you?" Arian cried. "It's no wonder I have that habit, seeing as how you've stalked me!"

"I do admit, it is quite entertaining to watch you become frazzled." Calif laughed as a bedroll was thrown at his head.

The upcoming days held similar conversations and they drove Arian crazy. She had never met anyone so infuriating and there were multiple times when she considered leaving him and going back alone. But then she always thought of her people and their needs, so she remained. It wasn't all bad, however. As she spent more time with Calif, the more used to his mannerisms she became. Calif turned out to be a good listener and seemed genuinely interested when she opened up about her village.

"What is it like?" Calif asked as they set up for camp.

"What?" Arian said, smiling as she braided her hair.

"Living in Mieru. You always get starry eyed when you talk about it." He attempted to show an example.

Arian laughed, shaking her head. "It's...nice."

"Nice?"

"Wonderful, really. I miss being surrounded by all those who love and support me. And I especially miss the little things."

Calif settled down, resting on his elbow. "Like what?"

"Children running and laughing, the way the sunlight hits the water at sunset, wandering about with family, the sounds of the wind against the lake..." Arian sighed, taking off her coat. "I miss it."

Calif's eyes suddenly widened.

Arian turned back, confused. "What?"

"Er... I didn't think Anax Sapiens had wings anymore."

Arian froze. Had she really just taken her coat off in front of Calif? During the previous nights on the road, she had been careful not to do so until he was asleep. She must've gotten carried away when talking about the village. She quickly put it back on.

"Calif, *please*, I'm begging you... Don't mention this to anyone, it's supposed to be a secret," Arian pleaded.

Calif sat up, mulling it over. "I suppose I won't... If you tell me what flying is like." He laughed as Arian sighed in relief.

Arian woke to the sound of Calif packing up. She stretched and got up and soon they were ready to set out.

"Thank you for helping me," Arian suddenly said.

"Of course, you're welcome." Calif's response sounded strained.

When she glanced in his direction, she noticed a strange expression on his face. Pushing the uncomfortable feeling evoked from that look aside, she asked, "You said we'll be there by this afternoon?"

Calif nodded stiffly. "Yeah. About that… I think we shouldn't go."

Arian stared at him incredulously. "Why not? After all we've done to get here, and you want to back out? For what?"

Calif looked away. "I was leading you into a trap."

Silence followed. Long, agonizing silence. "You… What?"

Calif met her gaze. "You heard me."

Chills ran up Arian's spine and she suddenly backed away, clumsily grabbing her satchel.

"Arian, wait!"

Arian took off, tears springing to her eyes. Of all the stupid things she had done, this was the worst. How could she have trusted him? How could she have gone right with a stranger into a secluded desert? *Stupid, stupid, stupid!*

Strong arms grabbed her from behind with sudden force. Arian thrashed, elbowing and kicking at him as he lifted her.

"Let me go, Calif!"

A deep, menacing laugh vibrated against her. "You found a feisty one, eh Calif?"

Chuckles echoed. Fear seized Arian and she fought harder, frenzied, until someone grabbed one of her antennae. She whimpered in pain as she was turned to face her captor. It was a large man with slit nostrils and yellow eyes.

"An Anax Sapien, eh? She'll be worth a handsome price." He grinned darkly, his yellow teeth showing.

"Let me go, please!" Arian screamed, tears of terror and pain streaming down her face. The man slapped her. Laughter filled the air, but one laugh was missing. Arian glanced over to see Calif looking grim.

"I'm sorry."

Betrayal pierced Arian's heart as she was forced screaming into a carriage. She was bound, handed to a Jinlee, and thrown inside the carriage. The windows were blacked out and the click of the lock sounded.

"Does it have wings like in the old tales?" someone asked.

Arian's heart froze.

"No, I checked myself. The rumors of them being gone must be true," came the voice of Calif.

Arian's panic lessened a bit until he added, "I'll be off now. I delivered, now pay."

As the clink of coins followed, and a new anger boiled within Arian. This was all because of her own stupidity. The carriage lurched forward and they began their journey. All Arian knew of her captors was that there were three of them now that Calif was gone, and that one was human, one was a Jinlee, and the other Yyw. On the fourth day they came to a stop and soon the carriage door was flung open. Arian flinched as the Jinlee dragged her into the light. They were in the forest in Ifran.

"Don't try nothing funny, bug eyes. We're going to someone civilized."

They trudged deeper into the woods, but it seemed unusually quiet. Just as Arian brushed the thought aside, a figure jumped down from the trees, sliced her bonds, and attacked the Jinlee.

"Get out of here!" the figure yelled as he locked swords with her captors. It was Calif.

Arian stumbled away, running back toward the road. The sound of footfalls followed her. As she ran faster, she decided it was now or never. She shed her coat, spread her wings, and took off. Someone beneath her cursed, but she didn't care to look down. Even though it was harder to fly in the trees and dodge low hanging branches, she was free! It was not until Arian found the road that she remembered Calif had just saved her life and was fighting his accomplices. She considered leaving him, but the thought made her stomach sink. Groaning, she turned and flew back to where she left the group. Calif had already slain the Jinlee and human, but he was battling the Yyw. After a few swings, Calif glanced up at Arian, making his opponent look, and then stabbed him. Arian's throat constricted at what she just witnessed, but she landed anyway.

"You came back," Arian mumbled as they stared into each other's eyes.

"So did you." Calif smiled a little.

"You're bleeding," Arian started, but Calif brushed it aside.

"I have bandages on me, don't fret about," he said as he pulled them out.

Once he finished, Arian walked toward him, studying his features. "Are you going to sell me?"

Calif shook his head, a serious look in his eyes.

"Good, because I need an escort," Arian stated, turning around. Calif began to say something, but she stopped him. "Don't you dare make a joke or I might change my mind."

He smiled and shook his head, and they walked back to the road heading toward Mieru. It was uncomfortable walking with the person who had betrayed her, but Arian couldn't deny that he had saved her twice and kept her secret. It was a lot of mixed feelings. Calif kept quiet for the most part, surprisingly. After several long days, they finally made it to Mieru. Arian practically ran the rest of the way when her home came into view. Calif lagged behind as Arian ran to her family and friends with open arms. She was welcomed with cries of joy, hugs and kisses, and she couldn't be happier to be home after all she had been through. As things settled down a bit, Arian noticed Calif wandering back toward the road.

"Calif!" she called, motioning him back.

"Is that the protector they sent?" Vermot wondered, squinting.

Before Arian could respond, Calif said, "Yes, I am here to help. I cannot stay long, but I can help you defend yourself during these bandit attacks." he flashed a quick grin and wink at Arian.

The villagers cheered, and soon Calif dove into a strategy. He proposed that they catch the thieves in the act of stealing before attacking so they could use the element of surprise. The men of Mieru offered to help and Calif ran them through his plan. They were going to hide and spy every night to watch the bandits' pattern before making a move.

It was not long before Calif rid Mieru of the thieves stealing their harvests, and the people came to have a liking for him. Apparently, the bandits had been known by Calif, and he was able to bribe them to leave after a brawl (which Calif won). It was not the most honorable way to rid Mieru of the bandits, but it seemed to work. Once the bandits were gone, Arian made it her duty to show Calif the village and how the Anax Sapiens did things. The children taught him some of their games and the women fed him. The men taught him how to harvest lacusweed, as best as possible for a human, and Arian taught him to weave baskets. It was a joyous occasion to show the ways of the Anax Sapiens to a human.

"So, this is the life of the Anax Sapiens. I'm not going to lie, it's amazing. Peaceful and simple, really," Calif noted on one evening.

Arian smiled, fondly looking around her. The moonlit sky stretched above them as the families danced and sang together around the fire.

"It is wonderful." Her gaze shifted to Calif. "You could stay here, you know. Move on from your past and live a simple peaceful life."

He smiled, staring into the distance. "As nice as that would be...I can't."

Arian blinked. "Why not?"

Calif shifted his weight, looking around him. "I like being on the move and exploring new things. Keeps it exciting." He looked her in the eye. "I'm sorry, Arian, but this isn't the kind of life for me. It sounds heavenly, trust me. But I know I'd get bored. Best if I move on."

"What if the bandits come back?"

Calif smiled. "Then I imagine you haven't seen the last of me."

The next day Calif bid goodbye to the Anax Sapiens. It was a more difficult parting than expected, but it was not surprising.

"Thank you for helping us." Arian tried to convey her sincerity in those words as Calif prepared to leave.

Calif gently embraced her. "You never know, I might show up one of these days to haunt you," he said with a glint in his eye.

Arian laughed, shaking her head. "I'll look forward to ignoring your taunts."

"Now where's the fun in that?" he asked, picking up his bag.

He waved to Arian and was soon overrun with Arian's cousins. As Arian watched him leave as more children hugged him, she decided that each person chose their own path in life. She had remained with her family, while Calif had gone. Perhaps someday he would return.

"Life is full of choices, and choices determine your life. That's what makes it an adventure," Lydis said suddenly.

Arian jumped, startled.

Lydis smiled, wrapping an arm around her niece's shoulder.

Arian thought about her aunt's words and smiled back. "I suppose you're right," she said as Calif's silhouette faded from view.

Alana Rae Christensen

Windkeeper

She was gone. The girl that had been there for the last twelve years, waiting on the docks when the traders came on the spring winds. She was gone.

Aup didn't know her name. He had never truly spoken with her. And yet, somewhere in his old heart he had begun to care for her, think of her like he imagined he would think of his grandchildren. Foolishness. Still, as he twisted the old tiller on his skirr so it nestled against the stone of the docks, he found his eyes searching for her slim figure and brilliant white hair among the usual crowd of fool children. The street rats were hoping to be taken onto a skirr as help, or to gain a free trip. The skirr slowed elegantly, and he pulled the sail in, then tossed a rope to the dock. Someone from the crowd, a vaguely familiar dark-haired girl, darted forward and caught it, tying it to a stone post with practiced motions. Aup quirked a gray eyebrow. Most of the urchins didn't bother with his skirr, noting its charred hull and the few barrels on its tiny deck, or more likely the lack of other crew. The girl always had, but then again, she wasn't exactly common.

Aup's skirr pulled against the rope before stopping, and he draped an ornate quilt over the side to protect the rare wood timbers from the rough-edged pier. His skirr was a small ship, barely ten yards long and a third of that wide, but it was good to him and he wasn't inclined to let it come to harm. Grimacing, Aup boosted himself onto a rough rock, surveying the outcrop of stone. It was one of several around the island, but while the others were perilously close to the Windkeepers outpost or the House of Trade, this was a small pier that led directly—and solely—into Understep.

The pier was an outcrop of stone, anciently hewn flat with rough tools then polished through near-constant use, some fifty yards wide and double that long. Small stalls for storage and trade, precariously layered, hunched in the center. They always looked on the edge of collapse, but Aup knew they wouldn't fall, just as those in Understep proper wouldn't. It had been a good thirty years since there had been a serious collapse there. Fools would be fools, but there was enough wisdom—or at least self-preservation—in the Understep gangs to prevent that.

He straightened slowly. The scent of the city washed over him like foul water; sewage and rotting food and unwashed bodies, contrasting with the sharp, smoky smell of the docks. He looked in the distance at the mountainous expanse of island stretching into the sky. Shanties, made of stone and fabric, heaped atop each other beneath a giant overhang extending from the mountain. Understep was a place of desperation and full of criminals, gangs, orphans, and refugees. The victims and predators of society lived on top of each other, making homes of fabric and pebbles because they couldn't afford wood. Aup didn't like remembering the time he had spent living like that. Stealing food every day, fighting for pennies, sinking deeper into desperation.

Further up was the rest of the city. Upper-class citizens, merchants, Windkeepers, skirr crew, and anyone who could, stayed there.

Searching the dock, Aup made eye contact with a muscled man standing in the midst of the crowd. The Agent of Trade was short in stature and had a perpetual squint. Just as the man started toward Aup's position on the dock, the dark-haired girl hopped into his skirr and disappeared from sight among the barrels. Aup frowned. Permission needed to be granted by the captain before anyone set foot on a ship. Since the Agent was approaching, he decided to investigate at a later time.

"Are you captain of this vessel?" the Agent asked, stopping in front of him.

Aup nodded as he stood on the dock for the first time in many months.

"It'll be ten cel for docking. Twenty more if you intend to trade."

Officially, the money went to the government, but they both knew over half would end up in other pockets. The price was fair, so Aup pulled out his coin purse and took out one ten-cel coin and one five. The Agent of Trade curled a lip but stalked away with his payment. Aup watched him go, then turned to find out what the scorching urchin was doing on his ship.

She headed past him, rolling his water barrel toward the pier. Aup frowned. She was pressing her luck by being on his skirr without permission, and she was trying to make up for it by taking on a burdensome task. She glanced at him out of the corner of her eye. So, she *did* realize she was running a risk and overstepping her bounds.

Aup limped toward his skirr. As the girl reached the edge of the skirr, rolling the barrel before her, she heaved it onto the dock and jumped after it. Averting her eyes from his scowl, she rolled the barrel past him, toward his reserved stall.

Aup narrowed his eyes. It wasn't exactly common knowledge that he kept a reserved stall. The pier 'authorities' knew, but the powerful docks gang was notoriously tight lipped. How had she known?

The girl pushed the barrel into the stone storeroom. Standing by the edge of the dock, Aup watched as she headed back to the skirr, going past him without pause. Interesting. He had expected her to stop and jabber about how he *had* to hire her, and how *amazing* of a worker she was, and other such nonsense.

As she jumped lightly to the deck, he was struck with a strange sense of familiarity. Something…

She glanced at him again.

It was *her*. He blinked, and he didn't know how he had missed it before. Her hair was jet black instead of white, but the shape of her face was the same. Those dark blue eyes were still clear, her cheekbones still high in her heart-shaped face. This was the same girl that had helped him unload his ship for the past twelve years, and he hadn't recognized her. It was unlike him. He squinted at her face and noticed it was dusted with powder makeup, like that used in the merchant houses. Her straight hair was cut short and died black along with her eyebrows. Was she trying to hide? She glanced at him again as she reached the edge of the skirr and paused.

"You noticed," she said softly, grinning.

"*Why* in the twelve suns?" he snapped, limping toward her.

Her almond eyes widened. "I needed to see if it worked. Sorry."

Aup frowned. What was she on about? "Why did you…" he gestured roughly at her, realizing that she also had on at least four layers of clothing, obscuring her slim form. "*Scorched corpse of reason!* What happened?"

Startled, she blinked at him and blushed. "I just— Why are you talking to me?"

"What?" She had wheedled him to engage her in conversation for *years* and now she questioned it?

"You've never said more than five words to me. I thought—" She blinked, shook her head. "Sorry. I don't understand. What's wrong?"

Aup's frown deepened. "Your disguise. Why, in the seven skies?"

She looked at him, setting her jaw. "I needed to know if it worked."

He was forced to take a deep breath. "The disguise. *Why?"*

"Oh. I needed a way to hide that I'm—you know." She looked away.

"Why would you obscure your Miea features, girl?" Some idiots would treat her better if she weren't 'foreign', but the makeup and dye had to cost a fortune. It cost too much for convenience, and the danger of thievery was too great. Something else was going on.

Her eyes narrowed a fraction as she lifted her chin defiantly. "Why did you need me to wear it before you spoke to me?"

"*What in scorched existence are you talking about?!"* She flinched as he growled. Fighting to contain his temper, he hoped she would give him a straight answer soon.

"Sorry," she said after a pause. "I thought—sorry." She winced, visibly biting her tongue.

Aup took a step back, narrowing his eyes. "You thought what?"

"Nothing." He shot her a glare, and she winced again. "It just seemed that you only would speak to me when I was disguised. I guess I jumped to conclusions—"

"You thought because you're Miea, I refused to speak to you?"

She swallowed, looked away.

He heaved a sigh. “I’m a trader. We can’t exactly afford to be discriminatory. I didn’t want to show favoritism. The gangs go after a person for that.”

The girl’s eyebrows pulled together. “You ignored me…to protect me? From the gangs?” She looked at him. “The gangs went after me years ago, when I was ten. They wanted to know where you stored Songleaf.” Her eyes went hard at the memory. “I told them you didn’t smuggle it, so they let me go. Eventually.”

Aup didn’t move. The gangs had gone after her. She had been *ten.* They had gone after her. They had gone after her *to get to him.* He clenched his jaw, fighting the urge to demand the name of the gang. Anything he did to help her would just paint a target on her back. ”Just the once?” At least they had given up.

She swallowed. “No. But it’s uncommon.”

“Reason’s *corpse!* Why didn’t you help another captain? They would have hired you after a few years.”

“It doesn’t matter. The gangs would have gone after me anyway. And I do help other captains on occasion, too.” She took a deep breath. “I need your help.”

“As I rule, I try not to help much. I’m not exactly the kind of help people search for.” He awkwardly stepped down into his skirr. It bobbed slightly under his feet, trembling in the tiny currents of air.

The distant hissing and popping of the Mar mixed with the calls of skirr captains, the cries of urchins, and the calls of vendors from numerous stalls. The girl hopped over the edge, landing beside Aup. He eyed her, before walking to the barrels loosely tied together in groups of five around the central hatch leading below deck.

The girl ran after him, grabbing the next barrel easily and tipping it over. It hit the planks with a thud, and she swiftly untied the rope attaching it to its fellows. “You’re exactly the kind of help I need.” She spoke quietly but with conviction as she rolled the barrel toward the pier.

“What do you need?” He tipped his own barrel onto its side and started pushing it toward the pier, grimacing. He was too old for this.

“The Windkeeper trials are tomorrow—”

“*No,*” Aup growled.

The idiot girl let go of her barrel and spun to face him.

"Why?" Her eyes were icy cold.

"The trials are a death trap."

"I'd pass. Besides, only two or three people die every year."

"Let's say you pass. Do you think you'd survive as a Windkeeper in training? Miea and smuggled into the course? It's illegal for you to set foot on their island."

"Since I'm Miea, they don't let me in the drawing. Because I'm not in the drawing, I can't so much as petition to go. But if I get on the island, and make it through the trials, I'm set. I'd learn to *fly.*"

"You'd be dead within a week. Besides, plenty of other captains sell passage to Windkeep island to needy idiots. Why did you come to me?" Of all the spitting schemes to want help with…

"They won't take me. And those other captains get caught more often than they get through. I need *your* help."

"Reason's corpse! I don't smuggle people. What makes you think I even know where their island is?"

"You were a Windkeeper once. You stole your father's skirr. You smuggled yourself into the trials. And you *passed.*" Aup opened and closed his mouth, speechless. The girl stalked closer one step at a time. "You were a trainee for barely a year. You earned your Wings and became a Windskater." Another step forward, and she was inches away and staring directly in his eyes. "Two years later you were training a Flight of your own. You know the way."

"They resented me for it. I was expelled."

"I don't care."

Aup cursed. "I'm not taking you." He turned away.

The girl set her jaw. "I'll find a way."

Spitting idiot. He turned around again. "What's your name?"

"Rikira."

"*Why* do you want to be a Windkeeper?"

"I…" she blinked. "I want to fly."

Aup narrowed his eyes. "And you're willing to risk death?"

"Yes." She was certain.

"Scorching corpse of reason!"

"You wouldn't be in danger, since they don't penalize people for trying to sneak in. It's tradition to pardon the captains. And I'd be wearing makeup, so I wouldn't look Miea."

"*No.*"

"Why?" Her eyes flashed.

"Because—"

"*Scorch*," Rikira cursed, going pale. She turned away from the dock with a sharp motion.

"What?" Aup demanded, looking around. Nothing had changed. Skirrs tied to stone posts, cargo being unloaded, the Agent of Trade wandering through the crowd. He looked back. The girl was terrified, breathing fast, fingers in fists.

"You won't help me get to Windkeep Island?"

"I won't. Why?"

She nodded, swallowed hard. "I'll find another way."

"Don't find *any* way! Windkeep Island is deadly, for more than the trials. You'd die."

"I—I don't have time to argue right now." She turned her face a little to the left, toward the crowd, watching. "I need to go."

"What's going on?" Aup demanded. "You're wearing a disguise, a very expensive one to maintain. Something's wrong. Tell me."

She laughed bitterly "You don't even know me."

"That doesn't mean I don't care."

They stared at each other for a tense second, and Rikira swallowed. "It's fine. I angered the wrong people, that's all."

"Who—" Aup cut off as he saw the Agent of Trade striding toward them, eyes narrowed. "Scorch—" he took a breath. "Tell me it's not the docks gang." In Understep, as in politics, the more wealth a group had, the more power, and the more power, the more danger they posed. The docks gang had controlled one of the city's commerce hubs for years. They were very, very powerful and very, very dangerous.

"It's not the docks gang?" Rikira offered unconvincingly, fidgeting.

Aup sent her a glare. "What did you *do?*"

"Does it matter? I need to go." Her eyes darted around, searching for an unobtrusive escape route, but the stone pier was bare between Aup's skirr and the Agent of Trade. He was currently engrossed in a quiet argument with a skirr captain, but that wouldn't last long enough for her to escape.

Aup cursed, paused, then growled. He was tempted to let Rikira try to escape through the crowd. If she ran, she might make it away from the docks without being noticed.

He wasn't going to abandon her like he had done in those dangerous years after he had been expelled from the Windkeepers and before he had inherited his father's skirr. Ironically, it had been the same one he had stolen as a child. He looked at the old ship—the masts, the barrels, the hatch. It had pulled him out of the blackness of Understep and away from the memory of his blood-soaked years as a Windkeeper.

He turned and looked at the Agent of Trade. If he defied the keepers of this port, he'd never be able to trade here again. He'd have to go to the other docks, find different ports.

The Agent of Trade turned away, leaning forward as he snatched coins from the captain's hand.

Aup made a decision.

"Get below deck," Aup said abruptly.

Rikira frowned. "What—"

"Get below deck," he repeated. She didn't move. "*Now!*" The girl jumped, then scrambled to the center of the skirr. She crouched behind the barrels, hidden from sight, working at the latch. Aup turned, grabbing the barrel he had been pushing, and heaved it onto the dock. Behind him, the hatch closed with a dull thud. Aup grabbed the barrel Rikira had been pushing. With a grunt, he forced it onto the stone pier.

"Captain," the Agent of Trade greeted him with a nod.

"Agent of Trade." Aup returned the bow of his head. He kept an even expression, looking up at the man. Standing on the edge of the dock, the official towered over Aup. It was somewhat disconcerting to Aup, especially since the man had a degree of authority over an organization more powerful than every other gang in Understep combined.

"Have you seen a girl by the name of Rikira?"

"The name doesn't sound familiar."

"No?" He tilted his head, eyes narrow. "She regularly helps you unload your skirr."

"Does she? Several urchins help, most days. You know how they are."

"A girl. About seventeen. White hair, Miea?"

"*Oh.* Her." Aup nodded to himself, hyper aware of the Agent's right hand, which rested on his sword. "She does help me unload. Most days I'm here, but I haven't seen anyone of that description in a few months. Why?"

The Agent of Trade looked like he had eaten something sour. "She stole something valuable."

"Did she?" Aup wrinkled his brow. What on earth had motivated her to do something so *idiotic*?

"Yes. She took a slave, one of my personal favorites. The Miea have no sense of propriety, wouldn't you agree?"

Aup grunted. "Depends on the Miea in question." So, she had saved a slave. He had done that, himself, a long time ago. It had gotten him expelled from the Windkeepers.

"Who were you speaking to, earlier?"

Aup swallowed. "Just an urchin. She wanted a position on my crew. I turned her away. You know how they are."

"Yes, as a matter of fact, I do." The Agent of Trade surveyed the skirr. "Where is she now?"

"She left a while back. Why?"

"Hmm, see, I don't think that she did."

Aup tried to maintain a steady expression. "What?"

"I was watching your skirr. She got on, and she never got off."

"I don't know what you're implying," Aup said firmly. "I paid the docking fee. I need to unload. If you would excuse me—"

"Then you don't mind if I inspect your skirr?" The Agent of Trade stepped down, into the skirr, before Aup could reply.

"Now wait a minute—"

"As Agent of Trade, it is my responsibility to inspect the skirrs which dock here. Are you impeding my responsibilities?" His voice was dangerous.

Aup's jaw tightened. "As captain, it is my right to request inspection by a different official."

"If you suspect corruption in the first Agent of Trade. Are you accusing me?" The man's grip on his sword hilt tightened, a spark of fury in his tone at Aup's defiance.

Aup swallowed, fingers closing into fists. "*Yes*. Now retreat to your post, and I'll go to the Trading Office for inspection." They'd fine him for smuggling spices, but the cost wasn't too steep. A good season would reimburse him for it. He could drop Rikira off along the coastline.

"I'll remain here and call my immediate overseer to conduct the investigation."

Aup took a breath, trying to remain calm. "Get off my skirr."

"*No*." The Agent took a step forward, looking around a group of barrels.

Aup growled, striding toward the Agent and grabbing his left arm. "I said, get off—"

The Agent of Trade drew his sword with a quick motion and

pointed the tip at Aup. "You're impeding my duties," he spat.

Aup assessed his chances in a millisecond. He had defied the gang. Whatever happened, he would have trouble from them. At this point, the Agent should have withdrawn his presence from Aup's ship. The law was on the skirr captain's side. Aup could act against the Agent, and it would technically be legal.

He doubted the law would see it that way.

Aup lunged forward before the Agent could react. As Aup grabbed the younger man's wrist, he drew from skills gained during his training as a Windkeeper and the two years he had spent fighting to survive in Understep. Aup twisted the man's wrist and the sword fell to the timbers with a clatter. The Agent recovered and buried a fist in the captain's side. Aup's breath escaped his lungs in a whoosh as he lost his grip. Desperately Aup threw himself at the Agent and they went to the ground. The Agent's head hit the timbers with a hollow smack and his eyes went vague for a split second. Aup growled and buried a fist in the Agent's nose. After being slammed against the deck for a second time, the Agent of Trade whimpered once, then went limp.

Aup collapsed away from the fallen man, body aching.

"Windkeeper!" Rikira's horrified voice made him lift his head, peering at her.

"What—are you—*doing*?" The scorching girl was supposed to stay below deck.

"I heard the fight. I came to help." She held out a hand and hoisted him to his feet. He leaned on her, groaning.

"Are you all right?" she asked.

"I'm not—as young—as I used to be," Aup gasped. He shook his head to clear it. Rikira steadied him before letting go and kneeling by the Agent of Trade. Aup figured the fallen man was either unconscious or dead.

"Alive," Rikira reported, feeling his breath exhale against her fingers. Aup grunted with relief. He looked at the docks and was surprised to find few onlookers gawking at the scene. A small crowd of urchins whispered amongst themselves and turned curious eyes conspicuously elsewhere when he looked at them. The brief confrontation had been relatively quiet, hidden from view by a stack of barrels and the rail of the skirr.

"You haven't helped my case, you know," Rikira said quietly. Aup swallowed as she continued. "The gangs went after me for helping you. The Docks gang went after me for freeing a slave.

You attacked one of their members to protect me. Now, I have a huge target painted on my back."

"I know," Aup said quietly.

"Earlier, you refused to take me to the trials." Aup opened his mouth to speak, but Rikira beat him to it. "Listen to me! You said that I wouldn't last a week as a Windkeeper. But you think I'd live longer here?"

"Yes," Aup snapped.

"Really?" Rikira took a step forward. "You saved a slave and were expelled from the Windkeepers. After that, you spent some time in the Understep, didn't you? Tell me. How long would you have lasted if you had attacked a member of the docks gang and stolen their property?"

Aup swallowed hard. Days. Maybe.

"You were a trainee of the Windkeepers," Rikira said. "You were associated with them. People were afraid of you. I'm no one. I'm *foreign*. No one will protect me. I'll be lucky if I last a day."

He took a shaky breath. "I can take you on as crew. That'd give you protection."

"You could never return here if I sailed with you. Windkeeper, most people in the order last long enough to retire. I don't understand why you won't help me."

Aup closed his eyes. "Don't call me that."

"What?"

"Don't call me Windkeeper. I'm not one."

Rikira gave him a look that seemed to pierce his soul. "What happened to make you hate them so much?"

Flying. Screaming. Falling. Battle in the air. Blood like fire, consuming his vision, pounding in his head.

"My friend…was murdered by a man who could fly." Her cries as she fell rang in his ears. The memory of her broken body, hanging in the air, filled his mind. He could still almost taste the smoke and blood on the wind. "I escaped." He remembered the days he spent running in terror. "They didn't believe me."

"Why?" Rikira breathed.

"All the Windkeepers were accounted for. They were convinced that no one else in the world could fly, so I had to be lying or deluded. The Windkeepers were going to throw me out as a madman."

"You were expelled for freeing a slave."

"My trial was the next day. I figured I had nothing to lose."

Aup paused. "How do you know?"

"The slave you freed—she was Miea, wasn't she?"

"Yes."

Rikira smiled. "My mother was saved by a Windkeeper. She never got to thank you, but she told me your name. I found you a year after she died."

"Twelve years ago," Aup said.

She nodded. "You saved her, all those years ago. I hoped you could save me as well."

"Taking you to Windkeep Island won't save you."

"Windkeepers don't murder people who offend them. They don't seek violence. Yes, they're arrogant, close-minded, even cruel. But so is everyone else. It's not a guarantee for a better life, but it's a chance. Please, Windke—Aup. Let me have the chance."

Aup grunted. "If I'm caught trying to smuggle a Miea fugitive onto the island, I'll lose everything I have." Rikira looked at him, pleading, and he sighed. "Fine. I know a way. Scorching girl. They could execute me for this. I barely know you!"

Rikira smiled, eyes glowing. "That doesn't mean you don't care."

Suzannah Maness

I Rode a Phoenix Once

Celia stared at the white board in the front of the room with a blank expression. She didn't want to be there. She couldn't handle the stress of it all. She was out of her mind worrying over this test, and even more out of her mind worrying over her ill mother. Her mother was ill. Medicine seemed to be helping, but no one knew how long it would keep working.

The teacher stood as the bell signaling the beginning of class rang.

"Welcome! I bet you're all excited for the test today. The test is open note, so I expect you to all get an A. I've basically handed you the answers."

Celia's stomach rolled. She didn't have notes. The past weeks had been a blur. Her mind had been so preoccupied that she hadn't focused in any of her classes, much less taken notes.

Her breathing quickened, panic seizing her. It felt as if a claw had grasped her heart and was slowly squeezing. Oh gosh, she couldn't take it! The words of her teacher faded into the background as she zoned out, her mind going to the one place she could escape her worries. A world where things always seemed to work out. A world where she was more than she could ever hope to be.

←→

Princess Celosia fiddled with the obsidian ring on her finger. This was taking too long. The physician should have been out by now. She needed to know how her mother was doing.

"Your Highness!" The court physician rushed into the room, causing Celosia to jump to her feet.

"Well? What news have you?" the trembling princess asked in tones that gave away her desperation.

"The Queen's life is in grave danger."

Celosia sucked in a breath. She had been hoping to hear anything but those words. "Do we— Do we know the cause?"

"She's been cursed."

Celosia had feared as much. Witches had become much more prominent in the past year, and it was no secret that many felt their rights weren't being met by the monarchy. A curse was worrisome indeed; there were so very few ways to break one. "Is there anything we can do?"

The physician's expression turned grim. "I fear there is but one way to break this specific type of curse, and Your Highness, you will not like it."

The princess braced herself. "Tell me."

"You must write it away using a phoenix feather quill."

The princess' mouth dropped open ever so slightly before she regained her composure, pursing her lips in a tight line. Phoenixes were incredibly rare, and incredibly dangerous. They were located in the east mountains, and only one flock remained. It would be nearly impossible to get a feather from one. To do so, so legend said, one must gain a phoenix's trust and ride it into the volcano. Then and only then would it grant you a feather.

"Celia!"

Celia's head snapped up at the sound of her teacher's voice. "What?"

Her teacher frowned at her. "We're starting the test. I asked you to get out a pencil five minutes ago."

"Sorry. I zoned out." She looked down sheepishly as her classmates snickered. To make matters worse her face insisted on pretending it was an oven.

"Clearly."

The laughter at her expense grew and she was certain her face had become warm enough to bake cookies. She hurriedly grabbed a pencil, her fingers fumbling. After several tries, she was finally sitting with a pencil in hand.

Celia silently cursed herself for her clumsiness, both with the pencil and with letting herself zone out like she did. Fantasies about curses and phoenixes weren't going to help her pass this test, not that she expected to pass it anyway.

After turning in her test, which she was sure she failed miserably, she sat and waited for the bell to release her. As she sat, she let her mind wander.

"We have to retrieve a feather. We must save my mother."

The physician looked at Celosia, his face revealing his shock. "I agree, but, who will you send to retrieve it?"

"We will send *no one. I will go."*

"Y-your Highness!" the physician stuttered. "But..."

Celosia held up a hand to silence him. "No buts. This is my mother, and I will do what is necessary to save her. Inform one of the maids of my departure so she may help me prepare."

The physician bowed, his eyes still wide, and his mouth hanging slightly agape, though if it was in awe or shock she couldn't tell.

The bell rang, and Celia didn't even hesitate to leave the building. It was friday, and she and her mother had a tradition of eating donuts on fridays. So as per usual, she headed toward the bakery the moment school was let out.

As she walked down Main Street, the scents of food greeted her, making her even more excited for that donut.

"Hello, Mr. Franklin," Celia greeted as she entered the bakery. Mr. Franklin smiled at her, his eyes crinkling around the edges. He was one of the nicest people Celia had ever met, not to mention he made delicious donuts.

"Celia! How are you today?"

Celia shrugged. "Okay I guess."

He looked at her with a worried expression. "How's your mother?"

She averted her gaze. "Not well. It hasn't gotten worse, but she hasn't gotten better either."

"Well, perhaps a donut is just the thing to help her."

She smiled slightly at his attempt to be optimistic. "I'm sure it is."

He handed her two donuts, a cream filled chocolate, and a glazed. They were the same ones she and her mom always got.

Celia pulled out her wallet to pay for the donuts when Mr. Franklin shook his head.

"They're my treat today. Wish your mother a good day from me, will you?"

Celia felt close to tears. "Of course! Thank you."

The whisper of a smile touched her face as she left the shop. Perhaps today wouldn't be too terrible after all.

Her next stop was the pharmacy to pick up her mother's prescriptions.

As she walked down the sidewalk, she was careful to step over each crack. She wasn't superstitious or anything, but it was a good way to occupy her mind. The cracks of the sidewalk reminded her of canyons and canyons reminded her of barriers. As she stepped over each crack she almost felt as if she were overcoming the struggles in her own life. A combination of that imagery and the monotony of her steps allowed her to escape once again, her story weaving itself into a new scene. .

Celosia had been traveling for a while now, and she hadn't been expecting the seemingly impossible trail ahead of her. From where she stood, she could see nothing but canyons keeping her from her destination.

"You can do this. The queen depends on you. You can do this. Do it for her," Celosia whispered the affirmation to herself over and over before taking a deep breath and facing what was in front of her.

There was no way to go over or around, so she would have to go down and then back up.

Throwing her fears and doubts to the wind, she turned backward and very very slowly began to climb down. Luckily, there were plenty of ledges to rest on, but it didn't make it any less nerve-racking.

She was almost all the way down when...

"Roar!!!" It was thunderous and sounded incredibly deadly.

She screamed at the unexpected noise, lost her grip, and fell the last few feet.

Honk! Celia zoned back into her surroundings at the noise. A car was heading straight for her, she froze. Hadn't she looked both ways before she crossed!? The moment didn't feel real, and she couldn't move.

"Get outta the way!" came a voice she vaguely recognized. She swallowed, knowing she was about to die.

"Oof!" Not a moment too soon, she was knocked out of the car's path.

After the initial shock died down, she looked up to see an annoyed looking boy, his blond curls dangling in front of his face. He had slight freckles across his nose. She had never noticed them before.

"Are you stupid or somethin'?" he practically yelled at her.

Her cheeks flared. "Get off of me, Edmund."

He rolled his eyes but moved off of her, offering a hand to help her up.

Begrudgingly, she took it. "Thanks."

"What were you thinkin,' Misty?"

"My name isn't Misty," she whispered.

His mouth fell open slightly, his cheeks turning pink. "Idiot," he muttered to himself. "I um...sorry. That's what everyone at school calls you."

"Why?"

He looked away from her quickly. "Doesn't matter."

"The fact that you're hiding it makes it matter."

He sighed. "Mist— Celia, believe me when I say that high-schoolers are stupid. They talk behind people's backs and make fun of them."

Celia narrowed her eyes at him. "That still doesn't answer my question."

To his credit, he looked ashamed. "It's because your eyes tend to mist over and you stare off into space." He shrugged. "Misty."

She nodded slowly, trying not to show how much the name hurt her. She had never sought after their approval, but the fact that they took her escape, her haven from the world, and turned it into a joke, that stung.

"Oh… Well, thanks for saving me."

He rubbed the back of his neck awkwardly. "Any time."

They stood in awkward silence before she remembered the donuts. She looked out into the street and huffed in frustration. They were flattened.

"You okay?" Edmund asked.

She looked away from him, willing for the tears to stay away. "That's none of your concern."

He put a hand on her shoulder. She shrugged it off.

"I'm just tryin' to help."

Don't cry! Don't cry!

"I need to go." She didn't look back at him as she crossed the street, this time properly checking both ways.

"See you at school!" he called after her.

She ignored him.

Celosia had expected to hit the ground, and was completely confused when she didn't.

"Gotcha."

She looked up to see a boy with blond curls, freckles, and sparkling blue eyes. She slapped him. He dropped her.

She quickly scrambled to her feet and gave him a sheepish smile. "I am incredibly sorry. You startled me." To her surprise, he laughed.

"I should have known that's what would happen if I attempted to save a damsel."

"Roooooooar!!!!!"

The two looked at each other as the thunderous sound returned.

"What was that?"

"A dragon," he muttered. "I came to slay it. I wasn't expecting to have to protect you as well."

"You don't need to worry about me. I'll just continue on my way."

"I thought girls were supposed to jump at the idea of being rescued. Shouldn't you be begging me to protect you?"

"I've never heard a rule about it."

He cocked his head to one side. "Now that you mention it, neither have I."

"Well, it was lovely meeting you, and I wish you the best of luck. I really must be going. I am on somewhat of an urgent mission." She began to walk away when he set his hand on her shoulder.

"Wait, do I at least get to know your name?"

She blushed. "Princess Celosia."

His eyes widened, and he bowed. "Your Highness, it is an honor. I am Sir Edmund." He reached for her hand and she allowed him to kiss it.

"Now, slay your dragon, sir. And after you have completed your task, you are welcome to come visit me at the palace."

He beamed at her and she hurried off.

"I'll see you at the palace, Your Highness!" he called after her.

She turned and waved.

Celia reached the pharmacy and entered. Behind the counter sat a woman with vibrant red hair that looked like it was on fire.

"Hello. Can I help you?"

"I'm here to pick up a prescription for Janet Harper."

"Just a moment." She retreated into the back and returned a few moments later. "You are Janet's daughter, yes?"

Celia nodded.

The woman gave her a sympathetic smile. Celia could practically hear the woman's unspoken thoughts. Celia's mother used to be able to pick up the prescriptions herself, and now Celia was here.

When Celia told Mr. Franklin her mother hadn't gotten any worse, she wasn't lying. Her mother could have come, but it was hard for her to move around, and so Celia had offered to pick it up for her.

"Here you are. Tell your mother hi for me."

Celia nodded and left the pharmacy.

Celosia stood at the base of the massive volcano, suddenly feeling very insignificant. She had traveled all the way here, but now that she was here, she had no idea what to do next. She, of course, needed to find a phoenix, but how did one go about doing that?

"Kawww!" Startled, Celosia looked up at the sky to the source of the noise. Her mouth dropped open in awe. Soaring above her head were five majestic phoenixes. They were absolutely breathtaking.

She looked around quickly, trying to find a path to higher ground. She scrambled upwards until she hit a dead end. She would have to climb.

She hiked up her skirts and reached for a hand hold. Inch by inch, she scaled the mini cliff. The longer she climbed, the more her arms began to shake and her fingers sting. She didn't dare look down, knowing that if she did, she wouldn't be able to continue. The more her arms ached, the more she pushed on. If she stopped now, she would fall to her death.

She placed her foot on what she thought was a sturdy hold, but she miscalculated, and her foot slipped. She shrieked from the pain that coursed through her arms as all her weight was placed on them. She frantically searched for a new foothold, but to no avail. Fear crept through her. She wasn't sure how much longer she could hold on.

The air around her became warm as her arms gave out, and for the first time in her life, she imagined the possibility of actually dying. The air whipped around her as she fell, her scream getting lost in the wind.

The princess screamed once more as something grabbed onto her, and she was soon floating in the air. She was flying! The moment was short lived as she was flung onto a ledge. She took deep gulps of breath, attempting to retrieve the air that had been knocked out of her by the impact.

Slowly, she turned to look at her attacker. She shivered, both in terror, and in wonderment.

She bowed her head to the awe-inspiring creature. It cocked its head to the side then stepped closer, staring at her with beady black eyes. It circled around her, poking her lightly with its beak every now and then. She giggled as it poked her side. Eventually it found her bag and nuzzled its beak inside before pulling out a vial of frankincense oil. It dropped the vial in her hand. She stared at it and then back into the phoenix's eyes.

"Do you want this?"

It blinked, not at all giving her an answer. She carefully took out the cork lid and held out the now open container.

The phoenix stepped closer, sticking a long, thin, tube-like tongue into the oil. It made a sound that was somewhere between a purr and a squawk as it enjoyed its treat.

Once it finished, she reached out her hand to stroked its head. It stepped back and she retracted her hand. She tried again, this time slower. It seemed to contemplate the situation before stepping into her touch. The feathers were soft and warm beneath her hand. She had never seen such a beautiful creature.

"Can I get a feather? I need it for my mom. You understand, don't you?" She whispered the words with reverence. As much as she wanted to save her mom, she wouldn't ask for something the phoenix wasn't willing to give. The phoenix stood up tall, turning its head to gesture to its back.

She stood as well. "Are you sure?"

It nodded.

She took a deep breath and approached the phoenix. Her hands shook as she climbed onto its back.

As soon as she settled, they took to the sky. It was a graceful, smooth movement, and it coaxed a laugh from her throat. The sensation of flying was thrilling.

The phoenix didn't spend any time flying around in circles or enjoying the scenery, it went directly toward the top of the volcano.

Even though Celosia knew what was coming, it didn't diminish her terror when they dove into the volcanoe's heart. She clung to the phoenix for dear life, and it made a sound that made it seem as if it were laughing at her. Lava sat at the bottom of the volcano, bubbling as if it were taunting her to submerge herself in its deadly depths.

The phoenix circled around the inside of the volcano before landing on a ledge, far above the magma.

Celosia slid off the phoenix's back, careful not to hurt the creature in any way. It looked into her eyes, it's message simple and clear. It would give the feather. Then, it burst into flames.

Celosia watched it burn with wide eyes. Once the flames died down, all that was left was a pile of ash and a single feather.

She gingerly grabbed the feather, and put it in her bag. She had done it.

As she turned around, she saw a staircase carved into the side of the volcano she hadn't noticed before. It was time to go home. Her mother was saved.

"Thank you," she whispered to the pile of ashes.

Celia walked inside the house, trying not to make a noise. If her mother was asleep, she didn't want to wake her.

"Celia? Is that you?" It seemed she was already awake.

"Yeah, Mom, it's me. I have your prescriptions." She made her way down the hallway to her mother's room. Once inside, she placed the prescriptions on the table next to her mom's bed and leaned over to give her a hug.

"Thanks for doing that, Honey."

Celia smiled. "Of course."

They sat in silence for a moment before her mom cast her a worried look. "Are you doing okay? With all of this? I know it's hard on you."

Celia hesitated before answering, her mind returning to her fantasies and the strength of Celosia in the midst of her adversities, the way Celia wanted to be.

"I'll be okay, eventually."

"Are you sure? I keep worrying that you'll revert further and further into your shell. I can't bear seeing you like this because of me."

"I can get through anything, Mom." Celia smiled to herself before her next words. "Because I rode a phoenix once."

Though her mom looked confused, Celia knew it was true. Even though it was all within her vast imagination, she knew that if Princess Celosia could make the best of a situation like that, then she could do the same in real life. Maybe things wouldn't go as perfectly as they did in her fantasies, but at least she could try her best to be okay with whatever was thrown at her next.

Once upon a time, a broken girl hoped for the best. Once upon a time, Celia Harper rode a phoenix.

Emma Charles

Miracles

"Adrian!" Aniya gasped, throwing the door open. The snow and wind from the storm outside swirled in around her, causing the fire to tremble.

Adrian surged to his feet, his book thudding to the ground. "Where?" he asked as he hurriedly pulled his worn leather boots on over his hole-ridden socks.

"The town square! I don't know what happened, but the cobbler's son is unconscious," Aniya said, worry filling her words. Adrian finished lacing up his boots and briskly walked to the door, Aniya following behind him.

"You go ahead," Adrian whispered, giving her a quick kiss. "See what you can learn."

Aniya nodded, pulled her dark cloak tightly around her, and ran out into the snow. Adrian threw his own cloak over his shoulders, and tied a mask over his face. Pulling up the hood, he ran out of the house, the door thudding behind him.

He let Aniya fade into the snow storm ahead of him, and he started to run.

His breath puffed in and out, seeming to grate at the edges of the mask, fighting for freedom. The mask was a necessary precaution, however. He couldn't let anyone see him heal. There would be a never-ending demand on his abilities, and that would take an enormous toll on him. If he didn't give his soul enough time to recover after each healing, he would slowly begin to die. A person cannot survive with less than half a soul.

Adrian loved the cold. He loved the feeling of running down a snow and ice covered street, his feet sure where others would slip, the crisp air blowing his snow white cloak up behind him, the ice cold kiss of each snowflake that touched his skin. The only sweeter kiss was that of Aniya.

The cold was his. His home, his shelter, the one constant in his life that had been there as long as he could remember.

Yes, he loved it, that frigid air. He could love it even when the ice hidden streets led to more accidents among the children, and the snow to accidents among drivers of wagons. Even through the deaths that the cold caused among those few souls who had strayed too far from home and gotten too cold too fast.

Not far now, he thought.

A moment later, he passed a pair walking away from the square. The woman stopped, looked at him, then whispered to the man, "It's the snow wraith."

Their name for him, his white cloak, his white mask, and his abilities. Their name for the face hidden deep in the folds of the hood.

The square was full of people. Talking, yelling, concerned. Adrian began to push his way through the crowd, but as the people saw him, they quickly cleared a path. In the center of the square, three figures kneeled around a smaller, paler one.

One of the people looked up and met Adrain's eyes. They gasped in astonishment.

"It's the snow wraith!" the man cried. "Away, away! Let him do his work!" The other two people, huddled deep inside their coats and cloaks, moved away at the man's words, blending into the crowd.

Adrian slid to the ground in front of the boy. A long, bloody gash ran from his left eye into his hair. His lips were pale, and his eyes closed, but he was breathing softly. The blood in his hair was beginning to freeze.

Aniya, come on... he thought.

"His name is Bryan," a person behind him whispered. The presence of the person disappeared as quickly as it had arrived, but it was all that he had needed. He could recognize that voice anywhere. Nodding his head in thanks, Adrian set to work.

He covered the boy's eyes with his hand then closed his own, ignoring the blood on the boy's face. Then he began to focus.

Feel the soul, find the tear or missing piece... It was easier the more you knew about the person.

A name on its own wasn't much to work with. But it would have to do.

Bryan.

Then he found it, a long, ragged tear.

Adrian began to syphon away small pieces of his own soul to fill the narrow gap, slowly healing it. Small piece after small piece. Too much at a time and he'd lose consciousness. And… There…

He opened his eyes and removed his hand. The cut was gone, and all that remained was the blood. Color had returned to the boy's lips, and his eyes slowly began to blink awake. Adrian was tired, maybe on the verge of exhausted, but he had healed far worse.

"Take him somewhere warm," Adrian whispered to the man who had recognized him, turning away from the boy.

"I will."

Adrian smiled at the relieved tone of the man's voice.

"All right, Bryan. Let's take you home."

Adrian stood and began to walk away, pulling his cloak around himself.

"That was the snow wraith, wasn't it, Da?" Adrian heard the young boy say sleepily. "Did he heal me?"

"Yes, Bryan. Now, let's get going. Your mother is worried sick."

Adrian was too far away to hear the boy's soft reply, but he could feel the happiness in the boy's father's laugh. His soft smile didn't fade as he continued down the street.

Adrian was sitting on the floor by the fire, reading and beginning to recover from the healing earlier that day, when Aniya returned.

"His parents were so grateful," she sighed, unlacing her boots by the door and hanging her cloak on the stand. "I wish we could tell the people it is you." She wandered over to where he was reading and sat by his side. She would frequently do that. Come to visit, and just sit with him for hours.

"You know why we can't," he replied, turning the page in his book.

"I know," she sighed. "What are you reading?"

"*The Sea of a Thousand Faces*," Adrian said, his voice soft.

"Are you very far into it?"

"A few chapters."

"Would you read it to me? I've always wanted to read that one."

"Of course. Would you like me to start from the beginning?" he asked, smiling at her.

"Not start at the beginning! What kind of monster do you think I am?" Her smiling sarcasm seemed to brighten the room even further.

Laughing, Adrain flipped back through the pages and began to read in a soft, clear voice, strong with the spirit of the book.

"Good so far?" he asked after a few pages.

"Of course." She leaned her head onto his shoulder.

Adrian continued, and the small room seemed to come alive at his words, dancing with the firelight. He told the story, one of death, pain, trials, to help with his own hurt. He had Aniya, he had his brother, but there would always be the lingering image of his mother, father, and sister lying in the cart next to the other bodies, and Adrian having been able to do nothing to save them.

His abilities had slowly begun to manifest over the following weeks and had strengthened as he used them.

But Adrian tried to push those feelings away, tried to focus on the warmth of Aniya's body next to him, the weight of her head on his shoulder, and the magic in the story. Beyond the tale of pain and suffering, the book also told the story of adventure, hope, and love.

Please, he thought toward Aniya, *Please, never leave me.*

"*And the group reached a crossroads. The leaf-littered ground seemed to beckon them forward into the woods, but they knew not which way to turn. And the voice came again,*" he read.

Whispering in Ranil's ear, the voice said, 'Choose wisely.'"

"Choose wisely," Aniya echoed.

←→

"Adrian! It's Lee! He slipped from the roof while tarring!" Aniya shouted. She was standing at the door, a look of fear and horror accompanying the tear tracks on her face.

"Lee?" Adrian looked to Aniya in terror, standing from his seat at the table.

"Yes! Come quickly! He's hit his head! He doesn't have very long!"

"Aniya." Adrian slowly sat back down. "If I healed that, I'd die. He might be dead already."

"Adrian!" Aniya sobbed, kneeling on the ground, desperate tears streaming from her face.

"I know," Adrian whispered, standing again. He walked to his boots and put them on.

"Wait!" Aniya gasped, looking up. "Don't do it! I wouldn't be able to go on without you!"

"I know," Adrian repeated, clasping his dark green cloak around his throat.

"Then… Where are you going?" She stood slowly, the skirt of her dress wet with melted snow.

"To say goodbye."

Lee lay in the snow, the red stain around his head a stark reminder that he was dead. A large group was gathered around the body.

"The mortuary workers are on their way," Aniya whispered, returning to Adrian's side.

"He's dead," Adrian breathed. "He's always been there for me. Always. Now he's gone. I couldn't have asked for a better friend, much less brother. He was going to be my best man…"

"I know," Aniya replied. "We can push back the wedding date…"

"No… No." The cold wind chilled the wet tracks his tears had left. "Life will move on, with or without Lee. I can't stop it."

"We both know there was nothing you could have done."

"I know."

Silence.

"But does this mean that I think my life is more valuable than his?" Adrian whispered.

"No," Aniya replied, drawing Adrian into a hug.

Lee's body was covered by a dusting of snow. The burial shroud.

The mortuary workers hadn't arrived yet. They were late. Just letting the body sit, slowly getting buried in its white tomb of snow.

The silence was filled only by the crackling of the fire in the hearth, and Aniya's knitting needles clacking together as she slowly created a blanket from the ball of blue yarn that lay in her lap.

Adrian sat next to her, watching the flames dance around each other, providing heat for them to survive, yet playing at the same time.

"Tomorrow," Aniya breathed. "Tomorrow. The day many people wait their whole childhood for."

"Did you not?" Adrian asked, continuing to stare into the fire.

"I have been waiting since the moment you asked. I was never in a hurry to grow up as a child…"

"With growing up comes the weight of many burdens. And understanding. Understanding things fully is a curse."

Death.

He had always understood death. The death of his mother, father, and now his brother. His parents' deaths had been slow things, over time, a result of the plague five years ago. This time, the pain had seemed so much sharper than all of the others. It had felt more real.

He looked over at Aniya, his fiancé, his love, his best friend. All he had left. She had stopped her knitting and met his gaze with eyes full of love.

"It will pass, as all things do," she said.

"Yes. It will."

"I miss him too." She returned to her knitting.

Adrian turned back to the fire.

"I know."

The cold bit Adrian's face as he raced through the streets. He didn't enjoy it this time. A man had come to his door, yelling that he was needed… But no one knew his secret except Aniya.

He was terrified.

He wore no cloak, just a white suit.

Adrian slipped. He never slipped. Not ever. One of his feet flew out from underneath him, and he landed on his stomach, the ice against his face, his breath puffing out in a white cloud.

Keep… Going!

Adrian stood and continued to run. To the town square. Tears streamed down his cheeks, and the cold wind seemed to freeze them as they fell. He heard someone whisper of the snow wraith, then another say it was just Adrian running late to his own wedding.

How wrong they were.

The square was crowded with people, packed around something next to the clock.

"Get out of the way!" he screamed, pushing people aside, his voice a raw roar fueled by fear. When they caught a glimpse of him, people backed away instantly, clearing a path to the body.

Aniya was laying in the snow, in her wedding dress. It was beautiful. Adrian had never seen it before, and now… Here it was.

"Aniya," he sobbed, collapsing by her side. He held his hand over her mouth, but he felt no breath. He felt at her neck for a pulse. Her skin was growing cold.

His tears dripped onto her face like blood. "I can't lose you…"

Adrian placed his hand over her eyes. He closed his own.

And then he looked into her soul. It would have normally taken a few minutes to find the missing section, but here… There was almost nothing left.

He began to push his soul into hers, desperately filling that gap. The world wouldn't be able to go on without Aniya's laugh.

Two words penetrated his mind.

Snow wraith.

Adrian removed his hand and opened his eyes. The last things he saw were Aniya's eyes blinking the snow off their lashes, and they meet his own, for just a moment. He had healed one last time, had healed in his white clothing, the white clothing of the snow wraith, and of Adrian.

Nothingness came, but he greeted it with a smile, for he had seen those eyes one last time. He had healed those eyes, and the soul that gave them life.

Aniya watched as Adrian collapsed to the ground beside her. She had met his eyes for a moment, and then…

Tears began to pour down her face.

She held his body in the cold for hours, trying to give back that soul that wasn't hers. They lay there, in the white snow, in their white clothing, together.

One last time.

But he would always be with her.

For he had given her his soul.

Trini Feng

Honor Bound

Whenever Kanlen walked on the street, he made sure his gait was awkward in any way. Unsteady, tottering, a skittish step here and there. Never practiced, never sure. Anything but that. Once he was certain of that part, he tossed in a few nervous glances and a slouched posture, and the look was complete.

Kanlen passed a small, nondescript building fashioned out of mismatched concrete bricks. He allowed himself to pause and raise his head. Kanlen's gaze hardened in defiance at the building's sign: *HERO CATALOG*. The words etched in brass sickened him, so he didn't look for long before continuing on his way.

What a silly place. Taverns and lounges were acceptable, but one specifically watching acts of grandeur to find the "next great hero" was ridiculous. Sure, the city of Tondyll needed something to pass the time, but did it have to be so shallow?

No, of course it did. That was what caught the most eyes. Kanlen had avoided any talk about heroes as much as he possibly could, but even he knew how common they were nowadays. He also knew that as soon as their popularity dimmed, they vanished as quickly as they had come.

Behind Kanlen, someone screamed. He froze, glancing around. Everyone on the street pointed up, some petrified in disbelief and others murmuring frantically. Something bright, almost like a tiny fireball, drifted in the sky.

Kanlen blinked fast to make sure he wasn't imagining things. He wasn't. The small white spirit bounced in mid-air, everything below its head wreathed in fire. It didn't make any noise—as expected, since it didn't have a mouth—but its two large black eyes twinkled with mirth.

And then, as Kanlen watched, it stared straight at him. Its eyes lit up, and a small fireball, not much bigger than a fingernail, came at him.

Kanlen threw himself to the ground. The fire sputtered out next to him, but when he stood up, the fire elemental was already racing away, set to hurt, destroy, and ruin.

Kanlen sprinted after it, but when the elemental passed right through the Hero Catalog's window, he skidded to a halt. For a moment, the elemental's plan didn't seem so bad. It would be better if the Hero Catalog was gone.

The grim thought crossed Kanlen's mind, and the longer it lingered, the more he realized its utter truth. With the Hero Catalog gone, the people who spent every waking moment there might actually find something useful to do with their lives rather than stalk others who simply had the common decency to act.

Would it even catch fire? Elementals avoided targeting the infrastructure of a building if possible. They preferred moving, living, breathing targets, like… the giant crowd inside the Hero Catalog.

*S*omeone screamed from inside the building.

How could Kanlen ponder whether it was worth it or not? People were in danger. He had never had a choice. He couldn't let someone get hurt while he stood listening to their cries for help. He threw open the door and rushed in.

The Hero Catalog had been renovated out of an old pub, and its cozy room, scattered tables, and creaky stools certainly matched that. People lined the walls and corners, none of them rushing to escape. At least three were injured, lying out in the open. Kanlen ran to the closest one, who was groaning and cradling his arm.

Kanlen took his arm, examining it. Nothing serious: a single scrape across and nothing more. No burn wounds. "What happened?" Kanlen said, and when the man didn't respond, he repeated the question. "*What happened*?"

"That fire thing attacked..." The man coughed. "Tried to get down... hit a table..."

"Can you stand?"

The man frowned and slowly shook out his legs. He put weight on them, almost crouching, and nodded to Kanlen.

He was perfectly functional, disregarding the minor scrape on his arm. Kanlen shook his head. "You need to go to the hospital. Tell them what happened. They'll get help."

The man slumped down and shook his head. He turned, pointing to the back corner.

"You're not listening. You have to *go*. It's dangerous here."

"He's a... hero." The man uncurled his balled fist, revealing a shining crystal. "He'll save me... I've got it all here..."

Kanlen gritted his teeth. He had hoped the crystal phase hadn't reached Tondyll yet. He took the crystal from the man's shaking fingers and hurled it away. "I need you to leave."

A new determination entered the man's eyes. "What's it to you?" He rolled over and crawled toward his crystal. "I'm not leaving until he's done."

Of course he wasn't. He was another fanatic, and they never listened to reason.

Kanlen followed where the man had pointed. Amidst the people crouching and hiding in corners, a boy holding a bucket of water scurried around the cramped space. He kept tossing the water into the air and running to the far wall to refill. Only when the boy threw the bucket against a wall and a small spirit flitted away, cackling, did Kanlen realize what he was trying to do.

He was chasing an elemental with water. Even worse, since he was running back to get more, the boy must've thought this was a good idea.

He was going to get himself killed.

Kanlen searched the nearby area before grabbing the narrowest stool available. Just as he did, a sizzle sounded from across the room, followed by a choked-out sob.

The fire elemental floated in the center of the room. It was at least smaller than Kanlen's head, so a direct hit would be difficult. Fortunately—or perhaps, unfortunately—it was focused on one target at the moment, back turned to Kanlen.

His senses sharpened, focusing on the elemental and his victim. All at once, it seemed natural to Kanlen, a duty he was bound to. Erase the evil, save a life. He charged toward the fire elemental, stool in hand. Before it could turn around, he rammed the stool leg straight through the elemental.

Its flames were the first to go, wicking off and petering out. Then the elemental dissolved into wisps of white that trailed into the air. Once the air had cleared, Kanlen dropped the stool and surveyed the elemental's next target: the boy with the water bucket. Now that he was closer, Kanlen realized they must've been around the same age, but the panicked expression on the boy's face made him look so much younger. His hands swiped at his burning sleeves, yet the water bucket still sat next to him, untouched.

Kanlen grabbed the water bucket and dumped it over the boy's arms. The boy spluttered and looked up, the fires extinguishing from his arms. Aside from the wounded look in his eyes, he seemed fine. Still, it was better safe than sorry.

Kanlen knelt in front of him. "Are you hurt?"

The boy frowned and rolled up his sleeves. Nothing burnt. He shook his head, springing to his feet. As he glanced around the room, he patted at his hair, drying it and ruffling it back up.

Kanlen turned, about to assess any injured people. He staggered back. Every eye was trained on him.

He took another step back, but he realized that wouldn't help. Kanlen shouted, "We need to get help!" He looked around, noting a few people that looked injured, and rushed over to them. "Do you need help? I can get—"

"Why would anyone need to get help?" a voice scoffed. Kanlen turned. A girl lingered in the corner, looking virtually unscathed. "You're here already, and that's all we need. A hero."

Hero. The word echoed through Kanlen's head.

He shook his head—as if that could block it out—and ran for the entrance. Kanlen swung open the door, sprinting down the street to the nearest hospital he knew. To get someone, *anyone*, who could help without anyone singing their praises to the whole world.

"Hey!" that same girl called. Footsteps pounded after him. Kanlen sped up.

"*Hey*!"

A hand grabbed Kanlen and pulled him back. He skidded, whirling around and meeting the face of his scoffer. Her eyes burned, a deep scowl set in her face, and strands of her cropped blonde hair blew about her face.

"Do you want to explain what in the world you're doing?" she spat.

Kanlen caught his breath before saying, "I'm not your hero." He paused and added, "I'm not anyone's hero."

"Please." She threw her arms up in the air. "If this is some extended form of modesty, I don't buy it. Did you see yourself back there? You ran right into danger and you handled it gracefully. Even helped others along the way. How is that not heroic?"

"If you want to take credit for that, you can. I don't want to be on the headlines later."

"That's not how it works. You can't just claim what others did as your own. People have to see *you* do it."

"So they can pretend they never saw me." Kanlen turned on his heel, walking away. "Destroy the crystals. Erase the evidence."

The girl caught up to him in a heartbeat. "Why would anyone do that? You know, people would kill to be in your position right now. To be admired, respected, and honored—all for something *you* did."

Kanlen stopped again. "That's exactly why! It's too much work. Everyone's looking at you, expecting something of you, and..." And he knew what happened if those expectations were let down once.

"What? Are you a little shy?" The girl sneered, and when Kanlen didn't respond, she huffed. "I can't believe you. Wasting an opportunity like this... I can tell you came from somewhere higher up."

"What does that have to do with anything?"

She fixed Kanlen with a look. "You never had to scrabble for anything that would get you off the ground. All that pressure that's scaring you? It's more important than you could ever imagine. We need *something*, anything, to make us look a little more important now compared to when we were born."

"Trying to become a hero isn't that stable," Kanlen said. "I don't imagine monsters attack every single day—"

"Not unless you pay them," an unfamiliar voice interrupted. Both Kanlen and the girl turned, and Kanlen's eyes widened. The boy, no longer with his signature bucket, stood in front of them, his fidgety expression gone.

Well. Almost gone. When they looked at him, he shrunk back and offered a nervous smile. "Sorry. I passed by, and I couldn't help but say something." He turned to Kanlen. "I have to thank you for saving me. My name's Casper."

Kanlen glanced away. "Kanlen, and anyone would've done it. What did you say about payment?"

The girl gaped. "You don't know? You're from Tondyll, right?"

"Been here all my life, but I've never walked into a Hero Catalog."

She shook her head. "That explains a lot." She paused, glancing at the other boy, who shrugged. "You at least know how everyone's worshipping heroes, right?"

All too well. Kanlen nodded.

"Well, you can guess what happens when that worship gets out of control. People want to become and make themselves heroes, and how do they do that? Defeating evil monsters that threaten the lives of others. It's a classic, and it's easy."

"It started as a forbidden black market of sorts," the boy said. "Just a few underground trades, exchanging money for a monster to attack a certain public place. Set a few crystals there to record the footage, rush in, and save everyone. It was so popular that it caught wildfire and spread."

"That's..." Kanlen stepped back, shaking his head. He knew people loved heroes, but to the extent of doing something like this? "No one's tried to stop it?"

"As long as you don't mess up, no one can prove anything or accuse you. It's dangerous, but if you're prepared, it works." The boy paused. "Come to think of it, the practice started somewhere in Bellona."

Bellona. A bustling city of hubbub and trade, the closest to Tondyll, yet it hid a heart of darkness. How did it continue as it did, ignoring all its crimes? How did the people there go on?

Kanlen remembered how packed the Hero Catalog had been, how he had tried to save the man who had only insisted that a hero was coming. This deceit was why, and Kanlen was the only one who cared. He hated it, but something had to be done. "I'm going there."

The girl blinked. "That was fast."

"I can't let this keep happening." Kanlen started walking back. "People will die if they haven't already. It's too dangerous."

Both the girl and Casper caught up with him. "You want to take away so many people's hopes and dreams, all because you think they're dangerous," the girl said.

"They deserve it." Kanlen's tone was unflinching. "It's not only dangerous but also wrong."

The girl sighed. "Well, good on you for being so moral, but not all of us can afford that. I take it this is another excuse to run away."

Kanlen didn't answer. The girl grinned.

"I don't blame him," Casper said. "It's harder than it looks."

"Like you can talk," the girl scoffed. "Throwing water around a room isn't brave."

Casper scowled. "Neither is sitting in a corner."

Kanlen sped up his pace, but the girl matched her steps with his. "Just so you know, I'll take you to Bellona," she said. "I'm not leaving you alone until you take what's yours. But I do think I have to tell you that you're going the wrong way."

"I'm telling my parents," Kanlen snapped, "and I doubt tagging along for that will be very entertaining. I'll meet you on the road."

The girl stopped in her tracks. "Fine, then." As Kanlen kept walking, she called after him, "Since I already know your name, I figure it's fair that I tell you mine. It's Petra."

Kanlen registered the words but barely cared, already at the front steps. He knocked on the door, waiting. Dreading. He didn't want to tell his parents what had happened, but he had to. Kanlen couldn't leave without at least one word of where he was going.

The moment the door opened, Kanlen stepped in, the words rolling off his tongue: "I messed up."

He recited everything that had happened to his parents, watching their calm expressions shift from surprise to disappointment, and, by the time he had said, "…and now I'm going to Bellona to see what I can do about it," a strange understanding.

Once he was done, Kanlen stopped to take a breath. He glanced up at his parents. "Did you know?" he said. "About the… mercenaries?"

"Of course we did," his mother said as his father shuffled away. "Every corner we turned, a new person would give us a new deal. I just didn't know it could happen here in Tondyll, too." She frowned, adding a new crease to her forehead. "I thought we were safe."

"We all did." Kanlen's father returned, holding something. He approached Kanlen. "I hoped you, of all people, would be safe."

Kanlen sighed. "So did I. I didn't want this to happen. I don't want to go. If I didn't have to, I wouldn't. But every time I think of that, I can't leave it alone. It's better if I do something with those thoughts."

"And that's admirable." His father dropped a token into Kanlen's palm. "I suppose with that kind of conviction, this couldn't have avoided you for long."

"It could've." Kanlen examined the token, an iron necklace. Attached to it was a small amulet that gleamed a faint blue. "If I had taken a different route, maybe walked a little faster, I never would've gone near that Hero Catalog."

"If it didn't find you today, it would've caught up with you eventually. Destiny likes to do that with its favored ones."

Kanlen swallowed before nodding. He wanted to feel as though he could've changed something to avoid this. He palmed the amulet. "What is this?"

"We recovered it from Merfocen," Kanlen's mother said. "One villager claimed it would ward off any beast that attacked. I suppose it did, but it did nothing for the desperate humans that came to loot his home afterward."

Kanlen winced.

"So don't get on any human's bad side," his father said in what Kanlen thought was supposed to be a light tone. "Easier said than done, of course."

"In general, avoid people when you can," Kanlen's mother said. "Get in there and get out."

"You don't have to tell me twice." Kanlen hung the necklace around his neck, hiding the amulet under his shirt. "Thank you."

"You just be careful," Kanlen's father said. "But I think you knew that already."

Kanlen nodded. "I will."

He couldn't think of anything else to say, nothing except trite, tearful farewells or empty promises that he'd return. His family had never been one for extra words, not if they could help it.

Kanlen walked out the door.

←→

The road to Bellona was short, and Petra pranced the whole way across it, smirking. Kanlen hadn't been at all interested in striking a conversation with her, but as they neared Bellona, the behavior was so irritating that he had to ask. "What happened?"

"Oh, Casper tried to come along, but I wouldn't let him." Petra's grin grew. "I knew he would only mess things up. You should've seen him before you came into the Hero Catalog."

So that explained his absence. Kanlen couldn't help but feel a pang of regret. Casper would've been slightly better company than this. He at least seemed to have some sort of sympathy for Kanlen.

As they stepped from the vibrant green grass onto cobblestone pavement, Petra said, "It is interesting. You seem cut out for heroism. Clever, capable, compassionate. So why are you avoiding it so much?"

Kanlen swallowed. "I guess… I'm scared."

"All right. Add *coward* to that list of traits, then. I think it's something more than that, though. What are you scared about?"

Her tone sounded almost sincere, such a contrast to what Kanlen had come to expect of her, that he was tempted to tell the truth. Still, he paused. He took in the narrow buildings towering over them, their limestone bricks smooth and glistening. It was far more captivating than anything from Tondyll, so different, so… *new*, but also dangerous; they could crack and fall down at any time. "Failure."

"How dramatic." Petra let out a sigh. "But isn't the reward enough to risk that failure?"

A reward? Kanlen tried to picture it: crowds surrounding him, his face on the front page, his name whispered throughout the land. That wasn't anything close to a reward. "Not really."

Petra whistled. "You're different; I'll give you that." She stopped at a small building that looked even more out of place with the neighboring skyscrapers. It looked eerily similar to Tondyll's rendition, except with a fresh coat of white paint, and the words *HERO CATALOG* were emblazoned in gold this time.

Kanlen said, "Why are we here?"

"Because it's the best place to get information," Petra said. "You have to know what you're walking into when it comes to this monster stuff. Better to make sure you do than chance it and pay."

"You're paying either way," Kanlen muttered.

Petra stared at him for a few moments before laughing. "And I thought you were just some stuffy rich kid. Come on." She sauntered past him, pulling open the door.

Kanlen gulped, feeling around his neck for the amulet before following her inside.

The place was packed. Kanlen could barely see an inch of the floor from where they stood. Long counters lined the rooms, crystals set up at perfect angles to project their footage. Some waiters even served refreshments, but a single look at the crystal screens and they too were entranced. A few main screens had been set up on the ceiling. They all played the same scene, a reporter addressing an incident that Kanlen had already seen one time too many.

"Earlier today in the village of Tondyll, a fire elemental attacked," a woman reported, the audio booming through the main crystals. "Thankfully, a brave hero stepped in and saved the day before things got out of hand."

The screen flipped to the on-scene footage. The fire elemental had burst into the Hero Catalog, terrorizing every person in its path. Then Kanlen ran in—frenzied, a little short of breath, but with a look of determination on his face.

Kanlen blinked. He hated admitting it, but the footage did make him look brave. Not too brave to border on the edge of arrogance, nor confused like Kanlen thought he must've looked like. Brave.

"You're famous," Petra muttered next to him begrudgingly, but he looked over at her and she smiled.

Once the fire elemental had evaporated, the screen shifted back to the reporter, luckily cutting out Kanlen's less brave getaway. "An anonymous source tells us that our new hero's name is Kanlen," the reporter continued. "It truly is remarkable. Fire elementals are rare and not easily beaten—"

Someone in the room shouted in disbelief. Kanlen glanced over to see a young woman pointing right at him, mouth wide open.

Slowly, a few others turned. It only took them a moment to realize who she was looking at, and less time than that for them to all utter similar gasps of shock. Many lingered on the screens before turning to the commotion. Soon, the whole Hero Catalog had frozen, everyone staring at Kanlen.

For a moment, Kanlen wondered if he should leave, but then the crowd surged forward.

A man approached first. "You… I can't believe what you did," he said breathlessly. "Elementals are so dangerous. Everyone who tried fighting them failed. But you…" He shook his head, too overcome for words, and walked away.

Without a single second to spare, a woman jumped in to take the man's place. She clasped Kanlen's hand. "You are so brave," she said. "You made it look easy."

Kanlen managed a smile. "I… thank you."

The woman beamed and trotted away. Another person came up offering their thanks. Then another, and another, and another. At some point, Petra muttered, "I'm going to question some folks," and sped away before Kanlen could say anything. He thought about calling her back, out of safety more than anything else.

But as Kanlen shook hands and smiled at a thousand strangers, he tried to picture Petra in the same situation. He couldn't. Acting kind bored Petra. In the short time he had known her, the kindest remark he could recall from her had barely passed for polite. Kanlen doubted she could accept even a few thanks before she burst. The same person who had mocked Kanlen for avoiding heroics could barely scrape by herself.

In fact, it wasn't as frightening as Kanlen had feared. Kanlen had never seen this many people happy. They were joyous approaching him and borderline gleeful leaving all because of his stunt, and there were likely more than just this Hero Catalog. All across the land, people were probably celebrating his defeat of the fire elemental. For once, he didn't shudder at the prospect.

There was even a certain monotony to it, repeating the same lines as the crowd thinned. Before long, Kanlen's attention drifted to the main screens on the ceiling. The scene had shifted, but Kanlen wasn't sure what it was until he caught a single phrase. "…the destroyed village of Merfocen…"

Whispers spread throughout the room. Kanlen stiffened. Those sitting at the tables ushered over the few people still standing, who followed without a second thought.

"Lavinia and Orson, parents of newfound hero Kanlen, seemed to have had their own time in the spotlight long ago," the same reporter said. "Until they were found sweeping over Merfocen, picking out what they could in the ruins. They claim beasts sieged the village and they tried protecting it, but their efforts were in vain. There is no proof that what they said is true. Darius, we turn to you now for your analysis."

"I've got our info," Petra whispered, slinking back to Kanlen's side. "We can go."

Kanlen ignored her, staring at the screen. She frowned, but then followed his gaze.

"It's clear that his intent is the same as his parents'," Darius, a man with a shock of red hair, said. "The fire elemental was likely hired by him for a hefty penny. He wants to get our guard down and strike with the same viciousness that Merfocen received. After all, his parents did the same thing. It runs in their blood."

"Kanlen?" Petra whispered, tugging on his sleeve. It didn't help. He was frozen to the spot.

It runs in their blood…

They had failed once.

He could fail again.

"Are you suggesting malicious intent?" the reporter asked.

"I'm not just suggesting it; I *know* it," Darius said. "His parents failed, and they raised him to try and be more sly about their intents. Can you expect anything more from the people who let a whole village die? Luckily, we discovered this before things got out of hand, or else—"

Petra tugged on Kanlen's sleeve harder, dragging him straight out of the Hero Catalog and onto the street. "Kanlen, can you hear me?"

When he didn't respond, Petra shook him. "Kanlen!"

He started. "W-what?"

"Good, you're awake. Come on. We're moving." She turned him around, practically dragging him across the street.

It took Kanlen a few moments to regain his footing, and an extra few to realize that Petra was still by his side. "You're… not leaving?" he asked.

She scoffed. "I know they were lying. Their evidence is so fake. You'd have to be some sort of idiot to believe that about your parents." Petra paused for a moment before adding, "Which a lot of people here are, to be fair."

"It was true," Kanlen said. Petra skidded to a halt. "I mean… no. My parents were warned about dangerous beasts attacking Merfocen. They got there right after the first wave. Most of the village was destroyed, but to make matters worse, the villagers looted and attacked one another out of desperation. While they were still weak, the beasts came for a second round. No one survived…my parents were still trying to dig bodies out of the wreckage when they were found."

"But they didn't plant the beasts there," Petra said. "Right?"

"Of course not."

"See?" Petra continued walking, faster this time, leaving Kanlen hurrying to catch up. "I was right."

"How did you know?" He would've thought that Petra, out of all people, would've believed everything they said about him.

"Because I saw you when you ran into our Hero Catalog, and I know you never intended anything malicious," Petra said, as if it was the simplest fact in the world. "You can't harm a fly. *Same viciousness*? Anyone who's known you for more than five seconds would know that you don't have a vicious bone in your body."

Kanlen sighed in relief. "Thanks." He paused before asking, "Where are the monsters?"

"A few blocks down. Underground. Any sort of plan?"

Kanlen almost stopped again. His look of panic must've said it all.

Petra smirked. "Good thing I'm here."

"What's your plan?" Kanlen asked.

"I don't have one, but I'm very good at improvising."

Kanlen was in no mood to die today, especially not in a monster-infested hole. "So maybe we could take a minute and *think* about this—"

"We shouldn't spend a single moment more out on the streets than we need to," Petra said. "News spreads quickly. This shutdown of the monsters for hire will clear your name, but before we're done, you're a target. We need to finish this. Now."

Kanlen shook his head. "What if I fail? They'll hate me even more."

"But the *right* people will know you at least tried." Petra stopped at a narrow door, holding it open for Kanlen. With no hesitation, she walked down the stairs. "Besides, monsters are predictable. They don't like being controlled. The humans in charge know that."

"If it's so easy, why has no one done it before?" Kanlen lowered his voice, but it still echoed off the walls. A musty smell infested the air, like that of a sewer.

"Because everyone's too scared to come here." Petra's steps softened. She hit the last floor, rolling a crystal between her fingers. After Kanlen came down, Petra whistled across the crystal's surface, and it emanated a dim glow. She set it on the floor before striding into the room. Kanlen followed.

The two were enclosed in a tight square with stone walls on all sides. Torches on the walls offered the only source of light, barely illuminating the iron bars of the cages beyond the walls. A faint scrabbling echoed in the darkness, sending a shiver down Kanlen's spine.

A footstep rang out behind them, and the room erupted into snarls and shrieks. A whistle followed, hushing the monsters, and Kanlen and Petra both turned to the sound.

There was a sigh, and then a figure emerging from the darkness. "You would not believe," Casper said, holding a whistle and leaning against the wall, "how hard it is to follow you two through Bellona."

Petra frowned. "Why are you here?"

"To stop you."

Petra rolled her eyes. "You have to have less than half a brain to think that the news is telling the truth."

"I know they aren't. My parents sent in the story themselves. It took some scavenging, but we needed dirt on you." Casper looked toward Kanlen. "There wasn't much else. You're too upstanding."

Kanlen fumbled for the amulet at his neck, trying to process Casper's words, but Petra wasted no time.

"You?" she shouted. "Why would you… he saved your life!"

"Yeah, and my parents almost killed me for it." Casper's look had transformed into a glare. "They saved up all that money for an elemental, and I went and blew it. If I didn't want their hard work to be a waste, I had to come out as the hero anyway. This was the easiest way. When people see Kanlen now, they'll see a lying criminal. When they see me, they'll see someone earnest and hardworking. It's not much, but they'll see future potential in me. That's more than enough."

"You're a sham," Petra spat. "Nothing but a crook—"

"You can never be a hero, Casper," Kanlen interrupted, his tone steady.

Casper almost stumbled back. "What?"

"You don't destroy fire elementals with water. You don't sabotage others for your own dreams. That's the opposite of a hero. They'll realize your act soon enough, and you won't have accomplished anything. Just ruined a few other lives along the way." Kanlen's eyes narrowed.

"You don't know what you're talking about," Casper hissed, stepping closer. "You didn't want this path! Why don't you give it to someone who wants—no, someone who *needs* it?"

Kanlen said it before Petra did. "You can't just claim what others did as your own."

"Watch me." Casper stepped right past Kanlen, facing the monsters instead. "Listen to me!" he shouted. "Your targets are those two!" He pointed.

Kanlen glanced at Petra, asking a silent question. Petra shook her head slowly. "We can't leave. They'll chase us through the streets if we do." She glanced at the cages, the creatures slowly awakening from behind the bars. Her eyes lit up. "Or…"

Kanlen frowned, but then he saw what she did: all the monsters stared at Casper, and he didn't even see the hate in their eyes.

Casper brought the whistle to his lips and blew, a short, piercing sound. A single cage rattled, and the lock slipped free. A beast stepped out, something akin to a dog as a lion was to a cat, its pelt as black as night and eyes beady red.

A long howl filled the air. The creature stalked toward Casper, not wasting a single glance in Kanlen's direction.

Casper only then realized what was happening. He waved his arms frantically, pointing toward Kanlen, screaming, "No! Over there!"

Kanlen clutched the amulet, almost stepping forward but freezing halfway through.

"Once they finish him, they'll come for us," Petra whispered. She reached back, scooping up their crystal. "Kanlen, we've got to go. We should barricade the door, tell the public—"

"And leave him to die?" Kanlen whispered back.

"Well, of course. He would've done the same for us."

Kanlen shook his head. The very thought was impossible.

The beast prowled closer. Casper's movements increased in speed, arms chopping the air like windmills.

Kanlen rushed forward, clasping the amulet around Casper's neck, and said, "Stay here. Distract them."

Casper whirled. "What? I thought you were—"

Kanlen couldn't stop to explain. He sprinted up the stairs, Petra at his heels. Behind them, the beast roared and Casper screamed.

A moment of silence passed before Casper's slow, confused voice drifted up: "Why did you…"

Kanlen tore open the door. Petra rushed through and slammed it behind her, locking it.

Petra stared at him. "What was that?"

"My parents said the amulet protects someone from beasts. Apparently, it does." Hopefully, Casper would figure it out soon. "Casper should keep it occupied for some time until we…" Until we *what*? What could they do? Kanlen needed to save Casper and beat the monster, but how?

Petra answered for him. "I'm sure there's old footage of someone beating something like that in the Hero Catalog."

The Hero Catalog. Kanlen didn't want to go back there, especially not after how he had left last time. He glanced at the crystal in Petra's hand. Those crystals had done nothing but hurt.

Except now, he realized. "That crystal will clear my name, right? Especially with Casper."

"It will, but it'll indict Casper, and we'll need people to restrain and arrest that fool."

"And we'll find those at the Hero Catalog, too." Kanlen sighed. Why did everything come back to that place? He felt he could never escape it.

"Yeah. You're okay with that, right? You can handle some heroics."

Clearing Kanlen's name, slaying a beast, rescuing and detaining Casper. Those were heroics indeed, yet Kanlen didn't feel quite as afraid as he thought he should.

For the first time, he felt… almost excited.

He nodded. "I'm ready."

Rylee Cundiff

The Counter Writer

I stood at the bus stop, jotting ideas in my notebook as a light drizzle of rain thrummed against the metal roof. "Well, what do we have here?" A voice asked from behind me, the snarky tone filling me with dread.

"N-nothing." I clutched my precious work to my chest.

Tony clicked his tongue. "Now, now, you know better than to lie to me." He grabbed a corner of the notebook and tugged, but I held on. "Give it up!" he snarled.

"N-no!"

He kicked my legs out from under me, my back slammed against the concrete. I gasped for breath. Tony's shoe pushed down on my chest as he took my notebook, waving its red cover in front of my face. "I'll give back what I don't use." He grinned and marched off, leaving me gasping for air on the ground.

The moment I got home I ran to my room, carefully pulling my journal from beneath the mattress. On the leather cover were the words "Halia's Book of Worlds" written in gold leaf. The pages rustled as I flipped to the last page I'd been writing. As I read the last paragraph, I froze in shock. Everything was all wrong. I'd written a tense scene between Amari, Raza and some soldiers ending in a shaky truce, but now it ended with Amari somehow stabbed by Raza's dagger. There were too few words to tell if Amari was dead. How was this even possible?!!! The paper showed no signs of the former scene I had worked so hard to build, and it was as though it had never been written. Rubbing my eyes, I reread each word carefully. A gasp escaped my lips. Swirling black lines spread across the paper forming one simple word: help. Closing my eyes, I pinched myself. This had to be a nightmare, it must be. Yet, when I checked again, nothing had changed. Hesitant, I traced the letters with trembling fingers. My breath caught in my throat. The inky black lines glowed with golden light as shimmering tendrils wrapped around my body. Tingling spread throughout my limbs. The world warped, growing dimmer until everything went dark.

Cold droplets pelted my face. A green canopy filled my clearing vision. The tingling subsided as I stretched my muscles; everything ached. *Where in the world am I?* I wondered. A girl was sprawled out barely five feet away, her ivory hair obscuring her face. A boy knelt beside her and bandaged her shoulder with trembling hands, "I'm so sorry Amari."

Amari.

The name echoed in my head—except that was impossible! But I knew it was true, I could feel it. My own character was sitting right in front of me! And if that was Amari, then the boy was… I gasped. The noise drew Raza's attention, his hand flying to his dagger. "Who are you?" He growled, standing protectively beside Amari. Oh, he sounded just like I thought he would! His voice so quiet yet strong. There was a flash of steel, the edge of Raza's blade suddenly against my throat. "Who. Are. You?"

The dagger scraped my skin. A trickle of warm blood brought me back to reality. "M-my name is H-Halia," I stammered.

"Whose side are you on?" I tried to speak but my lips remained still. "Well?"

Sensing Raza's fading patience, I struggled to say something, anything. Mustering all my willpower I managed one word, "Shade."

A spark flared in his amber eyes. "I can't believe that traitor is recruiting children."

Traitor? Realizing what must have happened, I mentally kicked myself. Whoever was rewriting my story must have changed the entire book! And I had just spoken a name that would probably get me killed.

Raza towered over me. "I'm sorry it has to be this way," he muttered, "but I can't have you reporting back to Mister Grumpy Shadow." Under other circumstances, I would have laughed at Shade's nickname, but a sense of doom filled my chest. I was going to die. Tears ran down my cheeks. My legs turned to mush as he raised his dagger.

"Raza, stop!" A voice called from behind him, but it was too late. Sharp pain shot through my head, my world once again spiraling into darkness.

My first thought was that I'd had a nightmare. That I would open my eyes and be back in my room, safe and sound. Then I heard the low murmur of voices, the words masked by the rustle of leaves and the sound of running water. I opened my eyes. Amari sat near the fire, the flames reflecting in her prism colored eyes. Raza leaned against a tree, while his messy brown hair was ruffled by the wind. His bronze skin seeming to glow in the firelight as he carefully whittled a stick with his dagger.

Everything came rushing back. My journal, the golden lights, fear. As I bolted upright, pain flared behind my eyes. Strong hands gripped my shoulders. I struggled to get away, my headache increasing with each movement. But they wouldn't let go. "It's all right, we're not going to hurt you," Someone whispered in my ear, the voice eerily familiar. Glancing over my shoulder I saw it was Amari. My panic ebbed slightly, at least she hadn't tried to kill me yet. Once I stopped flailing, Amari let me go, giving a reassuring smile. "I believe you know who we are?"

I nodded. "Y-you're Amari and R-raza is over by the f-fire. How did you know?"

"I had a vision, Halia."

My jaw hit the ground. "You saw my name in it?"

"No," Amari laughed. "Raza told me."

My ears burned with embarrassment. I should have guessed.

"Are you done yet?" Raza cut in. "It is rather boring sitting out."

I started, whacking my already pounding head on a log. Raza chuckled, "Don't worry, I am not going to hurt you."

"A-and I s-should believe y-you?"

"Of course."

I stared at him incredulously. "Y-you held a d-dagger to m-my throat!"

"And you're trying to hide your fear, but that stutter kind of undermines the effort."

Amari stepped in between us. "That's enough you two. Now Halia, drink this. It will get rid of your headache."

Shooting Raza one last glare, I took the cup from Amari. The scent of unknown herbs wafted up from the amber liquid inside. I took a hesitant sip—it was delicious! Smooth, sweet flavors with a hint of mint danced on my taste-buds. I finished in three gulps, the pounding in my head noticeably fading. "Thanks," I muttered.

"You're welcome." Amari smiled. "Besides, I know exactly how bad headaches can be, and Raza is very good at giving them."

We laughed, Raza's protest only fueling our amusement. It was weird I thought as our laughter died away, that even though I didn't completely trust Raza. I felt like I'd known him and Amari forever. Feeling oddly calm I crossed my arms. "Okay, I have lots of questions but first, why am I not completely overwhelmed by everything that's happening?"

Amari ground the tip of her boot into the dirt. "I may have put a little silklyn leaf in your drink." A memory flittered through my mind. Silklyn leaves are a herbal sedative found in mountainous regions. I sighed. "I'm sorry," Amari blurted out, "but I predicted your panic attack causing horrible consequences for everyone. And what we have to tell you is very important."

She paused, figuring out how to word the message. "Jaleer is in danger," she began. "It's being…altered. Allies are becoming enemies, usually peaceful creatures are destroying villages, and it seems nowhere is safe anymore."

I shook my head in disbelief. "What are you saying?"

"I'm saying that Jaleer is dying and I believe you're meant to save it."

"W-what?!" The world spun around me, "You m-must h-have the w-wrong g-girl."

"Nope, it was definitely you." Amari glanced at Raza. "Did I say something wrong?"

He shrugged. "I honestly don't think there's a way to share your news without some panicking."

I held my knees to my chest. "Please just let me wake up. Let this all just be a dream."

Amari placed a pale hand on my shoulder, her touch enough to confirm the truth. "You're not dreaming."

I couldn't breathe. The shadows deepened at the fringes of my vision, and I passed out.

Morning light warmed my face. Nearby birds welcomed the new day with their songs. A hand tapped my cheek. "Five more minutes," I mumbled, pushing it away. I bolted upright as ice cold water splashed my face, running down my shirt. Raza laughed, a now empty bowl sitting in his hands. Using a corner of the blanket draped over me, I dried my face.

Amari sat down beside me. "How are you feeling?"

"Like I lost my mind, but…" I grimaced, wondering why I was telling her this.

"You don't think we're real."

I rubbed my temples. "I don't know what to think."

"Just trust your gut. From my experience it won't lead you wrong."

Raza cleared his throat, his hand moving to his weapon. "Sorry to interrupt your little talk, but we have company."

The warmth seemed to be sucked out of the world as shadows poured out of the woods. In a blink, Amari had me on my feet, pulling me along behind her. "Catch!" Raza called, tossing a sword into the air.

Amari snatched it, yanking me to the side as an arrow flew past. Inky black particles melded into warriors, their purplish-black armor not making a sound. Raza ran beside us, daggers slicing enemy after enemy. Amari brought her sword down in a deadly arc, the shadow-men disintegrated—only to reform a moment later. We ran toward the river. Frigid water surged against my shins, promising a swift ride to anyone who lost their footing. Amari and Raza dove beneath the murky waves. I gaped at their foolishness. A hand shot up around my ankle pulling me under.

Bubbles exploded around me as Raza pulled downward. Rocks scraped my arms as we went down a short tunnel. I struggled, desperate for air. Light suddenly lit up the water around me. With my lungs on the verge of bursting, we finally broke the surface. I flopped gratefully onto the sand. There was air, amazing, wonderful air. The others stirred nearby. "Is everyone all right?" Amari asked.

"I'm fine," I rasped. Raza's muffled reply followed a moment later. We sat in silence for a minute, wearily watching the pond. To my relief, nothing followed.

I inspected our surroundings. We were in a well-lit cave, limestone walls formed a small pocket around the beach where we sat. Gathering my courage, I broke the thick silence. "W-what happened?"

Raza dusted sand off of his clothes, "Shade's ghouls found us."

"But why are you guys fighting? You're supposed to be allies."

"Because the world has been turned upside down, and Amari says you have something to do with it."

Heat burned in my cheeks. "I am not your enemy."

"Prove it."

Amari crossed her arms. "That's enough already. We have bigger problems at the moment, so please stop your bickering while we figure this out."

I reluctantly backed down, absolutely shocked when Raza did the same.

"Raza, I said she could save us, not that it was her fault." Amari pointed out.

Raza frowned. "Save us how? Within five hours our allies turn on us, we meet her and get attacked by Shade's ghouls. While *she* has been either unconscious or panicking the entire time. I don't think she even knows how to fight!"

His words pierced my soul. Raza, the character I'd created and thought of as one of my only friends in the world, was calling me useless. And it hurt more than I ever could have imagined. I fought back tears, but he was right. *What could a bookworm like me do to save a world?* I was just a liability, a chain holding them back.

"I'm sorry," I whimpered. "You're right, I am useless. I've never fought in my life."

I fled to the back of the cave, wishing that I was back home. "Halia, ignore Raza." Amari admonished, "When he gets stressed out, he takes it out on other people."

"That doesn't mean he's wrong."

"It also does not mean he's right." Amari held out a parcel wrapped in rubbery cloth. "I brought you something, it was with you when we found you, but I haven't had the chance to give it back until now."

Perplexed, I took it. "Thanks?"

"You're welcome." She stepped back to give me some space.

I turned my attention to the package on my lap, biting my lip as I peeled back the wrapping. My hands trembled at the sight of a familiar gold script.

It was my journal.

I hesitantly opened the leather cover, finding its pages still as scrambled as the last time I'd held it.

Ka-sploosh!

A vortex shot out of the pond's previously serene surface. Sirens emerged from within the disturbance, their colors mimicking those of a coral reef. Deadly weapons clear as glass sparkled at their sides. With a blood-curdling cry, they charged.

Shouts of fury filled the cavern. I ducked as a sword buried its glass-like blade deep into the stone where my head had been just moments before. I kicked a siren's shin, diving between another's legs. A melody played in my head above the roar of the battle. It was a tune like a familiar song, but it was changed almost beyond recognition. Instincts taking over, I yanked the pencil out of my hair, flipping my journal open to a blank page.

"What are you doing? We need to get out of here!" Raza snapped, intercepting an arrow aimed for my head. Unable to explain, I started to write. Words flowed from my mind, filling the page. Time seemed to slow down. The sounds of battle grew muffled. I became vaguely aware of the others faltering as I finished writing. Placing my hand on the words I'd written a golden light exploded from the page. Everyone froze. As the melody changed, my heart skipped a beat. I recognized it! It was the tune to which my writing always flowed—it was my song.

Weapons fell to the ground, all eyes resting on me. "What is your name, girl?" a siren asked.

I looked up. Her armor glistened like diamonds, and her perfect posture gave the impression she was not one to mess with. The coral crown resting in her midnight blue hair added to the feeling. "H-Halia."

She bent into an elegant bow. "I am Azzurra, princess of Lanara Bay. And I thank you on behalf of my kingdom for freeing us from our trance."

"Y-you're welcome," I squeaked, she was as formal and composed as I remembered describing her in my writings. Raza though had none of the same composure.

"How did you do that? Why didn't you tell us you could do that? You could have stopped the ghouls!"

"I-I..."

"Well?!"

Amari laid a hand on his shoulder. "Raza, take a deep breath. We'll figure this out together."

Raza muttered under his breath, but his posture visibly relaxed.

I slumped against the wall, adrenaline fading. "You should be safe here for now," Azzurra counseled, "though ghouls guard the exit."

Amari sighed. "I expected that we would not leave here unhindered. How many are we talking about?"

"Around a dozen."

Raza groaned, "Great! Another battle. Just do me a favor, tell the Fates I've been beaten enough for one day."

That earned an awkward chuckle from the crowd, easing the tension. "Could the girl free them too?" Someone asked. I searched the crowd but couldn't find the speaker. Exhaustion clouded my mind, my eyelids getting heavier by the second.

"I don't know..." My voice trailed off as exhaustion claimed me.

Amari shook me awake an hour later. "Halia we need your help getting out of here."

"Okay," I yawned, "what can I do?"

"Stop falling unconscious," Raza suggested sarcastically.

Amari pushed him away. “We want you to try and lift the trance on the ghouls.”

I mulled over it for a few minutes before shaking my head. “No.”

Their chorused dismay echoed through the cave. I held up my hands. “Please let me explain. Shade is their king. If I free the ghouls from their trance but he remains under its power who says it will make a difference? And if they rebel, he’ll kill them. I can’t—I won’t—do that to anyone.”

“But—” Raza tried.

I cut him off, “No. Nobody deserves a fate like that. We can find another way that doesn’t cost innocent lives.”

“You call them innocent? They tried to kill us!”

“They don’t have control of themselves!” I challenged, standing as tall as my five-foot-two height would allow. “Feel free to disagree, but I’m not doing it.”

Everyone fell quiet.

“What else can we do?” Amari asked.

I turned to Azzurra and her one remaining guard, “Can you use your magic to help us breathe underwater?”

“Of course,” she replied, confused. “But where would you go? Sadly, quite a bit of my kingdom remains entranced.”

“Oh no,” Amari gasped. Her eyes swirled with colors, her cry sounding like ten voices blending into one, “A battle will rise at the core in the blue moon’s light. Only if the clans stand united will Jaleer survive.” The moment the last word crossed her lips, she collapsed. Raza rushed to her side, gently rolling her over so she was laying on her back. Amari coughed, eyes fluttering open. “We need to go to the Roguewoods right away.”

While Raza scolded Amari for scaring him, I knew what I had to write.

We stood at the edge of the forest. The silhouettes of gigantic trees could barely be seen within the eerie mist as the cold pierced through my thin clothes. The sirens gathered near to us.

“Here,” Azzurra handed me a small, pearl-white shell attached to a silver chain. “When you need us, blow into the shell and we will come.”

I bowed. "Thank you."

"It has been an honor." She bowed her head, "Amari, Raza, I am truly sorry we did not meet on better terms."

"We share your regrets," Amari replied.

Raza gave a quick nod of agreement.

Giving a quick command, Azzurra and her guards dove back into the water, leaving behind a stream of bubbles. Raza turned his back to the river. "Well. Let's get this over with."

"Hold on a second." Amari pulled a small bundle of clothes out of her bag, thrusting it into my arms. "You should change. Your garments stand out way too much."

I stared down at my bright yellow shirt and jeans. "You're probably right." I stepped behind a tree, shivering as I slipped out of my clothes and into the faded brown tunic and trousers. Pulling a cloak tightly around my shoulders, I rejoined the group.

"Much better." Amari motioned to my face. "Now you just need to remove the things from your face."

"What?" I pushed my glasses up, suddenly realizing what she meant. "Oh-um… Those things are called glasses and I need them to see."

"Why? You have eyes."

"My eyes aren't very good," I blushed, "so I have to use my glasses or I'm pretty much blind."

Amari shrugged. "I still don't see how they help, but you can keep them if you need them."

"Now that we have that settled…" Raza interrupted. His tone nagged at me. "Can we please get going? I'd rather not get stuck in there," he motioned to the woods, "after nightfall."

Amari and I hastily agreed. The idea of staying there overnight was not appealing to anyone.

As our small crew marched deeper inland, the mist grew thicker. It soon became challenging to see a foot ahead of us. "Amari? Raza?" I called out, their fuzzy forms slipping out of view. When they called back, their voices sounded surprisingly distant.

"Hold still and keep speaking," Raza instructed. "I'll come to you."

Doing as he had directed, I found myself reciting the description of our surroundings I'd used in my story. "Branches sway like shadowy hands clawing at the sky. A mist seemed to imprison the landscape. Even the tiniest of noises echoed within its vast domain."

I screamed as something brushed my arm. A hand suddenly covered my mouth. "Shush," Raza hissed, "it's just us."

"Do-don't d-do." I stomped my foot, finding only thin air beneath it. "Th-AAAAT!!!"

The ground gave out from beneath me, my screams reverberating off unseen walls. Roots tore at my tunic. Mud flowed between my fingers as I clawed desperately for anything to stop my descent. Warm light flooded the shaft. The sound of shouts and cheers met my ears from below a moment before I hit cold stone. The air rushed out of my lungs and spots danced across my vision. I heard Amari and Raza land behind me with a thump. The world was suddenly silent.

"Well, what do we have here?" A deep voice broke the stillness. "Men, tie them up."

I struggled uselessly as my arms and legs were bound with rope. As a muscular man stepped forward, the sight of him filled me with dread.

Tikvah was just as I'd imagined with his shoulder-length brown hair and beard streaked with gray. His gaze traveled over our group, finally landing on Raza. Sorrow suddenly flared in Tikvah's steely gray eyes, vanishing just as quickly as it had appeared. "So, you've come home at last. It's taken you a long time to come to your senses, my son."

Everyone—even Amari—stared at him in shock. "Who said anything about me coming to my senses?" Raza challenged, fighting against his bindings.

"Then what…" Tikvah glared, grabbing Raza's chin so he was forced to meet his gaze. "Brings my rebellious, ungrateful child back home?"

"What I told you it would take—the end of the world."

"I've heard a lot of things," Tikvah crowed. His cruel, taunting smile sending chills down my spine. "But that tops them all!"

"You wouldn't say that if—" Raza's voice broke off as Amari went stiff beside him, her eyes shining with swirling colors. "They're coming!" she gasped.

Raza cursed under his breath, struggling against the rope with greater ferocity. Tikvah studied Amari, intrigued. "What does she mean by 'they're coming'?"

He had his answer much too soon.

The temperature plummeted. Ghouls materialized around the room cutting off all exits. Rogues and ghouls faced off for barely a second before they charged. Sparks flew as weapons collided. Men were thrown into the walls with a sickening crack. Ghouls disintegrated into inky black particles. My companions fought to get free. Their struggles increased when a stray arrow nearly hit Raza's leg. The arrow gave me an idea. Scooting awkwardly with my hands and legs bound, I inched toward the arrow. Halfway there, I doubled over. Disharmony surged around us; each note assaulted my mind relentlessly. Through the haze of pain, I watched as a man appeared in the middle of the fray. Shade had arrived. It was hard to discern him from the shadows, neither his silver hair or his eyes reflected the smallest bit of light.

"Hand over the girl," his smooth voice commanded.

Tikvah straightened clutching his shoulder, blood seeped between his fingers. "I'm not handing over anything. If you think you can waltz in here with your ghouls and take whatever you want, you're wrong."

Shade grabbed him by the throat, lifting him so his toes barely brushed the ground. "Say that again?"

"O-our prisoners are over there."

Shade dropped him, turning to face us. His silver eyes landed on me. "King has been looking for you. Though I don't know why a pathetic little thing like you is worth all the trouble."

A plan formed in my pain-riddled mind. "I-if you get me paper and a pen, I'll show you," I offered innocently. "Unless you're scared of my wordplay."

"I'm not scared of some childish game."

"Then bring me paper and a pen."

Shade motioned impatiently to one of his ghouls who returned a moment later, placing the requested supplies in front of me. "Um… I'll need my hands too," I pointed out.

Without a word, the ghoul cut me free. Shade crossed his arms. "If that's all you require, I suggest you start working. My patience runs thin."

I nodded, hurriedly setting to work. I had nearly finished when a scene played out in my head. I realized too late that I had written it down, the golden light once again lighting up the world. I heard Raza laugh as the glow faded. All the rogues' hair was now a bright neon pink. "Where am I?" Shade blinked. Analyzing his surroundings, he hastily checked to make sure his own hair was still silver. The look on the men's faces when they finally noticed the change was priceless.

"Who did this?!" Tikvah roared, cutting me off when I'd tried to respond to Shade. Snagging a sword, he marched toward me. "It was you. Change it back or I promise you're not going to live to see tomorrow!"

Amari stepped in between us. "I-it wi-will ch-change b-back," I squeaked from behind her.

Tikvah glowered. "Get out of my way."

"No," Amari said calmly. "Listen. Unless you want our entire world to perish you have to let her live."

"I don't care about the world."

"But if you care about your men, then we have a greater threat to deal with."

He faltered, looking at his band. "Explain."

By the time Amari finished, a grave silence had settled over us all. "I can't change the fact that the blue moon is tomorrow," Shade said, "but I can tell you what I know about who we're dealing with." He took a sip of water. "My scouts suddenly started disappearing. Only one returned, and all he would say was 'King is coming'. The very same night, a stranger appeared who called himself King. His power enwrapped us all, and everything after that is a blur. Then I saw the one thing that rivals his power, and she happens to be sitting right in front of me."

I shifted in my seat; everyone stared, making me uncomfortable. "Your story verifies what I'd seen in my vision," Amari conceded.

"It's not much, but it's more than we knew before," Raza said. "What we need now is a plan and a whole lot of luck."

I looked at everyone in the room. "I have some ideas for a plan, but I'll leave the decision to join us up to you."

Some men talked quietly amongst themselves while others gravely considered their options in silence. Shade was the first to step forward, followed by Tikvah. After that, a majority of their men joined alongside them. Maybe we were not completely doomed after all.

With the preparations for war nearly complete, tension in the camp grew as the moment to depart grew closer. I saw Raza standing alone sharpening his dagger. Knowing that if I didn't clear things up with him it would bug me for the rest of my life (which honestly might not be that long considering what we were about to do). I walked over, bracing myself. "Raza, c-can we t-talk?"

He shot me an exasperated look. "If you need a pep talk go bug Amari."

"That's not it. I wanted to ask why you don't like me."

Raza looked shocked. "Wh-why I don't like you?"

I nodded. He slid his dagger into its sheath, running a finger along the hilt. "When you appeared, my world turned upside down and I'd wanted someone to blame. When Amari connected you to it, I placed the blame on you."

"Oh…"

"But I was wrong."

I stared at him, confused. "About what?"

"You. I thought you were this lost child that would need cared for every step of the way. I figured that you could do absolutely nothing and would get us killed. You've proved me wrong multiple times. So, I'm sorry for placing the blame where it didn't belong."

I smiled at him. "I'm sorry as well. I've gotten us into a lot of trouble. Besides, I understand wanting to place the blame somewhere. Once, I got sick after eating eggs. I still won't eat them even though I know I didn't get sick because of them."

"That's the weirdest comparison I've ever heard," Raza chuckled. Though our laughter died away at the serious look on Amari's face when she joined us. "The sirens have arrived."

I nodded, the weight of everything that was about to happen settling on my shoulders. "I better go meet them."

"Azzurra, Shade, Tikvah," I greeted.

"Halia." Azzurra gave a small nod. "Our time is running short. I am not sure my people can get us there in time."

"If my plan works, they won't have to." I took a deep breath. "Tikvah, Shade, gather everyone."

They nodded. Within five minutes our army had formed a circle around me. "It's time," Tikvah announced.

Amari gave me an encouraging smile, "You can do this."

I hope you're right. Biting my lip, I opened my journal, flipping to the scene I'd written earlier that morning. With one last look at the expectant faces around me, I pressed my hand against the page.

The moon rose over the horizon, bathing the world in a blue-ish glow. An island took form in front of us, the sight of what awaited sent a chill down my spine. An army of beasts that seemed to be summoned out of nightmares cast shadows over the island's crystal surface. Battle cries rang out as the first wave of men engaged in combat. The chaotic beat pounded in my ears as I stepped onto dry ground, hastily activating a few pieces I'd written for this moment. I felt it pull energy from me as shields formed around my allies. Our enemies attacked them relentlessly as blades clashed. A heavy, metallic smell filled the air. Then I saw him. Even dressed in armor, his blond hair and taunting grin was unmistakable.

It was Tony.

"It's time we ended this." He smirked as our eyes made contact, reddish-black light emanating from his hands. "And I think a plot twist is the perfect way."

I watched in horror as allies turned on allies. Tikvah stabbed Azzurra in the back, Shade's body slowly deteriorated into black mist. Amari and Raza lay hand in hand, their eyes clouded over. I fell to my knees, a scream tearing from my lips. They were dead! He'd killed them!

Anger and grief seared through my veins. The disharmony pounded my mind relentlessly. This wasn't how it was going to end! I rose to my feet, writing my ending on my forearm. Each word chimed through the very core of the world. A blast of dark energy crackled through the air, trying to snuff out my light, but I refused to give in. Golden words formed in the air and pushed his darkness back. The force of our powers colliding leveled everything in its path. Each step felt like I was fighting hurricane winds. Tony's panicked shouts grew louder with each step.

I broke free.

Tony stumbled back, now trapped between a crystal boulder and me. I could finish him. He would pay for everything he'd done! Summoning my power, I was ready to strike when I looked at his face.

His eyes were filled with absolute terror.

Was I really going to do this? Did two wrongs ever make a right? I let the magic sputter out. Tony looked at me with wide eyes. "A-aren't you going to kill me?"

"No."

"Why wouldn't you after everything I've done?"

I thought about it for a second. "Because if I did, I'd be just as bad as you, and killing you won't bring my friends back. I just wish I knew why you did it."

Tony refused to meet my gaze. "I was jealous. Everyone said you were such a great writer and I wanted them to say that about me. When I ended up here, I finally had the power to be number one. I wanted to hurt you. But I… I never meant for things to go this far."

"But it did." My voice broke. "And we can't rewind time."

"Maybe we can," he got to his feet, "if we work together."

I stared at him. "W-what are you talking about?"

"We can fix everything," Tony offered his hand, "if you're willing to give me another chance."

I hesitated. *I've heard people say that everyone deserves a second chance. Now is my chance to give that gift.* Taking a deep breath, I took his hand as our magic danced across the world.

The glow slowly faded, revealing my friends' smiling faces. I ran forward and hugged them, tears streaming down my cheeks. "I am so glad you're back!"

"Of course, we had never truly left." Azzurra patted my head.

Before I could ask what she meant Raza nudged my arm. "Halia, your book's glowing."

I looked down at the gold tendrils sneaking out from between the pages. No, it couldn't be. Not now. I wasn't ready. Amari took my hands. Tears shone in her eyes. "It's time for you to go home."

I shook my head. "No, I can't leave now."

"You have no choice," Shade said gruffly.

"And besides," Raza grinned, "we have each other now. I'm sure we can hold down the fort until next time."

I wanted to scream that there might not be a next time, but the tendrils had almost entirely enwrapped Tony and me. Instead of fighting it, I forced a smile through my tears and looked at each one of them. "Goodbye. I will never forget any of you."

I had barely gotten the last words out as darkness closed around me.

When my vision cleared, I was once again alone in my room, my journal laid open in my hands. Five new words appeared on the page. Amari's voice rang in my ears.

"Until Jaleer needs you again."

AUTHOR BIOS

ALANA RAE CHRISTENSEN, AGE 16, loves to write, play flute, and drink hot chocolate. A HS junior in Utah, she reads everything she can get her hands on, from old sci-fi to Shakespeare, and plans to be a full-time author. She won the junior division First Chapter Contest in the Teen Author Boot Camp 2019 and is currently writing a novel.

ALEFIYA PRESSWALA, AGE 16, is a rising junior in high school with a love for all things writing, including creative writing and journalism. Alefiya is inspired by the people she meets and the places she travels and hopes to pass on this inspiration through her writing. In her free time, you can find her reading, painting, or baking new recipes.

AMANDA GRANT, AGE 17, is the creative type. She loves to write, play her flute, draw on her computer and art pad, and dance. This is her third time being published with Owl Hollow Press, and she certainly hopes it isn't her last. She has plans to be a mom, an author, and an editor in her future.

ARIANA HARRISON, AGE 18, is a quirky girl who often argues with herself over whether she should write or draw, since she hasn't learned how to do both simultaneously yet. When she's not sleeping or typing frantically, she can be found laughing at her own jokes, dancing in thunderstorms, or spending time with her loved ones.

DIÉRDRE KEPPNER, AGE 18, began writing at the age of twelve, taking it up after one of her older sisters, and has enjoyed it ever since. Well, other than the times where she's frustrated with her stories, but it's all worth it in the end…Right? She's the sixth child of thirteen, a hopeless romantic, and a firm believer in being kind.

ELIJAH LEWIS, AGE 15, is a born and raised Utahn who loves to read classical literature, play the piano, act, sing, bike, and, of course, write. He loves creating and thinking up stories, helping others, and in general being a good person.

EMILY CARLISLE, AGE 17, from New Mexico is a Latter-Day Saint teen author who fantasizes of world-travel. Writing or reading, she thrives on dreaming of space and the unknown, falling in love with the latest sassy fictional boy, and experimenting with film photography. Her plans for success would impress even the smartest evil mastermind and her determination could put any YA heroine to shame.

EMMA CHARLES, AGE 15, spends her time reading large fantasy books, writing into the early hours of the morning, and playing with her budgie Kaladin. She plans on one day being a full-time writer, with forensic investigation as her back-up plan. She also has a special love of medieval weaponry, dragons, and old science fiction.

JADE DAVIS, AGE 19, has been writing creatively for the past six years. In addition to avidly reading and writing, Jade loves to sing, dance, and study languages (her favorite being Latin). She most often spends her time in the company of books. She works at multiple libraries and loves the opportunity to share her passion for stories with others.

JOE ROGERS, AGE 13, is a freshman at MJHS. He is an aspiring writer that loves Star Wars, backpacking, his chubby dog and strange hats. This is his first time being published and he's very grateful for the opportunity.

KAITLYN HOWES, AGE 16, is an author working to improve her writing daily. After submitting, and winning, in many writing competitions she is still trying to get better. When not writing she is very interested in science and the outdoors. She spends as often as she can hiking through canyons and backpacking the mountains with friends and family.

KEN MEARS, AGE 17, is an author born and raised in Utah. He got his first book, *The Castaway Hero* published when he was just 15, and recently released the sequel, *The Dark Hero*. Ken plans to release two more books before graduating High School and runs a podcast called *Writers World* with his friend Melissa.

LENICKA LEE, AGE 18, is entirely too skilled at stumbling over her words, so she became a writer. When not writing, you can find her practicing jiu jitsu, snuggling her cat, beating friends at board games, or curled up with a good book. She looks forward to the opportunities ahead of her and sincerely hopes that writing fulltime is one of them.

LEXI ROGERS, AGE 18, loves to write; she has been published three times with Owl Hollow Press and once through Dixie State's annual journal. Lexi is excited to be published with her younger brother for the first time and she's very proud of him. Lexi hopes to continue to create adventures that she wishes she could live herself. She's grateful for this opportunity.

MEGAN RIANN, AGE 18, is a Creative Writing major from West Michigan. When she's not eating Argentinian empanadas or climbing the Great Wall, she enjoys watching superhero movies with her cat. Her favorite stories feature a dread pirate and a boy who never grows up. She's an active member of the writing community and can be found at www.authormeganriann.com.

MICHAELA WATTERS, AGE 19, was raised in Eagle Mountain, Utah. She's an aspiring author and accomplished artist. She loves Percy Jackson, Five Kingdoms, and anything related to the Arthurian Legends. No stranger to fiction/fantasy she enjoys Dr. Who, The MCU (Team Iron Man), BBC Merlin and Psych. She also loves sewing, crafting, and her job being a respite caregiver for special needs.

RYLEE CUNDIFF, AGE 16, is an aspiring author, avid reader and a dragon lover. Whenever she's not researching anything from the oldest mythology to futuristic technology she's with her three younger siblings or two dogs. She enjoys spending her summers in Wisconsin and winters in Arizona.

SARAH BARTHOLOMEW, AGE 16, lives in Provo with her stories and family. She loves Jesus Christ, Seminary, books, cleaning, and playing the piano. Despite having wonderful friends, she spends much more time with her laptop having adventures with her fictional characters. When she's not writing or playing the piano, she loves looking at art, admiring new books, and taking walks at night.

SHALIN HALE, AGE 17, is one of the nerdiest people out there. She plays Dungeons and Dragons at least once a week and spends the rest of her time drawing, writing, singing along to Broadway songs, and spending time with her family. When she isn't stuck in the house because of a pandemic, Shalin loves acting in her school's drama program.

SHION COOK, AGE 17, is an Oregonian who has always had a passion for the arts. She loves art, writing, music, acting and everything in between. A dream of hers is to perform for others through acting and singing. Shion is a sweet and caring soul who always has a joyous light about her, and befriends all she meets.

SUZANNAH MANESS, AGE 17, is a teenage girl who likes to escape to different worlds, those found in books, TV shows, movies, and those of her own creation. She is endlessly fascinated by human behavior and loves using that fascination to build characters one can relate to, learn from, or even fall for (yes, I'm talking about fictional crushes).

TRENTON MORRISON, AGE 17, is a professional bear wrangler. He spends his time watching corn grow, and yes, it is as entertaining as they say. He wants to shout out his favorite constellation, Orion. Also an amateur gamer boy and a part time pencil sharpener, he enjoys an elevated conversation.

TRINI FENG, AGE 15, is a high school sophomore who dreams up worlds while living in her own—the quiet suburbs of Illinois. She loves music of all kinds, from classical piano pieces to today's modern pop. In her free time, she dabbles in playing video games.

WILLOW SEYMOUR, AGE 18, from Las Vegas has been writing since before she could read. She would sit at the kitchen table with her mom, drawing pictures and telling the stories behind them. Since then, she's written dozens of short stories, worked on novels, become the president of her school's Creative Writing Club, and decided to go to college for Creative Writing.

FINALISTS

So many great stories—not enough space to print them all! Below are our talented *Write Your Own Adventure* finalists, whose stories deserve an honorable mention. Please visit owlhollowpress.com/TEEN-FINALISTS to read their tales:

ALLISON WILLIAMS, 18, *The Mermaid's Gem*
AMBRI ROBERTS, 17, *The Adventure of the Lonely Angel*
CHEYENNE INGALLS, 19, *Strange Companions*
JAYMELEE WOMACK, 15, *Essential*
KARA LLEWELLYN, 17, *After the Fall*
KATE OKABE, 17, *War of Hearts*
KIMBRIAH ALFRENAR, 17, *A World Without Color*
LIBERTY LUNDELL, 16, *Free Hugs*
MIRANDA EOFF, 19, *Dunes of Glass*
TOVIA VANDERBILT, 17, *Ms. Cleverly*

Editor Bios

Hannah Stiles Smith is an educator, has a BA in History, and has worked for years as an editor, helping bring fabulous books to their full potential. She spends her spare time escaping between the pages of a book, and a foray into publishing seemed like the best way to channel that energy. She lives in rural Virginia with her husband and four rambunctious children.

Nicole Brouwer was born and raised in Georgia by a family of Southern storytellers. In kindergarten, she wrote a story about a misjudged bush that won first prize in the MOSAIC creative writing competition and she's been hooked on writing ever since. Nicole graduated from BYU-Hawaii with a degree in Social Work, married a great guy from Holland, and is the happy mama of three busy children. She loves to travel and excels in people-watching and daydreaming. Nicole recently completed her debut novel, *The Lotus Ladies of London*, and is currently working with her dream agent, Jenny Bent of the Bent Agency, to prepare for submission.